MW00465544

MORNINGS

with

GOD

MORNINGS

with

GOD

365 DEVOTIONS TO START YOUR DAY RIGHT

JOYCE MEYER

New York • Nashville

Copyright © 2024 by Joyce Meyer

Cover copyright © 2024 by Hachette Book Group, Inc.

Hachette Book Group supports the right to free expression and the value of copyright. The purpose of copyright is to encourage writers and artists to produce the creative works that enrich our culture.

The scanning, uploading, and distribution of this book without permission is a theft of the author's intellectual property. If you would like permission to use material from the book (other than for review purposes), please contact permissions@hbgusa.com. Thank you for your support of the author's rights.

FaithWords
Hachette Book Group
1290 Avenue of the Americas, New York, NY 10104
faithwords.com
twitter.com/faithwords

First Edition: September 2024

FaithWords is a division of Hachette Book Group, Inc. The FaithWords name and logo are registered trademarks of Hachette Book Group, Inc.

The publisher is not responsible for websites (or their content) that are not owned by the publisher.

The Hachette Speakers Bureau provides a wide range of authors for speaking events. To find out more, go to hachettespeakersbureau.com or email HachetteSpeakers@hbgusa.com.

FaithWords books may be purchased in bulk for business, educational, or promotional use. For information, please contact your local bookseller or the Hachette Book Group Special Markets Department at special.markets@hbgusa.com.

Library of Congress Cataloging-in-Publication Data has been applied for.

ISBNs: 978-1-5460-2925-0 (paper over board), 978-1-5460-0691-6 (leatherbound), 978-1-5460-2926-7 (ebook)

Printed in the United States of America

LSC-C

Printing 1, 2024

INTRODUCTION

Starting our day with God is one of the most important things we can do, as far as I'm concerned. Even if you don't have much time in the mornings, and you prefer to pray and study God's Word at another time of day, at least take time to say "Good morning, God," and tell Him you love Him and need Him. A few words of thanksgiving are also good to help you start your day with the right attitude.

This devotional contains encouraging insights from God's Word for each day of the year. In these pages, you will find a lot of comfort, because we all need comfort at times, and we always need encouragement. When we are discouraged, we begin to shrink back from what we should do because we doubt we can accomplish our goals, or we think we are not valuable. But when we are encouraged, we are strengthened in our belief that we can press forward and successfully reach our goals.

Scripture refers to the Holy Spirit as the Comforter or the Helper (John 14:16), and I am glad He is always present in our lives to comfort us and encourage us. However, we must remember that He often works through people, so each of us needs to be encouraging to others. The best way to receive encouragement is to give it away, because God's Word teaches us that we reap what we sow (Galatians 6:7). Encouragement brings courage, confidence, and hope, and when we encourage others, it helps them to keep going in life.

I spend a lot of time alone studying and writing. Yes, I am on television and have the privilege of sharing God's Word at conferences. But on television I am being seen, not seeing anyone, and I have to walk by faith and believe that people are watching and being helped. Joyce Meyer Ministries has several offices in countries outside the United States, and recently our director in India sent a video of all the wonderful things that are happening through our ministry there. I was greatly encouraged by the video and felt strengthened to press on.

This year, let's set the goal of encouraging more people than we ever have. You may even feel led, with God's help, to encourage no less than three people every day in some way. You may want to compliment them, show appreciation, thank them for what they do, or share an appropriate scripture with them. Something as simple as a smile can encourage some people.

Our world is filled with people who are hurting. Often, those we think would never need encouragement are the ones who need it most. Encouragement is one of the spiritual gifts mentioned in Romans 12:8. But even if we don't have the spiritual gift of encouragement, we can still encourage people. We may simply have to make more of an effort than those who are naturally gifted. Paul instructs all of us to encourage and edify one another (1 Thessalonians 5:11).

I pray you will learn and be comforted and encouraged by this daily devotional and that you will consider giving one to people you know and love.

One of the best ways to stay connected with God is to "pray your way through the day." Start your day with Him each morning. Talk with Him about everything as though He is your best friend who is with you all day long, because He is. God loves you very much, and He never tires of hearing your voice.

BEGIN YOUR DAY WITH GOD

*In the morning You hear my voice, O Lord; in the morning I prepare
[a prayer, a sacrifice] for You and watch and wait [for You to speak
to my heart].*

PSALM 5:3

Starting each day right is important. We are more likely to be
satisfied with the outcome of any day if we begin it in a positive
way than if we get up dreading what lies ahead of us. I encour-
age you to start each day as I do—with God. Spend as much
time with Him as you can, based on your schedule. The only
way to get your day off to a good start is to start it with Him.
Talk to Him, ask for His help and guidance in all you do, and
submit your day to Him for His direction. Take in God's Word
in some form through studying it, reading it, listening to it, or
watching someone teach or preach it. Whether it's one verse of
Scripture or an entire chapter in the Bible, it will help you.

Going to God first, before we do anything else, is a way of
honoring Him and saying with our actions "Apart from You,
Lord, I can do nothing" (based on John 15:5). You might even
consider lying in bed for five minutes after you wake up and
using that time to talk to God about your day. This is an espe-
cially good idea if you have small children or a busy household
that is active from the moment you get out of bed. If you do
only have a short time in the morning, make an effort to spend
more time with God later in the day.

David knew that God heard his voice in the morning, and
he watched and waited for God to speak to his heart (Psalm 5:3).
I hope you'll do the same.

Confession: *I start my day with God, and I wait and watch for Him
to speak to my heart.*

GOD'S COMFORT AND ENCOURAGEMENT

Even though I walk through the darkest valley, I will fear no evil, for you are with me; your rod and your staff, they comfort me.

PSALM 23:4 NIV

We all go through hard times, but the good news is that when we do God is always present to comfort and encourage us. When times are tough, remember that they won't last forever. God will not allow more to come on you than you can bear (1 Corinthians 10:13).

You don't have to be afraid, no matter what you may face today, because God is with you, and He loves you deeply and unconditionally. You may not know how you can turn your situation around, but God does. He always has a good plan for you, and temporary problems don't have the ability to cancel those plans.

What you are dealing with is temporary, but God is eternal, and He will never leave you or forsake you.

Confession: *I will not fear because God is always with me.*

YOU'RE STRONGER THAN YOU THINK YOU ARE

Fear not, for I am with you; be not dismayed, for I am your God; I will strengthen you, I will help you, I will uphold you with my righteous right hand.

ISAIAH 41:10 ESV

When we are going through difficult times or have unexpected problems, we often say to ourselves, "I can't take this." But you are stronger than you think you are, because God has promised to strengthen you.

When we look back over our lives, there are many very difficult things we have done that initially we thought we couldn't do. It is good to remember those times when God helped you and be confident that He will do it again. I encourage you not to allow fear of the unknown to control you because even though you don't know what will happen, God does, and it will end well.

Make a decision to trust God when you don't have the answers, knowing that He is good and faithful and will never fail you.

Confession: *I will not fear the unknown because God knows all things, and He will always take care of me.*

TAKE TIME TO BE REFRESHED

So repent [change your inner self—your old way of thinking, regret past sins] and return [to God—seek His purpose for your life], so that your sins may be wiped away [blotted out, completely erased], so that times of refreshing may come from the presence of the Lord [restoring you like a cool wind on a hot day].

ACTS 3:19 AMP

If we are following Jesus and His way of doing things, we will be energetic instead of tired and worn out all the time. We will live in peace, and we will experience contentment. He leads us beside the still and restful water, and there He restores our souls (Psalm 23).

Jesus and the disciples were ministering to people in great need. There were so many people coming to them that they had no time to eat or rest. So what did Jesus do? He said, "Let's go off by ourselves to a quiet place and rest awhile" (Mark 6:31 NLT). Amazing! Jesus walked away temporarily from valid needs in order to take care of Himself so He could finish what God had sent Him to do.

When you can't do everything, choose the best thing for the present time. Jesus knew it was better to let the needs of the people wait momentarily so He and His disciples could rest and eat. This allowed Jesus to be properly prepared to meet their needs in due time.

When you can't do it all, remember there is a time for all things—and everything is beautiful in its time (Ecclesiastes 3:11). Being in God's timing is equivalent to being in His will. If you are doing something in God's timing, it will be beautiful and fulfilling.

Confession: When I can't do everything, I choose to do what is best at the present time.

CAST YOUR CARE ON GOD

Casting the whole of your care [all your anxieties, all your worries, all your concerns, once and for all] on Him, for He cares for you affectionately and cares about you watchfully.

1 PETER 5:7

The word *cast* means to pitch or throw, and that is exactly what you can do with your problems. You can cast (pitch, throw) them on Jesus, knowing that He cares for you and wants to help you anytime you are hurting or have anxieties, worries, or concerns.

The amplification of today's scripture tells us to cast all of our cares on Him once and for all. That means that once we have cast them on Him, we should not take them back, even though the devil will try to worry us with them. Once you have cast your cares on Jesus, if they try to come back, just say, "I don't have that problem anymore; Jesus has it, and I am free from worry."

It is comforting to know that we don't have to try to take care of things we don't know how to take care of. If you know what to do, by all means do it; but if you don't, give it to the Lord because all things are possible with Him (Matthew 19:26).

Confession: *I refuse to frustrate myself trying to solve problems that only God can solve.*

MAKE WISE CHOICES TODAY

Who is the man who reverently fears and worships the Lord? Him shall He teach in the way that he should choose.

PSALM 25:12

You and I can choose our thoughts, words, attitudes, behaviors, and activities each day. We cannot always choose our circumstances, but we can choose how we respond to them. God has given us free choice, and we can manage our emotions instead of allowing them to manage us.

When we use our freedom to choose to do God's will, He is honored and glorified. When we choose to manage our emotions, we live with the stability and focus we need to carry out His will for us. We can choose to accomplish something worthwhile and to make each day count.

In his book *The Secret of Guidance*, F. B. Meyer wrote:

> Perhaps you live too much in your feelings, too little in your will. We have no direct control over our feelings, but we have over our will...God does not hold us responsible for what we *feel*, but for what we *will*...Let us, therefore, not live in the summer-house of emotion, but in the central citadel of the will, wholly yielded and devoted to the will of God.[1]

Most of us know people who live entirely by their feelings, and the result is that they are wasting their lives. This could change quickly if they would make different decisions, ones that are in agreement with God's will. Don't waste today by letting your emotions rule you.

Confession: *I do not waste my life by living by my feelings.*

LIVE A BALANCED LIFE

And He said to them, [As for you] come away by yourselves to a deserted place, and rest a while—for many were [continually] coming and going, and they had not even leisure enough to eat.

MARK 6:31

Most of us try to do too many things and too much of some things, even good things—and this usually becomes a bad thing. We should only do what we can do peacefully, and when we lose our sense of peace, we need to do whatever is necessary to get it back.

We make our schedules, and only we can change them. So instead of running frantically through life trying to please everybody, we can learn to say no at the proper time. If I ask a crowd of people how many of them feel they have too much to do, almost everyone raises their hand. God never intended for His people to live under excessive stress and pressure. Life is to be thoroughly enjoyed, and that isn't possible if we constantly feel pressured by a schedule that causes us to rush frantically through the day. Remember: God will never give you more to do than you can do peacefully.

Part of living a healthy, productive life is developing an ability to schedule your life so that you are well balanced in all areas. That is why when I plan my day, I almost always schedule time for relaxation and enjoyment as well as time for work.

You will enjoy your life much more if you take proper time for yourself. The best gift you can give your family and friends is a strong, healthy you.

Confession: I take time to take care of myself on a regular basis.

THE LORD WILL
TAKE CARE OF YOU

The Lord is my shepherd; I shall not want.

PSALM 23:1 ESV

It is very comforting to know that our Lord will always take care of us. He meets all our needs if we trust Him to do so. I love to meditate on the one line of Scripture we read today because it is so encouraging to me.

You can depend on God to meet your financial and physical needs as well as your emotional needs, including the need for wisdom when making decisions and the strength to do whatever you need to do each day. Because He has promised that we shall not want, we don't have to live in fear concerning what will happen to us.

Are you going through a difficult time right now? If so, remember that the Lord is your shepherd, and a good shepherd always watches over, protects, and takes care of his sheep. Don't waste your time and energy trying to figure out how to solve your own problem. If God shows you something you can do, then be obedient and do it. But if you don't see the way out, remember that, Jesus *is* the way (John 14:6). You can trust that He is working in your life right now, even if you don't see anything happening or changing.

God often works mysteriously and in secret. Then suddenly your breakthrough comes, so stay focused on Him and expect something good to happen.

Confession: *God is working in my life, and I expect something good to happen.*

TODAY'S PLANS AFFECT TOMORROW

Commit to the Lord whatever you do, and he will establish your plans.

PROVERBS 16:3 NIV

Each day is different and presents us with different responsibilities and challenges, so we get to plan each one accordingly. Some days I may work all day; other days I may be with family or friends all day. Planning variety in our schedules is very important if we don't want to get bored with life.

I am training myself to plan each day intentionally because I want to put my time into things that will bear good fruit. I refuse to waste my life. I only have one life, and I don't get another one here on earth when this one is over, so I want it to count.

I have looked at the week, the month, and the year ahead of me. I have specific ideas about what I need to do this week and this month. For the rest of the year, I have a vague idea of what I need to do and accomplish, where I need to be, and what I have to do to get there. I have long-range and short-range goals, and I hope you do too. But we still have to take life one day at a time if we want to enjoy it and not feel overwhelmed. What we choose today is part of what we want to happen in the days to come, even in the distant future.

I think that when people have no plans, they have no direction. Have a plan and work your plan, but always be open to letting God change your plan if He chooses.

Confession: *I make plans and set goals, but I also remain open to letting God change them if He sees fit.*

DECIDE TO OVERCOME TEMPTATION

But we do [strongly and earnestly] desire for each of you to show the same diligence and sincerity [all the way through] in realizing and enjoying the full assurance and development of [your] hope until the end.

HEBREWS 6:11

Make up your mind ahead of time to finish what God has given you to do, no matter what temptations you face. Whatever situation challenges you most, decide now to set your mind for victory over it. Talking to yourself ahead of time is one way to do this. Consider making statements such as these:

- "I will believe the best of everyone."
- "I will not complain about anything. I will be thankful for all I have."
- "I will eliminate unnecessary stress from my life."
- "I will think positive thoughts and speak positive words."

As you speak to yourself in these ways, you build a foundation from which to resist the temptations you face. When they come, you'll hear the messages you've recorded in your mind, and making the right decision will be easier than it would have been had you not decided in advance how to handle temptations.

Recognizing your weaknesses and temptations is wise, and firmly setting your mind to overcome them is the pathway to victory.

Confession: *I overcome temptation by setting my mind in advance to gain victory over it with God's help.*

BE STILL AND REST
IN THE LORD

He makes me lie down in green pastures. He leads me beside still waters.

PSALM 23:2 ESV

We all have many things we could worry about, but we can choose to trust God instead. Worry does no good, but it does steal our peace, joy, and energy. The psalmist David tells us we can rest in God.

It has always interested me that Psalm 23:2 says God "makes" us lie down in green pastures. This means we have to learn how to rest, and if we don't use wisdom and do it on our own, He will *make us* rest.

If we want to be healthy, rest is part of the cycle of life. Work is good, but so is rest. I find that one of the main things that refreshes me is quiet. Our world today is very noisy. All the phone calls, texts, emails, social media alerts, traffic, and the busyness of life can be overwhelming. I encourage you to rest and take time each day to merely sit and enjoy some quiet time. Even ten minutes can work wonders.

God loves you very much, and He wants you to be healthy and feel energetic each day.

Confession: *I live a balanced life—I work, play, worship, and rest. I am healthy and have plenty of energy for each day.*

I AM BLESSED IN THE PRESENCE OF MY ENEMIES

You prepare a table before me in the presence of my enemies. You anoint my head with oil; my [brimming] cup runs over.

PSALM 23:5

Our enemies may be people who hurt us, or they may be people through whom the devil works to reject, abuse, or discourage us. He also works independently by putting into our minds thoughts that will cause us to be hopeless and afraid. But Jesus has given us authority over the devil (Luke 10:19). We can resist him, and he will have to flee (James 4:7). In addition, we can cast down the thoughts that don't agree with God's Word (2 Corinthians 10:5 NKJV). We should always believe what God's Word says above anything we think or anything other people say if it doesn't agree with God.

At times we have to stand our ground for a while as we wait for God to deliver us. But today's scripture teaches us that even in the presence of our enemies, God will take care of us and meet our needs. He will give us a fresh anointing of the Holy Spirit, which energizes us, and even in the midst of trouble he will give us an abundance of overflowing joy.

During times of trouble, be careful not to focus on the trouble but instead focus on God. What we focus on, think about, and talk about becomes the largest thing to us. We should always remember that God is greater than any problem we have. Greater is He that is in us than he that is in the world (1 John 4:4).

Confession: *God will take care of me and meet my needs, even in the midst of trouble.*

After you have suffered for a little while, the God of all grace [who imparts His blessing and favor], who called you to His own eternal glory in Christ, will Himself complete, confirm, strengthen, and establish you [making you what you ought to be].

1 PETER 5:10 AMP

No one's entire life is like one big, long sunny day. At some point, we all face storms—unexpected illness, job loss, financial crisis, marital difficulties, problems with children, or other stressful scenarios. I have faced many storms in my life. Some have been like quick afternoon showers, and some have seemed like category 4 hurricanes. If I've learned anything about weathering the storms of life, it's that they don't last forever, and that, if possible, I shouldn't make major decisions in the midst of them.

When storms arise in your life, keep your mind and emotions as still as you can. Thoughts and feelings often run wild during a crisis, so we need to be careful about making decisions. We must remain calm and discipline ourselves to focus on doing what we can do as we trust God to do what we cannot do.

I often say "Let emotions subside before you decide." Next time you face a storm, do your best to let things settle down before you make major decisions. This may not be possible, but if it is, put significant decisions on hold until your storm passes. If you can't wait, at least calm your mind and emotions, and ask for God's help before deciding what to do.

Confession: *When possible, I let storms subside before I decide.*

POSSESSING GOD'S PROMISES

But charge Joshua, and encourage and strengthen him, for he shall go over before this people and he shall cause them to possess the land which you shall see.

DEUTERONOMY 3:28

After Moses died, Joshua was given the position of leader of Israel and the job of taking the Israelites into the land God had promised to give them. I can imagine how Joshua may have felt. He was Moses' assistant and had seen Moses do mighty and astounding miracles, so he may have felt incapable of standing in Moses' place. But God told Joshua that just as He had been with Moses, He would be with him (Joshua 1:5).

God is with you also. No matter what kind of challenge you are facing, He will enable you to get through it. What is impossible with human beings is possible with God (Luke 18:27). It is not easy to go through things when we feel like giving up, but I encourage you to keep asking God to strengthen you, and He will. Sometimes the most powerful prayer to pray is "God, help me!" There have been days in my life when I think I have said these words at least a thousand times.

God wants you to possess and experience His promises in your life, just as He wanted the Israelites to believe and experience them centuries ago. He wants you to help others possess His promises too. Before Joshua completed the job God had given him, He declared that Joshua would do it. You, too, will possess all that God has in His plan for you.

Confession: *God is my strength, and I will possess all the good things He has planned for me.*

GOOD NEWS

And with many other words John exhorted the people and proclaimed the good news to them.

LUKE 3:18 NIV

John the Baptist exhorted the people, which means he encouraged them to take action. He may have encouraged them to believe the message he was preaching about Jesus, to repent of their sin, or perhaps not to give up during their times of struggle. He proclaimed the gospel, which is the "good news," to them.

Today I say to you that the good news is that God loves you unconditionally. He is for you, not against you; you have favor with Him; your sins are forgiven; and, as a believer in Jesus, you are a joint heir with Him. You share His inheritance (Romans 8:17).

Good news nourishes the bones (Proverbs 15:30). I love good news. Each day I pray for and declare that I will receive some kind of good news, and I encourage you to do the same thing. James said we have not because we ask not (James 4:2), so perhaps you are not getting good news because you are not asking for it and expecting it. When your phone rings, someone may be calling with good news, or when you get mail, it may be good news. John preached good news, Jesus preached good news, and I pray that I will always preach good news. Even if a message corrects you, it is still good news because it will help you change and grow.

Confession: *I am expecting good news today.*

RENEWING YOUR MIND TAKES TIME

But his delight and desire are in the law of the Lord, and on His law (the precepts, the instructions, the teachings of God) he habitually meditates (ponders and studies) by day and by night.

PSALM 1:2

Renewing your mind isn't like renewing your driver's license or library card, which can be done quickly and infrequently. It's more like refurbishing an old house. It doesn't happen quickly; it takes time, energy, and effort and needs regular attention.

You can't renew your mind by thinking godly thoughts one time. You need to think godly thoughts over and over again, until godly thoughts come to you more easily and naturally than ungodly ones. You need to discipline yourself to think properly and guard against falling into old thought patterns, because this can happen easily. When it does, don't feel bad about it; just start thinking in godly ways again. You will eventually reach the point where wrong thoughts actually make you uncomfortable and no longer fit into your thinking processes.

The ongoing process of renewing the mind extends to every aspect of your thinking, including the way you think about yourself, your finances, your health, your family, time management, vacations and recreation, your job, your future, or other areas. Don't assume you have renewed your mind simply because you feel confident your thinking has changed in one area. Celebrate your progress, and keep pressing on.

Confession: *I renew my mind continually, realizing that it is an ongoing process.*

BE SAVED FROM THIS CROOKED GENERATION

And Peter solemnly testified and continued to admonish and urge them with many more words, saying, "Be saved from this crooked and unjust generation!"

ACTS 2:40 AMP

If Peter felt the people of his day were living in a crooked generation, what would he say about the world today? Every generation seems to think theirs is the most sinful. They may be right. Evil continues to grow and will do so until it gets so bad that God says "Enough" and sends Jesus to earth for the second time—this time to take God's people home to live with Him forever.

We should be aware of the wickedness in the world and remember that the Bible says we are in the world (John 17:11), but that we should not be like the world (Romans 12:2).

I encourage you, as Peter exhorted the people of his day, to be careful due to the wickedness around us. We cannot afford to be lazy, lukewarm Christians (Revelation 3:16). We must be active and on fire for God for our own benefit. The more we stay plugged into God's Word and His people, the safer we are from the perverseness around us.

Be on your guard. Watch and pray (Matthew 26:41), for the days are evil (Ephesians 5:16), and the time is short (1 Corinthians 7:29). We do not have to be afraid, because we are more than conquerors (Romans 8:37), and we will spend eternity with Jesus.

God will always take care of you.

Confession: *God protects me in the midst of evil.*

ENCOURAGE YOURSELF

David was greatly distressed, for the men spoke of stoning him because the souls of them all were bitterly grieved, each man for his sons and daughters. But David encouraged and strengthened himself in the Lord his God.

1 SAMUEL 30:6

What if all the people around you were preparing to stone you, as they prepared to stone David, and you had no friends or allies with you? What would you do? David encouraged himself in the Lord. I imagine he did so by remembering previous times when God had delivered him from dangerous situations, or he may have remembered some of the promises in God's Word.

We all have times, as David did, when we need to encourage ourselves because there is no one else to do it. Remind yourself of how good God has been to you and of His promise to never leave you or forsake you (Hebrews 13:5). He has told us that we can do all things through Christ who strengthens us (Philippians 4:13).

When your mind says that you are not going to make it, speak aloud and say what God says: "I am more than a conqueror through Christ who loves me" (see Romans 8:37). "I am strong in the Lord and in the power of His might" (see Ephesians 6:10). The devil works diligently to make us feel overwhelmed, unable, and incapable, but he is a liar.

Confession: *I will daily encourage myself by remembering all God has done for me.*

NEVER GIVE UP

But the people, the men of Israel, took courage and strengthened themselves and again set their battle line in the same place where they formed it the first day.

JUDGES 20:22

Israel had gone out to battle against the Benjamites, and they followed God's instructions to let Judah lead in the battle; yet "the Benjamites came out of Gibeah and cut down twenty-two thousand" men of Israel that day (Judges 20:21 NIV). I am sure that felt like a defeat, but the Israelites didn't give up.

As our verse for today says, they encouraged themselves and did again what God had previously told them to do. They were not going to let the loss of one battle determine the outcome of the war, and neither should we.

We may not always have victory in everything we do, but if we won't give up, victory will come. Even Jesus had to place His hands on a blind man twice before his sight was fully restored (Mark 8:22–25). At times, I have felt that I obeyed God and followed His instructions, yet my problems remained. I have learned to just keep doing what God is leading me to do until the devil gives up. As of the writing of this book, I have been in ministry for forty-six years, and I often say that my greatest testimony is "I am still here doing what God told me to do."

Confession: *I will never give up, no matter how long it takes.*

GOD'S EYES ARE ON YOU FOR GOOD

For I will set My eyes upon them for good, and I will bring them again to this land; and I will build them up and not pull them down, and I will plant them and not pluck them up.

JEREMIAH 24:6

Everything God has planned for you is good, even if you are not seeing all of it right now. It is important for us to believe in God's goodness. When we go through difficult times, the devil wants us to believe that God doesn't love us and that He is not good. But hold firm to your faith in the goodness of God.

God is a master builder, and He is building us up and planting us where He wants us. All of God's plans for us are good, and He intends to give us blessings and favor. Psalm 145:9 says, "The Lord is good to all, and His tender mercies are over all His works [the entirety of things created]."

Many of the tests and trials we encounter are intended to help build our faith. Faith only grows as we use it, just as a muscle does. The more we use it, the stronger it gets. If you are facing a difficulty at this time in your life, keep declaring that the Lord is good and has a good plan for you. Be sensitive to the Holy Spirit, and if God is leading you to do or not to do something, be quick to obey Him. Anything He asks of us is always for our good. Why? Because He is good.

Confession: *God is good, and He has a good plan for me.*

BE A VICTOR, NOT A VICTIM

But thanks be to God, Who gives us the victory [making us conquerors] through our Lord Jesus Christ.

1 CORINTHIANS 15:57

If in the past you have suffered things that still affect you today, you may feel like a victim, but God wants you to be a victor. Try this: Lie in bed for a few minutes after waking up and think some specific thoughts on purpose, such as: *This is the day God has made and given to me as a gift. I will not waste it! My past is behind me, and nothing from the past can affect me unless I allow it to. God is on my side, and I choose to live this day energetically, enthusiastically, and passionately. By God's grace, I will get up and do things that have purpose.*

Be prepared to do this day after day, and you will soon begin to see results. It takes time to renew the mind, so don't be disappointed if you do not see change immediately. It is great if you do, but be prepared not to give up. Beginning each day with this mindset helps you get your day off to a good start.

Many people lie in bed each day and think, *I don't want to get up. Nothing good ever happens to me. I hate my life, and I dread facing another day.* I woke up daily for many years with this type of thinking. I made myself miserable with my thoughts. I was unaware that I could do anything about my life, so I remained a victim. But if we believe and obey Him, God gives all of us the victory through Christ, so we do not have to live as victims.

Confession: *I am not a victim. I am victorious in Christ.*

ENCOURAGE THOSE WHO ARE WEARY

[The Servant of God says] The Lord God has given Me the tongue of a disciple and of one who is taught, that I should know how to speak a word in season to him who is weary. He wakens Me morning by morning, He wakens My ear to hear as a disciple [as one who is taught].

ISAIAH 50:4

God wants to use you to speak a word of encouragement to those who are weary, and He wants to use others to do the same for you. We need to encourage one another. Encouragement gives us the courage to press forward in reaching our goals and not to give up on trusting God.

Ask God daily who you can encourage, and He will show you. He will put someone on your heart. Even something as simple as a short text message saying "God put you on my heart today, and He wants you to know that you are important to Him" can turn what may be a bad day into a good one for the person you reach out to. Not only will it bless them, but you will be blessed in the process. It is more blessed to give than to receive (Acts 20:35). God told Abraham that He would bless him and make him a blessing (Genesis 12:2). That's what He wants to do for each of us.

Confession: *I will speak an encouraging word to someone today, and it will bless them and bless me.*

WORDS ARE POWERFUL

And Judas and Silas, who were themselves prophets (inspired interpreters of the will and purposes of God), urged and warned and consoled and encouraged the brethren with many words and strengthened them.

ACTS 15:32

It is amazing how powerful words are. Proverbs 18:21 says that the power of life and death are in the tongue. With words, we can heal, or we can wound. God has given us a great ability to encourage with our words, and we all need encouragement. I want to encourage you today by telling you that you are stronger than you think you are, and you can and will make it through any trouble that comes your way.

Don't project the outcome of your situation based on what it looks like right now; trust that it will end well. God has a plan for your escape to a safe place full of fruitfulness and good things. It is very important to have hope, to expect something good to happen to you. The devil wants us hopeless, but "hope deferred makes the heart sick" (Proverbs 13:12). Without hope, our strength fades, and we tend to give up. So stay full of hope because God is on your side, and He will not fail you if you continue trusting Him.

Confession: *I am strong in the Lord and full of faith, and I am expecting good things.*

YOUR SINS ARE FORGIVEN

If we confess our sins, he is faithful and just and will forgive us our sins and purify us from all unrighteousness.

1 JOHN 1:9 NIV

We have all sinned. We are all in need of God's forgiveness, and He is ready to give it. All we need to do is admit our sins and ask for and receive His forgiveness. According to Romans 3:23–24, "all have sinned and fall short of the glory of God, and all are justified freely by his grace through the redemption that came by Christ Jesus" (NIV). Yes, all have sinned, but through faith in Christ all are justified freely by His grace.

The devil wants you to focus on your sin, but God wants you to focus on His forgiveness. It is wonderful not to have to carry the burden and guilt of sin through our lives. The moment we are aware that we have sinned, we can immediately be washed totally clean and made just as though we never sinned by believing God's Word and acting on it.

Have you been burdened with the weight of your sin? Have you been carrying a load of guilt over wrong things you have done in the past? If so, today I have good news. You can pray right now, and not only will God forgive you, but He will forget your sins and remember them no more (Hebrews 8:12).

Confession: *My sins are forgiven, and there is no condemnation, because I trust God to justify me freely by His grace.*

ARE YOU HAVING TROUBLE WITH YOUR MIND?

For who has known or understood the mind (the counsels and purposes) of the Lord so as to guide and instruct Him and give Him knowledge? But we have the mind of Christ (the Messiah) and do hold the thoughts (feelings and purposes) of His heart.

1 CORINTHIANS 2:16

If you are having trouble with negative or destructive thoughts, the first thing you need to know is that everyone does from time to time, so you are not alone in this battle. Our minds are the devil's main target because he knows if we think something long enough, we will become what we think (Proverbs 23:7). But we have the mind of Christ (1 Corinthians 2:16). We hold the thoughts, intents, and purposes of His heart. Christ's mind is in us, but we have to develop it.

Our minds are renewed by studying and meditating on God's Word. When you feel your mind is under attack with worry, fear, or anything that is against God's Word, you can replace the wrong thought with one that is right according to what He says in His Word.

I had very negative thoughts for a long time, and God has helped me over the years to renew my mind. Now I am very positive. You can have control over your thoughts, but it will take time to change the old ways of thinking into new ones. I encourage you not to become discouraged in the process. No matter how many times you fail, just start again, and soon you will find that you are making real progress.

Confession: *I have the mind of Christ, and I think according to God's Word.*

GOD IS WATCHING OVER YOU

Are not two sparrows sold for a penny? And not one of them will fall to the ground apart from your Father. But even the hairs of your head are all numbered. Fear not, therefore; you are of more value than many sparrows.

MATTHEW 10:29–31 ESV

A sparrow is a very small bird that God watches over. Surely, if He watches over the sparrows and nothing can happen to them without God's notice and consent, He will watch over us. If He has counted even the hairs on our head (Luke 12:7), He surely cares about every little thing in our lives.

Take a few moments and think about the fact that right now God is watching over you. There is nothing happening to you that He is not fully aware of. When we are hurting, we often feel very alone, but we are never alone, because God is always with us and watching over us.

You are very precious to God. He says in Isaiah 43:4, "Because you are *precious* in My sight and honored, and because I love you, I will give men in return *for* you and peoples in exchange *for* your life" (italics mine).

God gave His only Son, Jesus, to redeem you from sin and death, and He will surely meet every need you have. Don't base your faith on what you feel; base it on God's Word. Nothing can happen to you without God knowing it, and He will strengthen you and use any difficulty to work good in your life (Romans 8:28).

Confession: *I am very precious to the Lord. He knows everything about me and my life and will always take care of me.*

SUCCESS BEGINS IN THE MIND

Then Jesus said to the centurion, "Go your way; and as you have believed, so let it be done for you." And his servant was healed that same hour.

MATTHEW 8:13 NKJV

Success in every aspect of life begins with a thought, and so does failure. Consider the successes and failures you have experienced. What kinds of thoughts were you thinking before and during your greatest achievements? And what kinds of thoughts filled your mind before and during your biggest failures or missteps? Can you see how much influence the mind has over your life and how it has worked either for you or against you?

Many times, we succeed because other people encourage us, and we think about their affirming comments to the point that we believe them. Anyone who has ever been told "You can do it!" knows how easy it is to turn those confidence-building words into a thought. When "You can do it" becomes "I can do it," then "it" happens—whether it's scoring a point in a ballgame, making a good grade on a test, getting a job, losing weight, or buying a house. When we believe or think we can do something, then somehow, some way—even if we face challenges—we still manage to get it done.

The words others speak to us and the words we speak to ourselves become ingrained in our thinking to the point that they influence our decisions, and we tend to follow where our thoughts lead us.

Confession: *I pay attention to the positive words other people speak to me, and I speak positive words to myself.*

THE GOD OF ALL COMFORT

Blessed be the God and Father of our Lord Jesus Christ, the Father of sympathy (pity and mercy) and the God [Who is the Source] of every comfort (consolation and encouragement), Who comforts (consoles and encourages) us in every trouble (calamity and affliction), so that we may also be able to comfort (console and encourage) those who are in any kind of trouble or distress, with the comfort (consolation and encouragement) with which we ourselves are comforted (consoled and encouraged) by God.

2 CORINTHIANS 1:3–4

When you need comfort, go directly to God in prayer and ask Him for it. He is the source of true comfort. We have a bad habit of running to friends or other sources who are not always able to help us, but the Holy Spirit is the Comforter. As a believer in Jesus Christ, the Holy Spirit lives in you, so comfort is closer than you might think.

I have learned to ask and depend on the Lord to comfort me the moment someone hurts me. I am sure we can all look back over our lives and wonder how we ever got through all the things we have had to endure. The answer is that the strength and comfort of God helped us. He comforts us inwardly, and when we are strong inside, we can handle anything that comes against us from the outside.

Once we have experienced God's comfort, we are also able to comfort and encourage others who are hurting with the same comfort we received from the Lord.

Confession: *I receive comfort from God, and I give comfort to others who need it.*

GOD ENCOURAGES THOSE WHO ARE DEPRESSED

But God, who comforts the downcast, comforted us by the coming of Titus, and not only by his coming but also by the comfort you had given him. He told us about your longing for me, your deep sorrow, your ardent concern for me, so that my joy was greater than ever.

2 CORINTHIANS 7:6–7 NIV

We all feel down at times, but God is ready to help us when we are depressed or feel we are sinking emotionally. When you first start getting that sinking feeling, don't wait and let it get worse; immediately ask God to comfort you. He comforted Paul by sending Titus to encourage him, and He often comforts us through other people. Anytime someone gives you even a simple compliment, don't take it lightly. Instead, ponder it and receive it graciously, because compliments are meant to encourage us. Look at it as God working through that person to help you.

You can encourage someone else today with a compliment that is as simple as "That color looks really good on you," or "I like your hairstyle." Reaching out to others with help and encouragement helps us keep our minds off of our own problems.

Confession: *Today, I will be the best encourager I can be.*

COMMIT YOUR WAY
TO THE LORD

Commit your way to the Lord [roll and repose each care of your load on Him]; trust (lean on, rely on, and be confident) also in Him and He will bring it to pass.

Are you the type of person who wants your own way? I have to say that I wanted my way for many years, and I still do at times. It took me years and much help from God to learn to respond in mature ways when things didn't go as I wanted. I had to learn not to become angry, withdraw from others, and feel sorry for myself when I didn't get my way. This is why I still remember my first Bible, a gift from Dave's mother when he and I married. It was a white King James Bible, and she wrote in the front of it: "Commit thy way unto the Lord; trust also in him; and he shall bring it to pass" (Psalm 37:5 KJV).

I didn't understand this verse at the time, and I doubt my mother-in-law realized just how perfect it was for me. But I've remembered it often because I have needed to commit *my* way to the Lord frequently through the years, trusting Him to do what He wants to do in my life instead of insisting on having what I want and trying to figure out how to get it.

Learning to commit my way to the Lord took a while, but I am learning daily that committing my way to Him is vital if I want to live a happy, fulfilled life. As you surrender to God and obey His Word, I am confident He will bring to pass all the good things He wants to do in your life too.

Confession: *I do not demand my own way, but instead, I commit my way to the Lord.*

BREAKING STRONGHOLDS

The weapons we fight with are not the weapons of the world. On the contrary, they have divine power to demolish strongholds. We demolish arguments and every pretension that sets itself up against the knowledge of God, and we take captive every thought to make it obedient to Christ.

2 CORINTHIANS 10:4–5 NIV

In today's Scripture passage there is a key word: *strongholds*. Strongholds are thought patterns that are based on lies and that enable the enemy to dominate certain areas of our lives.

If the enemy can trap us in mental strongholds, he can work all kinds of destruction. God doesn't want us held captive in fortresses of the enemy's lies, so He teaches us through His Word how to destroy them. This process is called renewing the mind, which simply means learning how to think the way God wants us to think.

Millions of people are trapped in miserable lives because they believe lies. They may believe that they have no value and wonder why they were even born. They may have a stronghold of rejection in their lives. This thinking leads to an expectation of being rejected, so they end up behaving in ways that can cause people to be uncomfortable around them and end up rejecting them.

We can tear down any mental stronghold through the power of God's Word as we renew our minds according to it.

Confession: *I refuse to be held captive in mental strongholds, because I know and believe God's Word, which breaks the strongholds in my mind.*

SHARE YOUR FAITH

For I long to see you so that I may share with you some spiritual gift, to strengthen and establish you; that is, that we may be mutually encouraged and comforted by each other's faith, both yours and mine.

ROMANS 1:11-12 AMP

When we share our faith with one another, we are all encouraged. According to God's Word, He gives each person the measure of faith they need to do whatever He asks them to do (Romans 12:3). But doubt is always lurking around, trying to hinder our faith. Faith is something we have, but we must use it. The more we use it, the stronger it grows. The less we use it, the weaker it becomes.

Be careful about the kind of people you spend your time with. Being around unbelieving and negative people can have an adverse effect on you, especially if you are going through a difficult time and need your faith to be active. Faith is in you, but you must release it. You can do so by praying, speaking faith-filled positive words, and taking faith-filled action, led by the Holy Spirit.

Share with others how comforting it can be to live by faith, and encourage them to continue trusting God at all times.

Confession: *I trust God and believe He will always help and strengthen me in every situation.*

HAVE YOUR SOUL REFRESHED

Come to Me, all you who labor and are heavy-laden and overburdened, and I will cause you to rest. [I will ease and relieve and refresh your souls.] Take My yoke upon you and learn of Me, for I am gentle (meek) and humble (lowly) in heart, and you will find rest (relief and ease and refreshment and recreation and blessed quiet) for your souls.

MATTHEW 11:28–29

Jesus invites us to come to Him when we feel weary or overburdened and to receive His rest, relief, and refreshment. The more time we spend with the Lord in fellowship, in the Word, or merely being aware of His presence, the more refreshed we become.

Prayer doesn't have to be labor; it can be as simple as telling the Lord that you love Him and need Him. Sitting quietly in His presence will refresh your soul. Psalm 16:11 says, "You will show me the path of life; in Your presence is fullness of joy, at Your right hand there are pleasures forevermore."

Slow down, breathe deeply, and let your soul find its rest in Jesus. Don't worry, because He will always take care of you if you trust Him to do so.

Confession: *When I feel frustrated, worried, or burdened with cares and anxieties, I will take time to go to Jesus and be refreshed in His presence.*

HIDE GOD'S WORD IN YOUR HEART

I have hidden your word in my heart that I might not sin against you.
PSALM 119:11 NIV

I have learned that when I am tempted to sin, the best thing I can do is turn to God's Word. I may know specific verses that will help me deal with certain situations, or I may need to search for them in a concordance or on the internet. Once I find those scriptures, I read them, meditate on them, and declare them aloud.

For example, if I struggle to forgive someone who has hurt or offended me, I know where to go in God's Word to be strengthened against the temptation to stay angry with that person. Satan constantly tries to deceive us and draw us into sin. We need to resist him immediately, as Jesus did when tempted in the wilderness, by saying "It is written…" (Luke 4:4, 8, 10) and speaking in faith what God's Word says.

In today's scripture, David said he had hidden God's Word in his heart so he would not sin against Him. When we regularly and diligently study God's Word, we hide it in our hearts, and it comes to the surface when we need it. One of the ministries of the Holy Spirit is to remind us of what we need to know when we need it (John 14:26), and He does this with God's Word when we battle temptation. Helping us to recall His Word is one of the ways God speaks to us.

Confession: *I hide God's Word in my heart, and the Holy Spirit reminds me of it.*

FINDING GOD'S WILL
FOR YOUR LIFE

*Paul, an apostle of Christ Jesus by the will of God, and Timothy
our brother.*

COLOSSIANS 1:1 NIV

Notice that Paul says he is an apostle "by the will of God." This
is important because, as Christians, we want to follow God's
will. People often ask, "How can I know if I am walking in
God's will for my life?" Here are two simple ways:

1. You will enjoy it. God's will for you will not cause you to
be miserable or excessively stressed. You may face challenges as
you pursue it, but if it is God's will for you, He will give you the
wisdom and grace to overcome any difficulty, and you will find
joy in doing it, and be passionate about it.

2. You will be equipped for it. Also, when we are in God's
will, we will be good at what we are doing. God gives us the
skills and abilities to fulfill His will for our lives. You may have
to work, study, or prepare in other ways to carry out His call,
but you'll have an aptitude for it and feel at ease in it.

Finding God's will for your life is not difficult: You simply
try things until you find what is comfortable for you. "Com-
fortable" doesn't necessarily mean easy. You will likely have to
work hard, but you will know in your heart that it is what you
are supposed to be doing, and it will bring you peace and joy.

Confession: *God has a unique purpose for me, and I trust Him to
guide me as I step out in faith.*

JOY RESTORED

May the God of your hope so fill you with all joy and peace in believing [through the experience of your faith] that by the power of the Holy Spirit you may abound and be overflowing (bubbling over) with hope.

ROMANS 15:13

If you have lost your joy and peace, I encourage you to take some time today to think about your thoughts and what you believe. Emotions are directly connected to thoughts. If our thoughts are negative, hopeless, and discouraging, we will feel negative, hopeless, and discouraged.

Your joy and peace can be immediately restored by changing your thinking to agree with God's Word. He wants us to abound (be overflowing) with hope. Hope is an expectation that something good is about to happen. God's Word teaches us to wait on Him (Psalm 130:5), and we are to wait expectantly.

If someone told you they had sent you a surprise package in the mail, how would you feel while you were waiting for it? You would be excited to see what it is. You would be watching for it to arrive, and your joy would be full. We should expect even more from God than anyone on earth can offer us because He has many wonderful surprises in store for us. Get your hopes up and expect them to be fulfilled.

Confession: *I am expecting something good to happen to me today.*

FRUITFULNESS IS BETTER THAN BUSY-NESS

I am the vine, you are the branches. He who abides in Me, and I in him, bears much fruit; for without Me you can do nothing.

JOHN 15:5 NKJV

Today people are very busy, but that doesn't mean they are busy doing what will bear good fruit for God (meaning to make a positive difference in the world and to bring honor to Him, or to be productive) in their life. God has not called us to be busy, but He has called us to be fruitful (John 15:4–5).

Today's scripture says that if we abide in Him, we will bear much fruit. *To abide* means to live, dwell, and remain in. Meditating on God's Word is part of the abiding lifestyle. We cannot have only a one-hour visit with Jesus on Sunday morning during a church service, not think of Him until the next Sunday, and expect to live a fruitful life. The abiding lifestyle means that we include Him in everything we do and acknowledge Him in all things. We talk to Him, think about Him, and think about His Word throughout each day.

God's Word rules. This means that when a decision needs to be made, we make the one that agrees with His Word. There are two words that can never go together in the life of a Christian: "No, Lord!" If He is our Lord, then our answer must always be yes.

Confession: *I abide in Christ and acknowledge Him in all I do.*

GOD UPHOLDS THE UNIVERSE

He is the radiance of the glory of God and the exact imprint of his nature, and he upholds the universe by the word of his power. After making purification for sins, he sat down at the right hand of the Majesty on high.

HEBREWS 1:3 ESV

When we ponder the universe and how marvelous it is, we may wonder what keeps the Earth spinning perfectly on its axis or how the sun, moon, and stars stay in the sky without falling. The world did not come into being because of a big bang that occurred billions of years ago, nor are humans evolved from primates. God created the world, and we are created by God in His image (Genesis 1:27).

Satan has perpetrated the theory of evolution because if we believe we are no more than animals, then we will continue to act like animals and feel that we have no real value or purpose. But if we know that God has created us in His image and that He has a plan for our lives, we will live with purpose and joy.

Jesus is the perfect image and imprint of God's nature. If you want to know what God is like, just look at and study Jesus. He keeps this world going correctly by the power of His Word. Since His Word has that much power, surely it can keep us maintained, upheld, and guided.

Put your trust in God. He alone is completely reliable. God loves you and desires to take care of you even as He cares for the rest of His creation, and He will if you let Him.

Confession: *I count on God to uphold the universe and to take care of me.*

MAINTAIN A GENTLE TONGUE

A gentle tongue [with its healing power] is a tree of life, but willful contrariness in it breaks down the spirit.

PROVERBS 15:4

Our words are some of our most important tools, and we need to manage them properly. The power of life and death is in the tongue (Proverbs 18:21 NIV). Our words reveal what is in our hearts, and what we think of another person will always be revealed eventually by what we say.

Words are free, but the way we use them may cost us. Blaise Pascal said, "Kind words do not cost much. Yet they accomplish much."[2] We should slow down and think before we speak—Proverbs 12:18 says, "There is one who speaks rashly like the thrusts of a sword, but the tongue of the wise brings healing" (NASB). And James 3:8 tells us that "no human being can tame the tongue. It is a restless evil, full of deadly poison" (NIV). Who then can help us? Jesus can.

There are two scriptures I pray frequently. The first is Psalm 141:3: "Set a guard, O Lord, before my mouth; keep watch at the door of my lips." The other is Psalm 19:14: "Let the words of my mouth and the meditation of my heart be acceptable in Your sight, O Lord, my [firm, impenetrable] Rock and my Redeemer." I know that I cannot control my tongue by merely trying to. I need God's help, and so do you.

Confession: I declare that I have a gentle tongue and that God puts a watch over my mouth so I will not sin against Him.

NO NEED TO BE AFRAID

For God did not give us a spirit of timidity (of cowardice, of craven and cringing and fawning fear), but [He has given us a spirit] of power and of love and of calm and well-balanced mind and discipline and self-control.

2 TIMOTHY 1:7

Being afraid of something can't stop it from happening, but placing your faith and trust in God can. Fear is not from God. So many people suffer from fear, especially in these days in which we are living.

Fear brings torment, and that is exactly what the devil wants. He wants to torment us. But you don't have to let him succeed if you remember that God has given you a spirit of power, love, and a calm and well-balanced mind. Fear is a liar, and most of what it threatens never happens. Even if something we fear does happen, God is with us, and He will deliver us and help us (2 Corinthians 1:10). I encourage you not to waste your days in fear. When fear knocks on your door, answer with faith.

Confession: *I will not fear, because God is with me.*

GOD'S GOOD PLAN FOR YOU

For I know the thoughts and plans that I have for you, says the Lord, thoughts and plans for welfare and peace and not for evil, to give you hope in your final outcome.

JEREMIAH 29:11

Perhaps you have been going through a difficult season and find yourself wondering what the future holds for you. Will it just be more of the same, or is something good coming soon? According to God's Word, He has a good future planned for you, a plan that will bring peace and welfare, not evil.

When trouble comes, one of the most comforting things we can do is believe that it won't last forever. I'm sure you can remember difficulties you have had in the past and realize that they eventually ended. You will also have victory over the problem you face today. You may have to be patient, and the path through this challenge may not be easy, but be assured that God is watching over you. Humble yourself under His mighty hand, and in due time He will exalt you and lift you up (1 Peter 5:6).

Confession: *I believe that God has a good plan for my future, and He will bring it to pass in His perfect timing.*

GOD'S GLORIOUS INHERITANCE

By having the eyes of your heart flooded with light, so that you can know and understand the hope to which He has called you, and how rich is His glorious inheritance in the saints (His set-apart ones).

EPHESIANS 1:18

God wants your heart to be filled with light, so you can surely know that good things are planned for you. He has a glorious inheritance stored up for you. God wants us to look at the future with a heart and mind full of hope (the expectation of good things). Doing this will keep you out of depression and despair, especially when life is difficult.

I don't know all the good things God has planned, but today's scripture says they are glorious, which means the most excellent that He has to offer. I think what we will experience in the future is so amazingly wonderful that we would not understand it, even if the Lord tried to explain it.

Life is often hard and unfair, but the difficulties we experience now will be nothing compared to the glory that is to come. Because this is true, we can live full of hope and trust in God, and we can rejoice, knowing that our future is secure.

Confession: *I wait with hope and enthusiasm for the glorious inheritance that is mine in Jesus Christ.*

YOU ARE SPECIAL

*I praise you because I am fearfully and wonderfully made; your
works are wonderful, I know that full well.*

PSALM 139:14 NIV

You are unique. No one else on the planet is exactly like you.
God picked your hair color, skin tone, height, bone structure,
and every other tiny thing about you. The devil wants us to
compare ourselves with other people and think we are flawed if
we are not like they are, but that is absolutely not true.

God delights in you. He loves it when you talk to Him. God
doesn't always like everything we do, but He always, always
loves us completely.

I encourage you to begin to think of yourself in a positive
way. Don't think in a proud and haughty way, but see yourself
through Jesus as your heavenly Father does. You are the apple
of God's eye (Psalm 17:8 NIV).

Confession: *I am special to God. He carefully created everything
about me, and I am free to be myself without comparing myself to
others.*

LIVE BY GOD'S LAW

Therefore know that the Lord your God, He is God, the faithful God who keeps covenant and mercy for a thousand generations with those who love Him and keep His commandments.

DEUTERONOMY 7:9 NKJV

Years ago, US Air Force captain Edward A. Murphy was frustrated with a technician who made a mistake. He noted that "If anything can be done wrong, this man will do it." Such thinking became known as Murphy's Law: "Whatever can go wrong will go wrong."[3] People have elaborated on this to say that nothing is as easy as it looks, everything takes longer than you expect, and things go wrong at the worst possible moment. Who could enjoy life if they lived according to Murphy's Law? They would always expect the worst, so they would probably get it.

The world may expect Murphy's Law to operate in their lives, but we need to embrace God's law instead, also called "commandments" or "statutes," which completely disagrees with Murphy's Law: "Nothing is as difficult as it appears" (see Philippians 4:13); "Everything is more rewarding than it seems" (see Colossians 3:23–24); and "If anything good can happen to anybody, it will happen to me" (see Jeremiah 29:11).

Negative thinking produces a negative life. How much more could you enjoy your life if your thoughts agreed with God's law, not Murphy's? God wants you to enjoy life thoroughly and live it to the fullest (John 10:10). I challenge you to live by God's law and consistently fill your mind with positive thoughts.

Confession: *I choose to live by God's law and to think positively, not negatively.*

ENJOYING GOD

Rejoice in the Lord always. I will say it again: Rejoice!

PHILIPPIANS 4:4 NIV

I love the idea that "Man's chief end is to glorify God, and to enjoy him for ever."[4]

Do you know that we can rejoice in the Lord and enjoy Him? Perhaps you tend to focus more on duty rather than on delight in your relationship with God, or performance rather than pleasure. The idea of enjoying God may seem foreign to us because it is something we have not been taught. God is life, and the Bible tells us in multiple places that He wants us to enjoy life. Jesus said that He came to earth so that we might have and enjoy our lives (John 10:10).

You were created for someone, not just for something. You are living on earth because God wants you to be alive, and He has a plan for your life. God not only loves you; He likes you. He likes every little quirk about you—your funny-looking toes, your very curly or stick-straight hair, and all the other things you may not like about yourself. The more we learn to enjoy God, the more we will enjoy ourselves, and that releases us to enjoy life.

Confession: *I enjoy God, myself, and my life.*

NO REGRETS

Do not [earnestly] remember the former things; neither consider the things of old. Behold, I am doing a new thing! Now it springs forth; do you not perceive and know it and will you not give heed to it? I will even make a way in the wilderness and rivers in the desert.

ISAIAH 43:18–19

We have all made mistakes, but God doesn't want us to live in regret, always thinking about the things we should not have done. When we repent of wrongdoing, God not only forgives us, but He forgets what we did (Jeremiah 31:34).

Paul said one of the most important things he wanted to do was to forget what was behind him (Philippians 3:13). I can just imagine how difficult that may have been for him at times, because before he met Jesus, he persecuted Christians, put them in prison, and delighted in their being sentenced to death. Once he encountered Jesus on the road to Damascus (Acts 9), his life changed completely.

God can take the most awful things we have done and work them for our good (Romans 8:28). If nothing else, we learn not to do what we did again, and we gain experience that can benefit others. Living in regret will prevent you from going forward, so it is time to turn your back on the past and move forward into the good plan God has for you.

Confession: *I do not live with regrets over the past, but I look ahead to the good things God has planned for me in the future.*

THERE IS NOTHING GOD CANNOT DO

But Jesus looked at them and said, With men this is impossible, but all things are possible with God.

MATTHEW 19:26

Hopelessness is a terrible feeling. But with God, we always have hope, no matter how difficult our situation is. God can heal a body, restore a relationship, soften a hard heart, restore finances, and do anything else that needs to be done.

Sometimes the only thing that stands between us and the miracle we need is believing. The Lord wants us to believe He can do all things. As long as we keep praying and believing, we will see many things come to pass—things that we previously thought were impossible. What is impossible for us or other human beings is possible with God (Matthew 19:26).

Jesus said that in the world there would be tribulation, and then said to cheer up, for He has overcome the world (John 16:33). I encourage you to keep your hopes up and always believe for things that seem impossible.

Confession: *I believe that God can do anything, because nothing is impossible with Him.*

STAYING ENCOURAGED WHILE YOU WAIT

For you know how, as a father [dealing with] his children, we used to exhort each of you personally, stimulating and encouraging and charging you to live lives worthy of God, Who calls you into His own kingdom and the glorious blessedness [into which true believers will enter after Christ's return].

1 THESSALONIANS 2:11–12

Just as you and I need encouragement, the early Christians needed to be encouraged as they waited for the return of the Lord. The Amplified Bible, Classic Edition, indicates that Paul's exhortations were "stimulating" to the Christians as he encouraged them. To be stimulated means to have levels of activity increased, or to have an increased interest. It is like a tonic for our weary souls.

I want to encourage you today by reminding you that Jesus is coming again. We should be spending the time we have on earth preparing ourselves and others to meet Him. I so look forward to the day when I will see Him face-to-face and know Him even as He knows me.

When you feel weary, remember that you are not alone. While you encourage others, ask God to send people to encourage and stimulate you.

Always remember that you can do whatever you need to do through Christ, who is your strength (Philippians 4:13).

Confession: When I am weary and long for the Lord's return, I go to Him to be refreshed.

STRENGTHENED IN THE MIDST OF EVIL

And that we may be delivered from perverse (improper, unrighteous) and wicked (actively malicious) men, for not everybody has faith and is held by it. Yet the Lord is faithful, and He will strengthen [you] and set you on a firm foundation and guard you from the evil [one].

2 THESSALONIANS 3:2-3

I grow weary of all the evil in the world today, and I would imagine that at times you do too. Yet you and I are living during this season of world history for a purpose. In order to fulfill that purpose, we must stay strong. Paul reminds us that the Lord is faithful, and He will strengthen us.

God will set us on a firm foundation—one that is not shaken, no matter how much the world around us shakes. Regardless of how much the world changes, God is always the same (Malachi 3:6). We can totally depend on Him.

I pray that God will deliver and protect you from evil and perverse people, and that He will send across their path those who may lead them to Christ. Always remember that while we wait, God will protect us from the evil one. The enemy may win an occasional battle, but he will not win the war.

Confession: *I trust God to protect me from evil and use me to help those who are living in the dark to see the light of the glorious gospel of Jesus Christ.*

YOU HAVE A NEW HEART

A new heart will I give you and a new spirit will I put within you, and I will take away the stony heart out of your flesh and give you a heart of flesh.

EZEKIEL 36:26

Many people have a hard heart and are not even aware of it. I had one as a result of being abused during my childhood and then during my first marriage. When people are hurt often enough, they may form a hardness around their heart so they will no longer feel pain when others mistreat them. Some signs of a hard heart include a lack of compassion for others, being rude or suspicious, struggling to hear from God or obey Him, and difficulty in believing His Word.

When we receive Christ as our Savior, He gives us a new heart, and we need to learn how to behave differently than we behaved before we invited Him into our lives. I found that the more I studied God's Word—especially what it says about His love—the more my hard heart melted. As God healed my broken heart, I became more sensitive to the pain of others and had a desire to help them when they were hurting.

A little bitterness or resentment can easily sneak into our heart, and we may feel justified in having it, but it is very dangerous. As soon as you sense that something is ungodly in your heart attitude, deal with it right away. Realize that God has given you a new heart, and ask Him to help you learn how to operate out of it. A good prayer to pray is based on Psalm 51:10: "Create in me a clean heart, O God; and renew a right spirit within me" (KJV).

Confession: *I don't allow bitterness or resentment in my heart, because I deal quickly with ungodly attitudes.*

CULTIVATING THE FRUIT OF THE SPIRIT

But the fruit of the [Holy] Spirit [the work which His presence within accomplishes] is love, joy (gladness), peace, patience (an even temper, forbearance), kindness, goodness (benevolence), faithfulness, gentleness (meekness, humility), self-control (self-restraint, continence). Against such things there is no law [that can bring a charge].

GALATIANS 5:22–23

If Jesus Christ is your Lord and Savior, His Holy Spirit lives in you and gives you the ability to go through every situation with love, joy, peace, patience, kindness, goodness, faithfulness, gentleness (meaning humility), and self-control—the fruit of the Holy Spirit.

The fruit of the Spirit does not simply appear in your life when you become a Christian. It starts with a tiny seed that is planted when you give your life to Christ, and it develops over time as you work with the Holy Spirit to learn how to live as a Christian. The more you cultivate the fruit of the Spirit, the stronger and more mature it becomes.

The first word in the list of fruit is *love*, and the last word is *self-control*. I look at love and self-control as bookends that hold all the other fruit in place. Each fruit comes from love and is a form of love but is also held in place by self-control. If you concentrate on developing the fruit of love, you will also demonstrate joy, peace, patience, kindness, goodness, faithfulness, and gentleness. At times, you may not feel like expressing these qualities, but self-control will enable you to show them.

Confession: *I express love and demonstrate self-control.*

GUILT-FREE LIVING

Then I acknowledged my sin to you and did not cover up my iniquity. I said, "I will confess my transgressions to the Lord." And you forgave the guilt of my sin.

PSALM 32:5 NIV

Once we have repented for sin, we should not feel condemned or guilty. Jesus bore our sins *and* the guilt attached to them. Guilt is a heavy burden that I carried for years, even though I had asked for forgiveness and believed God had given it to me.

God finally helped me to understand that my guilty feelings were my way of trying to pay for what I had done wrong. We don't have to pay because Jesus paid our debt in full and cleansed us from all sin (1 John 1:7 ESV).

I encourage you today to let go of any burden of guilt you may be carrying. If you have admitted your sin, repented, and asked for forgiveness, that's all you need to do. I believe that guilt will draw us into sin rather than strengthening us against it. Guilt weakens us spiritually and makes us more vulnerable to sin. It can also cause illness and make us difficult to get along with. Jesus died to set us free from sin and all the guilt attached to it. Be encouraged today in knowing that Jesus wants you to be free and enjoy your life.

Confession: *Once I am forgiven for sin, I refuse to carry a burden of guilt, because it is not God's will for me to do so.*

YOU'RE STRONGER THAN YOU THINK YOU ARE

Yet amid all these things we are more than conquerors and gain a surpassing victory through Him Who loved us.

ROMANS 8:37

In the world, we encounter tribulation and trouble (John 16:33), but our faith in God and reliance on Him assures that He is always with us, and we have no need to be afraid. We are "more than conquerors," and I believe this means we have the assurance of victory in every battle before it even begins.

I don't know right now what may come up in my life next week, but I am not afraid, because I know that even though I may have to go through something I'd rather avoid, it will end well and the victory will be mine. You can have this same assurance.

God loves you, and as long as your trust is in Him, you have no need to fear evil. You are more than a conqueror.

Confession: *I am more than a conqueror through Christ, who loves me, and I will not be afraid of trouble.*

GOD ALWAYS FINISHES WHAT HE STARTS

And I am convinced and sure of this very thing, that He Who began a good work in you will continue until the day of Jesus Christ [right up to the time of His return], developing [that good work] and perfecting and bringing it to full completion in you.

PHILIPPIANS 1:6

God chooses us according to His foreknowledge, and He begins a good work in us. Most of us struggle at times and feel we are not making any progress. We may even feel we are going backward in our spiritual growth. Today's scripture is a great one to go to when you feel this way because He who began a good work in you, meaning God, will bring it to completion. He doesn't tell us how long it will take, but He never fails to finish what He started.

Part of how long the good work takes depends on how responsive we are to the teaching and correction of the Holy Spirit. Correction is not a bad thing; it is really just direction about how to do the right thing. If we receive it graciously and thankfully, we can grow much faster than if we are stubborn and rebellious. God's way is always the best way. Submit to it quickly, and your walk with Him will be much easier.

Confession: *God has begun a good work in me, and He will complete it.*

DECLARE SOMETHING GOOD

In the morning, Lord, you hear my voice; in the morning I lay my requests before you and wait expectantly.

PSALM 5:3 NIV

I don't feel enthusiastic when I first wake up, and perhaps you don't, either. I have to stir myself up to intentionally have an upbeat, positive attitude toward the day. As believers, we don't have to live by our feelings. With God's help, we make choices we know will bring good results, and we invite our feelings to go along if they want to. Most days my feelings get on board and go along with me, but there are days when they don't. Those are testing days, and when we're tested, we have an opportunity to grow spiritually and develop godly character.

Most days, before getting out of bed, I declare that something good is going to happen *to* me and that something good will happen *through* me that day. I pray for and expect the day to be blessed. I pray for energy, enthusiasm, zeal, and passion—and then I get up.

Don't start your day feeling guilty about yesterday's mistakes and failures. Receive God's mercy and forgiveness for the past and expect good things to happen to you and through you today. If you feel bad about yourself, it will drain your energy, and that won't help you make today count.

It is important that you start your day right, and making sure you don't have a bad attitude toward yourself is part of doing that. Believe that God loves you, that you are important to His plan, and that He will show His goodness to you and through you today.

Confession: *I declare that something good is going to happen to me and through me today.*

THIS TOO SHALL PASS

What is impossible with men is possible with God.

LUKE 18:27

Do you have a miserable past? Are your current circumstances negative and depressing? Are you facing situations that are so bad it seems you have no real reason to hope? I boldly say to you that *your future is not determined by your past or your present.*

Believe that all things are possible with God and have a positive expectation regarding the future. God made everything we see out of nothing (Hebrews 11:3). Therefore, He can take difficult circumstances and turn them around for good. Give your problems to Him. Cast all your care on Him and release the burden of worry (1 Peter 5:7). All God needs to work is your faith. Put your faith in Him and prepare to be blessed.

Confession: I believe all things are possible with God. I put my faith in Him, and I am excited to watch Him work in my circumstances and turn them around for good.

HOW TO GROW IN FAITH

When Jesus heard this, he was amazed and said to those following him, "Truly I tell you, I have not found anyone in Israel with such great faith."

MATTHEW 8:10 NIV

When Jesus entered Capernaum, a centurion (Roman soldier) approached Him and said his servant was lying at home paralyzed and suffering terribly. Jesus said He would go and heal him, but the centurion said, "Lord, I am not worthy to have you come under my roof, but only say the word, and my servant will be healed" (Matthew 8:8 ESV). Jesus replied that He had not seen such great faith from anyone in Israel.

The Bible mentions people with "no faith," with "little faith," and with "great faith." How can we have great faith? If you have no faith, try putting even a little faith in Jesus and watch how He works in your life. If you have little faith, it can grow into great faith as you exercise it. The more you use your faith, trusting God to do things you cannot do, the more you will see Him work. Each time you do, it will be easier to trust Him for more and more.

I began my walk with God with little faith and great fear, but after more than forty-five years of studying His Word and having experience with Him and His faithfulness, I have great faith that all things truly are possible with God. Be encouraged that God has big plans for you. All you need to do is trust Him.

Confession: *I will invest what faith I have in God and watch Him make it grow into great faith. I believe God can do anything and that He has wonderful plans for me.*

BE STILL AND KNOW THAT HE IS GOD

He says, "Be still, and know that I am God; I will be exalted among the nations, I will be exalted in the earth."

PSALM 46:10 NIV

It is often difficult to be still because our flesh is full of energy and wants to do something. It wants to solve its own problems and get the credit for doing so. I have done this many times, and it simply isn't effective. I only end up frustrated and confused about why I have tried so hard and nothing I've done has worked. Does this sound familiar? God doesn't tell us to try to figure things out ourselves; He tells us to *believe,* to put our trust in Him and ask Him to work in our lives.

James 4:1–2 teaches us that we become frustrated because we try to do things ourselves. But actually, we have not because we ask not. Ask God for what you want and need, and He will give it to you on His schedule, or He may even give you something better. He doesn't always work on our timetable, but His timing is always perfect. Be patient (which means to wait with a good attitude), and while you wait, keep saying, "God is working in my life."

While you are waiting for your breakthrough, be a blessing to other people. By doing that, you will be sowing seed for the harvest you are expecting.

Confession: God is working in my life, and I will see amazing things. I will wait on Him because I know He is faithful.

MEDITATE ON GOOD THINGS

Make me understand the way of Your precepts; so shall I meditate on and talk of Your wondrous works.

PSALM 119:27

Instead of meditating on your problems, meditate on God's goodness and on the victories He has given you in the past. If you know how to worry, you know how to meditate. *To meditate* simply means to roll something over and over in your mind. Proverbs 23:7 teaches us that we become what we think in our hearts. I like to say, "Where the mind goes, the man follows." In practical terms, this means that if I think about ice cream long enough, I will get some and eat it.

Our thoughts are powerful, and they precede our words, emotions, and actions. If we want to change our behavior, we must first change our thoughts. Romans 12:2 teaches us that our minds must be renewed, and 2 Corinthians 10:5 teaches us to "take captive every thought to make it obedient to Christ" (NIV). If we want to see something good happen in our lives, we cannot continually think about the bad things that have happened or that are going on right now.

We can reject wrong thoughts and replace them with "God thoughts." Ask the Holy Spirit to convict you each time you are thinking something that is not pleasing to Him, and keep at it until you begin to see a change.

Confession: *My mind is continually being renewed by God's Word, and I think thoughts that add power and blessing to my life.*

MAINTAIN A GOOD ATTITUDE

Finally, brothers and sisters, whatever is true, whatever is noble, whatever is right, whatever is pure, whatever is lovely, whatever is admirable—if anything is excellent or praiseworthy—think about such things.

PHILIPPIANS 4:8 NIV

When negative things happen to you, determine to keep a positive attitude in the midst of them. If you make this decision and meditate on it during life's good times, then when difficulty arises, you'll be prepared to maintain a good attitude. For example, if an unexpected bill presents itself, make up your mind that you won't complain about needing to tighten your belt financially for a few months to make up for it. Instead, decide to view the challenge as an adventure and find creative ways to cut costs and to enjoy life without spending money.

I recently heard about John, who was struggling financially but was also determined to keep a good, positive, and thankful attitude. John worked in a restaurant, and one day a customer had a heart attack while eating there. John had some medical training and administered CPR to keep the man breathing and his heart beating until the paramedics arrived. The man whose life was saved happened to be very wealthy, and he gave John five thousand dollars as a way of saying thank you for saving his life. The good attitude John maintained through his financial struggle opened the door for God to work miraculously in his life.

No matter what you may be facing today, choose to have a positive attitude—and watch what God can do.

Confession: *I am determined to stay positive when negative situations arise.*

GOD LEADS US
IN RIGHTEOUSNESS

He leads me in the paths of righteousness [uprightness and right standing with Him—not for my earning it, but] for His name's sake.

PSALM 23:3

God teaches us the right way to live and gently guides us into a life of righteousness. When we are born again we are made right with God through Christ (2 Corinthians 5:21), but this gift of righteousness needs to be worked into our daily lives. We need to learn to obey God and live as He wants us to live, and we have the Holy Spirit to help us do that.

We don't have to earn righteousness; it is a work that God does for His name's sake and an act of His grace. Our part is to learn and follow the leading and guidance of the Holy Spirit day by day and let God change us into the image of Jesus Christ. We must learn to walk in the Spirit, not in the flesh, as we may be accustomed to doing.

This is a process that takes time and diligent commitment, but even while we are changing, God still views us as righteous through our faith in Jesus. You can be encouraged today that you don't have to struggle to do what is right; you only need to spend time with God and His Word, and trust that He is changing you from glory to glory (2 Corinthians 3:18).

Confession: *I don't have to earn God's righteousness. All I need to do is walk in the righteousness that has already been given to me through faith in Christ.*

YOU CAN DO HARD THINGS
WITH GOD'S HELP

Ah, Lord God! Behold, You have made the heavens and the earth by Your great power and outstretched arm. There is nothing too hard for You.

JEREMIAH 32:17 NKJV

Has God ever asked you to do something you felt you were totally incapable of doing or unqualified to do—or something you felt would be too hard? Let me assure you that if God asks you to do something, you can count on Him to give you the strength to do it. As today's scripture reminds us, nothing is too difficult for Him. We are in Him, through Christ, and He empowers us to do everything we need to do—even things that are hard.

Over the years, I have watched God enable me to do things I didn't know how to do, didn't feel qualified to do, and felt incapable of doing. But each time He has given me strength, ability, and power to do them. Often, I didn't feel any ability, even when I stepped out to do what He asked of me; but then the power came. God didn't part the Jordan River until the priests carrying the Ark of the Covenant put their feet in it (Joshua 3:13). And, in obedience to God, Moses had to hold out his staff before God parted the Red Sea (Exodus 14:16).

We don't always *feel* capable of doing what God asks us to do, but when we step out to do it, He will always be waiting to give us what we need.

Confession: *I can do hard things when necessary because God helps me and gives me strength.*

WAIT ON GOD

The Lord is good to those who wait for him, to the soul who seeks him. It is good that one should wait quietly for the salvation of the Lord.

LAMENTATIONS 3:25–26 ESV

Are you waiting for God to do something in your life? I'm sure you have learned this, but I want to remind you that God rarely moves according to our schedule. What we think of as slowness isn't slow to God (2 Peter 3:9). He is much more interested in excellence than in speed. He is in the process of fashioning us into people who represent Him in excellent ways. He wants people who are always available to Him and ready to do as He asks. Since this is the case, He does not always move quickly to change us. A masterpiece is never created in a hurry.

Patience is a prerequisite of spiritual maturity. We need to slow down, enjoy our journey through life, and embrace the process God takes us through as He makes us who He wants us to be, even though it often takes longer than we would like.

One reason we find waiting so difficult is that we tend to focus on what we want more than on what God wants. But we can choose instead to focus on God and use our waiting periods to grow in Him. God is good, and He withholds nothing good from us unless He sees we are not ready for it or that it would not be best for us. As you wait for Him to move in your life, keep thanking and praising Him for using this time to make you who He wants you to be and to equip you to represent Him with excellence.

Confession: *I wait patiently on God, knowing He is preparing me to represent Him in an excellent way.*

THE POWER OF ENCOURAGEMENT

Now may our Lord Jesus Christ Himself and God our Father, Who loved us and gave us everlasting consolation and encouragement and well-founded hope through [His] grace (unmerited favor), comfort and encourage your hearts and strengthen them [make them steadfast and keep them unswerving] in every good work and word.

2 THESSALONIANS 2:16–17

Who do you look to for encouragement? Your friends or family? Your coworkers or neighbors? Or God?

Over the years, I wasted a lot of time getting angry with Dave because he didn't encourage me when I thought he should have. But I finally learned to go to God first. He will either encourage me Himself or work through another person to give me the encouragement I need.

Encouragement is powerful because it gives us the courage to press on when we become weary or discouraged. Always give away what you hope to receive. Make it a habit to encourage someone each day. This will not only make them feel better, but it will make you feel better too.

God loves you. He has a good plan for your life, and He will enable you to do anything you need to do.

Confession: *I will encourage someone each day, and God will always encourage me while helping me to do anything I need to do.*

BE CONTENT, PART 1

Not that I am implying that I was in any personal want, for I have learned how to be content (satisfied to the point where I am not disturbed or disquieted) in whatever state I am.

PHILIPPIANS 4:11

When we feel discontented, we also feel discouraged. Paul writes in today's scripture that he learned how to be content. One thing that helps us be content is to think about all we have, not what we want but don't have.

God will give you what is right for you at the right time. When we are not content, all we do is delay being able to receive our desires. I believe discontentment also dishonors God. We say we believe He is in charge of our lives. If this is true, being discontent says we don't like the way He is taking care of us.

God's timing is always perfect, but we often have to wait longer than we would like for some of His blessings. As humans, we are impatient, but God is never in a hurry. He would rather things be done right than quickly. Be encouraged that God is working in your life, even if you don't feel it or see it. When the time is right, *suddenly* you will have a breakthrough. Who knows? It could happen today!

Confession: *God is working in my life, and I am content to wait on Him.*

BE CONTENT, PART 2

That's why I take pleasure in my weaknesses, and in the insults, hardships, persecutions, and troubles that I suffer for Christ. For when I am weak, then I am strong.

2 CORINTHIANS 12:10 NLT

Just as the joy of the Lord is your strength (Nehemiah 8:10), contentment is also strength. A content and satisfied person cannot be easily tempted by the devil. Paul writes of being content with his weaknesses and troubles because he was assured that God would strengthen him in the places where he was weak. This is a powerful attitude that is available to us all.

Trust that God will always give you His strength to fill up your weaknesses, no matter what happens in your life. Believing He will compensate for our weaknesses allows us to live without fear and to enjoy the various seasons of our lives.

Being content doesn't mean that we never want change, but that we are satisfied to the point where we are not disturbed or disquieted. It means we can enjoy what we do have while we wait for what we want.

Confession: I am content and strong in the Lord. No matter what happens, I believe God will give me His strength to fill up my weaknesses.

BEING FULLY SATISFIED

As for me, I will continue beholding Your face in righteousness (rightness, justice, and right standing with You); I shall be fully satisfied, when I awake [to find myself] beholding Your form [and having sweet communion with You].

PSALM 17:15

When we don't feel satisfied, we often seek wrong things to satisfy us and then feel frustrated when they don't. Things cannot satisfy us for long. We may get something we want and think we have finally found what will fill the emptiness in our soul— only to find after a while that we feel just as empty as ever. Only Jesus can satisfy completely. I love our verse for today. I think it is beautiful and comforting. When Jesus is the first thing on our mind after we wake up, it usually indicates that we have reached a place of spiritual maturity that helps us be content in all situations.

Seek first the kingdom of God and His righteousness and all other things will be added to you (Matthew 6:33). If you are discouraged with your life right now, ask yourself what you have been seeking. Keeping God first is the wisest thing we can do. He is a jealous God and will not allow us to be satisfied as long as anything else occupies the place that belongs to Him. Don't seek God for His presents (what He can do for you); seek Him for His presence.

Confession: *I seek God first before anything else because only He can fully satisfy.*

A HUMBLE ATTITUDE

Let this same attitude and purpose and [humble] mind be in you which was in Christ Jesus: [Let Him be your example in humility].
PHILIPPIANS 2:5

Humble people are happy people. They are not in competition with anyone else, they are not jealous of what others have, and they are satisfied to wait for God to do what He knows is best in their lives.

We all want things, but the humble person waits on God instead of trying to make things happen themselves. Humble yourself under the mighty hand of God, and in due time He will exalt you (1 Peter 5:6). Humble people get the help they need from God, but He resists the proud (James 4:6). God wants us to lean on Him and trust His timing in our lives.

Jesus is to be our example in humility. He never tried to defend Himself or prove He was right when people accused Him falsely. He trusted His Father with His reputation. Don't worry so much about what people think of you. Humble yourself and let God exalt you at the right time.

Confession: *I humble myself, and God exalts me at the right time. I wait on Him, because His timing is always perfect.*

TOUGH TIMES DON'T LAST FOREVER

He changes the times and the seasons; He removes kings and sets up kings. He gives wisdom to the wise and knowledge to those who have understanding!

DANIEL 2:21

Seasons change. This is true in the natural world, and it is true in the seasons of our lives. Difficult times do not last forever. We may have "off" days, tough weeks, bad months, or even a year with more than its share of troubles, but every negative experience does come to an end.

Some of the trying situations we find ourselves in seem to go on far too long. When this happens, we are usually tempted to complain or become discouraged. Instead, we need to promptly adjust our attitude and ask God to teach us something valuable as we press through the situation at hand. According to James 1:2–3, God uses trials and pressure to produce good results in our lives. He always wants to bless us. Sometimes His blessings come through unexpected circumstances we may view as negative, but if we will keep positive attitudes in the midst of those situations, we will experience the positive results God wants to give us.

If you are going through a difficult time right now, let me remind you that this probably isn't the first challenge you've ever faced. You survived the last one (and probably learned some valuable lessons through it), and you will survive this one, too. Your trials are temporary; they won't last forever. Better days are on their way. Just keep your attitude "up" instead of "down," and remember that this is just a season and it will pass.

Confession: *I keep a positive attitude when I go through negative experiences.*

GOD'S LOVE BRINGS COMFORT

This is how God showed his love among us: He sent his one and only Son into the world that we might live through him. This is love: not that we loved God, but that he loved us and sent his Son as an atoning sacrifice for our sins. Dear friends, since God so loved us, we also ought to love one another.

1 JOHN 4:9–11 NIV

Anytime we need to be encouraged or comforted, it is helpful to remember how much God loves us. Everyone in the world wants to be loved, and God loves us unconditionally and at all times. He loved us when we were still in sin (Romans 5:8). We cannot earn or deserve His love; we can only thankfully receive it as a gift. Take some time right now and roll the thought that God loves you over and over in your mind.

God's perfect love casts out fear (1 John 4:18). If we know that God loves us, we can live without fear because we believe He will always take care of us. If you have children, wouldn't you always help them if they were in trouble? Yes, you would help them, and God feels the same way about us. Are you facing a discouraging problem in your life right now? If so, then meditate on how much God loves you. I believe this will cheer you up and comfort you.

Confession: *I believe that God loves me with a perfect love and that He will always help me, even if I don't deserve it.*

FREEDOM FROM WORRY

Therefore humble yourselves [demote, lower yourselves in your own estimation] under the mighty hand of God, that in due time He may exalt you, casting the whole of your care [all your anxieties, all your worries, all your concerns, once and for all] on Him, for He cares for you affectionately and cares about you watchfully.

1 PETER 5:6–7

We can worry if we want to, but it does no good. In fact, it does a lot of harm. It makes us unhappy and causes stress, which can lead to sickness. It distracts us and makes us difficult to get along with. But if we will cast our care on the Lord, He will take care of us.

Worry is work. It is our way of trying to figure out how to solve our problems. But it doesn't help. It is interesting to me that today's Scripture verses say that there is a connection between humility and not worrying. Casting our care on God is a way of humbling ourselves. We cannot solve our own problems. God wants us to lean on Him and trust Him to give us the answers we need. However, there is something we can do to replace worry—and that is to pray. One sincere prayer can accomplish more than a year of worry.

Confession: *I will not worry, but instead I humble myself under God's mighty hand, cast all my care on Him, and trust Him to take care of me.*

YOU ONLY HAVE ONE LIFE

Let Your hand become my help, for I have chosen Your precepts.
PSALM 119:173 NKJV

As you start your day today, remember that many people live their lives without doing much they intend to do because they get busy doing things that don't accomplish what is truly important to them. "I'm busy" has become the standard excuse for everything we should have done but didn't do. If you see people you once heard from regularly but don't return your calls anymore, they will probably say, "I'm sorry I haven't called you back. I've just been so busy."

What if God never answered us and gave the excuse of being too busy?

I truly wonder how many people, at the end of their lives, feel they lived the life they were meant to live. How many have nothing but regret about what they did or didn't do during their time on earth? You only have one life, and if it isn't going as you want it to, now is the time to make changes.

When we live unproductive lives, we should take responsibility for them. God gives us free will. This means we have the ability to make choices in every area of life. If we don't follow the Holy Spirit's leading in our choices, we will end up with regrets. Today's scripture is a prayer for God to help us when we choose to live according to His will.

God has a will and purpose for you. Use your free will to choose His will to enjoy the best life possible.

Confession: *I ask the Holy Spirit to help me make good choices about how I spend each day, and I follow His lead.*

TODAY IS THE DAY TO DO WHAT YOU NEED TO DO

He who observes the wind [and waits for all conditions to be favorable] will not sow, and he who regards the clouds will not reap.

ECCLESIASTES 11:4

Today's scripture reminds us to be diligent to do the things we need to do. Most of us have a lot to do. The desire to accomplish all we need to do is noble, yet procrastination tempts us and it is very deceptive. When we procrastinate, we never say to ourselves, "I am not going to do this thing I need to do!" We merely tell ourselves we will do it later. But later often becomes later and later, until the task never gets done. It's natural to want to put off doing less enjoyable things in favor of doing the things we do enjoy, but this is not a habit of a successful person. Successful people stay focused and finish their tasks.

We all procrastinate to some degree, and this indicates a struggle with discipline and self-control. To do what we need to do at the time we need to do it requires discipline, and Hebrews 12:11 says, "No discipline seems pleasant at the time, but painful. Later on, however, it produces a harvest of righteousness and peace for those who have been trained by it" (NIV). We need to focus on the fact that discipline brings a harvest rather than on the fact that it seems unpleasant.

People may think they are buying time today by procrastinating, but putting things off is like using a credit card—it's fun until you get the bill. Procrastinators will ultimately have to deal with the problems created by not doing things in a timely manner.

Confession: *I do what I need to do in a timely manner, and I do not procrastinate.*

THIS WORLD IS NOT OUR HOME

In My Father's house there are many dwelling places (homes). If it were not so, I would have told you; for I am going away to prepare a place for you.

JOHN 14:2

It is easy to get so caught up in the realities of daily living that we forget the most important reality of all: This world is not our home. First Peter 2:11 states that we are "aliens and strangers and exiles [in this world]." Though we have temporary earthly citizenship, our true home is in heaven, where Jesus has prepared a place for us.

People in the early church believed that Jesus would return soon. This was one reason they wanted to make sure they used their time for what was truly important and had lasting value. The reminder that Jesus was coming soon also helped them make good choices regarding their behavior. For example, Paul writes, "Let all men know and perceive and recognize your unselfishness (your considerateness, your forbearing spirit). The Lord is near [He is coming soon]" (Philippians 4:5). I think we all know that if we believed Jesus would return one week from today, we would make lots of changes in our lives. Why not live as if He might come next week, because according to Matthew 24:36, no one knows the day or the hour of Christ's return.

Our present life is not the final chapter; it is merely the opening one. We are simply preparing for the wonderful life to come. Enjoy this life on earth, but be sure you are ready for the next one, which is eternal.

Confession: *I live as though Jesus may return at any minute, knowing that this world is not my home.*

NOT GUILTY

*But He was wounded for our transgressions, He was crushed
for our wickedness [our sin, our injustice, our wrongdoing]; the
punishment [required] for our well-being fell on Him, and by His
stripes (wounds) we are healed . . . The Lord has caused the wick-
edness of us all . . . to fall on Him [instead of us].*

ISAIAH 53:5–6 AMP

Until I was in my fifties, I suffered from a continual sense of
guilt. I even felt guilty about feeling guilty, because I knew it
wasn't what God wanted for me. I didn't feel right if I didn't
feel wrong! My guilt started when I was very young and my
father started abusing me sexually and warning me not to tell
anyone. I assumed it had to be wrong if I couldn't tell anyone,
and this started a tormenting cycle of guilt in my mind.

When people feel guilty, they can't really enjoy anything.
God wants us to enjoy our lives, but we can't do this if we don't
know how to enjoy ourselves and if we continually find fault
with ourselves. God has provided total forgiveness and guilt-
free living in Jesus. Our debts have been paid. Our sin and
the guilt that comes with it have been removed. The devil uses
guilt to deceive us and prevent us from receiving the fullness of
God's love.

God helped me break free from the torment of guilt by teach-
ing me what His Word says about it and helping me believe His
Word more than I believed how I felt. Although complete free-
dom took some years, I made steady progress, and so will you if
you believe God's Word more than you believe guilty feelings.

Confession: *I agree with God and declare myself "not guilty."*

DON'T WORRY; STAY PEACEFUL

And [Jesus] said to His disciples, Therefore I tell you, do not be anxious and troubled [with cares] about your life, as to what you will [have to] eat; or about your body, as to what you will [have to] wear.

LUKE 12:22

Jesus has given us His peace (John 14:27), so in reality we have peace, but to experience it, we have to stop allowing ourselves to get upset. How do we do that? One thing that helps me is to talk to myself. My conversation might sound something like this: "Joyce, being upset and worried will not do you any good. It won't solve anything, so why waste your time doing it? Just calm yourself down and trust God to solve this situation." I might have to do this again and again if the worry is persistent in coming back. But it works for me.

Of course, we should replace our worrying with praying. Prayer releases God's power into any situation, and if we truly believe in the power of prayer, it removes our burdens from us and puts them in God's hands. Learn to enjoy a life of peace, which is only possible when we learn not to worry.

Confession: *I have peace inside of me, and when worry tries to steal it, I resist and keep myself calm. God has all my answers, and He will help me because He loves me.*

WHAT TO DO WHILE YOU WAIT ON GOD

Wait on the Lord: be of good courage, and he shall strengthen thine heart: wait, I say, on the Lord.

PSALM 27:14 KJV

It is difficult for us to do nothing when we are waiting on God to either deal with our problems or show us what to do about them. When we must wait for some reason, we want to be doing something. Are you waiting on God to do something in your life right now? Here are some things you can do while you wait:

- Pray.
- Keep a good confession. Speak God's Word and let your conversation agree with your prayer.
- Stay positive. Express your thankfulness for everything God does for you, and do not complain.
- Be patient. Continue being kind to others even when you are hurting.
- Don't be jealous, envious, or resentful of people who are not having problems.
- While you are hurting, keep your commitments, if at all possible.
- Trust God and declare your trust in Him.

While you're waiting, also remember the times you have needed God to intervene in your circumstances, and He did. God is faithful, and as you wait on Him, you will not be disappointed.

Confession: *I wait on God to solve my problems, and He will not disappoint me.*

BE GENEROUS

And God is able to bless you abundantly, so that in all things at all times, having all that you need, you will abound in every good work.

2 CORINTHIANS 9:8 NIV

God wants His people to be extremely blessed so we may always have what we need to help others and give to good works. God doesn't bless us so we can be selfish and simply gather more and more goods for ourselves, or to see how big our bank account can get.

It is wise to save money for the future, and it is also good to spend some of your money on yourself. But giving to others and being a generous person is God's desire for each of us. Dave has said for years concerning finances to "save some, spend some, and give some" within your borders. Then God will stretch your borders so you have more to distribute into each category.

Proverbs talks a lot about *prudence*, which means good management. We are stewards, managing God's finances. We are not owners and should always remember that. We are taking care of God's money for Him, and we should always do what He wants us to do with it.

Confession: *I love to give into every good work, and God enables me to do so abundantly. I am a good steward of God's resources.*

AS WE THINK, SO WE ARE

For as he thinks in his heart, so is he.

PROVERBS 23:7 AMP

The longer I study God's Word, the more I realize the importance of our thoughts. Today's scripture is one I have referenced many times and is very important to understand. It teaches us that what we think about determines who we become. This is encouraging to know, because it tells us we can change our lives by simply changing the way we think. Romans 8:5 also helps us understand this:

> For those who are according to the flesh and are controlled by its unholy desires set their minds on and pursue those things which gratify the flesh, but those who are according to the Spirit and are controlled by the desires of the Spirit set their minds on and seek those things which gratify the [Holy] Spirit.

The mind is the forerunner of our actions. In other words, the decisions we make and the actions we take are direct results of our thoughts. If our thoughts are negative, life will not go well for us, because we will view it negatively, and we will not be happy or optimistic. On the other hand, if our thoughts are positive, we can expect many things to go well for us—and when something doesn't, we will find ways to use it for good. When we think positively, we are happier people, and we enjoy life much more than those who are negative. This is a very simple principle, but it is important to remember each day, especially when we are tempted to despair or feel hopeless.

Confession: *I think positive thoughts, and I live a positive life.*

YOU HAVE EVERY SPIRITUAL BLESSING

Praise be to the God and Father of our Lord Jesus Christ, who has blessed us in the heavenly realms with every spiritual blessing in Christ.

EPHESIANS 1:3 NIV

Today's verse gives us the good news that we have already been blessed with all the spiritual blessings that are available from God. Spiritual blessings are different than material blessings. A person may have great material wealth and be at the pinnacle of worldly success, yet be bankrupt in terms of spiritual blessings such as salvation, peace, joy, contentment, wisdom, fellowship with God, and true spiritual power.

We often waste years trying to obtain things that mean much less than the spiritual blessings He has already given us because we are His children. The more we realize what God has already done for us through Jesus, and the more we receive it by faith, the more we are able to find real joy in each day. Our true life is not found in our circumstances, but inside of us. Jesus says that the kingdom of God is within us (Luke 17:21). This means that we will never access spiritual blessings and the things of God by looking to external surroundings or resources; we will find them in our hearts.

You will find this kind of thinking to be much better than trying continually to find something to make you happy and then being disappointed because somehow what you thought you wanted evaded you once more, or you got what you wanted but it didn't make you happy like you thought it would.

Confession: *I have every blessing I need to have a great day today.*

PRAY BOLDLY

Let us then fearlessly and confidently and boldly draw near to the throne of grace (the throne of God's unmerited favor to us sinners), that we may receive mercy [for our failures] and find grace to help in good time for every need [appropriate help and well-timed help, coming just when we need it].

HEBREWS 4:16

If there is anything in your life right now that causes you to need comfort and encouragement, today's scripture should give it to you. It is wonderful to know that even when we have sinned, we may still go to God's throne and ask for the help we need because of God's amazing grace and magnificent mercy.

We always need to ask God to help us resist temptation, because we cannot do it on our own. But when we sin, we should always be quick to repent. This means we should admit our sins, be willing to turn away from them entirely, and go in the right direction. Forgiveness is a wonderful gift, and we should be thankful for it each day. It allows us to go to God without a guilty conscience and boldly ask Him to help us in our time of need. The amplification of today's scripture says that we will have "well-timed help, coming just when we need it."

Confession: *When I sin, I quickly repent and ask God to help me resist temptation in the future. Because of God's mercy, I pray boldly, asking God to help me.*

GOD'S LOVE NEVER CEASES

The steadfast love of the Lord never ceases; his mercies never come to an end; they are new every morning; great is your faithfulness.
LAMENTATIONS 3:22–23 ESV

It always encourages us to know that God loves us. But it is *powerful* to think that there is never one moment in your life when God does not love you, and that His mercy never ceases.

God wants you to enjoy your life and not live in fear that He is angry with you about every little mistake you make. Learn to receive God's mercy, and don't be so hard on yourself. God is faithful, and we can trust everything He says in His Word. Don't mediate on everything that is wrong with you and how far you have to go to meet God's standard. Instead, think of how far you have come and celebrate your progress.

Confession: *God loves me at all times, and His mercy never ceases.*

ENJOY TODAY AND DON'T WORRY ABOUT TOMORROW

But seek first his kingdom and his righteousness, and all these things will be given to you as well. Therefore do not worry about tomorrow, for tomorrow will worry about itself. Each day has enough trouble of its own.

MATTHEW 6:33-34 NIV

If we seek God and His ways first—before anything else in life—then He promises to add to us the other things we need. Because of this, we don't have to worry about tomorrow. Anxiety causes us to waste today worrying about what will happen in the future. But just as God provided the Israelites manna one day at a time (Exodus 16:4), He gives us what we need one day at a time. God wants you to trust Him today to provide what you need for tomorrow.

Worry causes a great deal of stress, and that stress can eventually make us sick. Worry is a total waste of time. Can you think of even one problem you have ever solved by worrying? I can't. God wants our faith, not our worry. Perhaps you have never thought of it like this, but worry is pride, because when we worry, we are saying, "If I think about this long enough, I can find a way to solve my own problem." God resists the proud and helps the humble (James 4:6). Cast your care on the Lord, enjoy today, and trust Him for tomorrow's needs.

Confession: I put God first in my life, and He provides everything else I need, so I don't waste my time worrying.

ASK GOD FOR BIG THINGS

Now to Him Who, by (in consequence of) the [action of His] power that is at work within us, is able to [carry out His purpose and] do superabundantly, far over and above all that we [dare] ask or think [infinitely beyond our highest prayers, desires, thoughts, hopes, or dreams].

EPHESIANS 3:20

Today's scripture invites us to ask God for big things. I would rather ask God for a lot and get half of it than ask for a little and get all of it. The first thought we have when it comes to asking God for something big is "I don't deserve it." And that is correct; we don't deserve it. But we ask in Jesus' name, and when we do, we present to God all that Jesus is, not what we are.

Today's scripture allows us to dream big dreams and ask God to partner with us in bringing them to pass. I once asked God to let me help every person on the planet with His Word. This request sounded foolish even to me when I prayed it, but now our ministry reaches multiple millions through various media outlets. What if I had asked God to let me help ten thousand people? Had I done that, perhaps I would be helping only ten thousand today.

As long as our prayers are in line with God's will and are not selfish, we can ask for more than we can even imagine and watch God do big things.

Confession: *I am not afraid to ask God for big things, because He is a big God and is able to do more than I can even imagine.*

I CAN DO WHATEVER I NEED TO DO WITH GOD'S HELP

*I have strength for all things in Christ Who empowers me [I am
ready for anything and equal to anything through Him Who infuses
inner strength into me; I am self-sufficient in Christ's sufficiency].*

PHILIPPIANS 4:13

No matter what you are facing, you can do it. You don't have
to live in fear or dread, because God will empower you. Live
with the attitude that you are ready for and equal to anything
through Christ.

Fear and dread are draining. But faith and courage are
empowering. Think strong, and you will be strong; think weak
and incapable, and you will be weak and incapable. God never
asks us to do anything without giving us the power and abil-
ity to do it. Add your faith to His promise, and you are sure to
have a victory. I'm sure you have faced situations in the past
that you thought you would not make it through—but you
did. Remember those experiences when situations looming in
the future seem like they will require more than you are capa-
ble of. You have what it takes to do whatever you need to do
because you have Jesus on your side.

Confession: *I can do whatever I need to do in life through Christ
who strengthens me.*

CHEER UP

I have told you these things, so that in Me you may have [perfect] peace and confidence. In the world you have tribulation and trials and distress and frustration; but be of good cheer [take courage; be confident, certain, undaunted]! For I have overcome the world. [I have deprived it of power to harm you and have conquered it for you.]

JOHN 16:33

In today's scripture, Jesus tells us to cheer up if we have tribulation, trials, or distress. That may sound like an odd thing to say to people who are hurting, but He said it because joy has power. The joy of the Lord is our strength (Nehemiah 8:10). At times when we have trouble, Satan brings it for the sole purpose of stealing our joy. I heard a preacher say one time, "The devil doesn't want your stuff; he wants your joy."

You might wonder how you can have joy when your circumstances are painful or troublesome. I know that it is more challenging than when our circumstances are good. One of the ways to have joy at all times is to think of what we have in Jesus. This earth is not our home; we are merely passing through. Before long, we will be in heaven, living in the manifest presence of God—a place where there are no tears, no pain, no miserable circumstances, no death, no grieving or mourning. The pain you have now won't last forever, but remaining joyful can help you get through it.

Confession: *My joy is in the Lord. He gives me joy that nothing can take away from me.*

PRAY WHEN YOU FACE TEMPTATION

And He came out and went, as was His habit, to the Mount of Olives, and the disciples also followed Him. And when He came to the place, He said to them, Pray that you may not [at all] enter into temptation. And He withdrew from them about a stone's throw and knelt down and prayed.

LUKE 22:39–41

Everyone will be tempted in various ways at times. The Bible says that temptations must come, but woe to him through whom they come (Luke 17:1). Why does temptation have to come? One reason is that our faith is strengthened as we resist temptation. Satan tries to lure us away from God by tempting us to sin. He may work directly in his attack, or he may work through a person or circumstances.

Jesus gives us one simple instruction in today's Scripture passage: Pray that we will not fall into temptation. Notice that He doesn't say to pray that we won't be tempted, because as I said, we will all be tempted. Even Jesus was tempted to try to avoid going to the cross. Three times He asked His Father to remove the cup if possible (Matthew 26:39–43). But He also said, "Nevertheless, not as I will, but as You will" (v. 39 NKJV). Each time, He went away and prayed. I am sure He was praying for the strength to resist the temptation. Temptation is part of life, but you can resist it in the strength of God. If you know of areas in which you are weak, I recommend that you pray about them regularly, not merely when you feel tempted.

Confession: *I can resist temptation through praying and receiving God's strength to resist.*

GOD WILL MEET ALL YOUR NEEDS

And my God will liberally supply (fill to the full) your every need according to His riches in glory in Christ Jesus.

PHILIPPIANS 4:19

Paul makes the promise in today's scripture to the people who were partners with him in ministry, and it is as relevant to us today as it was to them. He told them in Philippians 4:15–18 that they were the only ones who had received from him and also given back to him. He wanted them to know that he did not seek their gift but the fruit that would increase to their credit.

We often hear this scripture quoted as though God will meet all our needs, without realizing that we need to be faithful in giving to Him. I can truthfully say that in over forty-five years of ministry, God has met all our needs. There have been lean times, but a bill never went unpaid. I believe it is impossible to outgive God. What we give to His kingdom work and to help other people with a cheerful attitude and right motive, He multiplies back to us.

Always remember that if you do the part God asks you to do, He will never fail to do His part.

Confession: *I believe God will meet all my needs, and I support those who minister to me.*

KNOWING WHO YOU ARE IN CHRIST

In him we have redemption through his blood, the forgiveness of sins, in accordance with the riches of God's grace that he lavished on us. With all wisdom and understanding, he made known to us the mystery of his will according to his good pleasure, which he purposed in Christ, to be put into effect when the times reach their fulfillment—to bring unity to all things in heaven and on earth under Christ.

EPHESIANS 1:7–10 NIV

Many Christians spend their lives trying to get things that already belong to them in Christ. For example, they may try to gain right standing with God through good works and behavior, yet they end up disappointed because they repeatedly fail. However, when they see the truth of the gospel and realize that because they are in Christ, God already views them as being in right relationship with Him, according to 2 Corinthians 5:21, their struggle ceases and joy increases. They can learn to rest in Christ's finished work at Calvary. While hanging on the cross, Jesus said, "It is finished" (John 19:30), and He meant that He had become the "atoning sacrifice" (payment) for all our sins— past, present, and future (1 John 2:2; 4:10). He fulfilled the law, and the door was now open for anyone who would believe to enjoy an intimate, personal relationship with God.

You grow in the knowledge of who you are in Christ by studying God's Word and allowing it to transform your thinking.

Confession: *I freely receive the righteousness Jesus died to give me.*

KEEP ASKING

For everyone who keeps on asking receives; and he who keeps on seeking finds; and to him who keeps on knocking, [the door] will be opened.

MATTHEW 7:8

If there is a promise in God's Word, don't stop asking to receive it. Let today's scripture encourage you to refuse to give up. Continue asking, seeking, and knocking, and you will receive, find, and see doors open for you.

I prayed for my father's salvation for more than forty years. Finally, at the age of eighty, he received Christ and was baptized. It seemed as if it would never happen, but it did.

Even Jesus, who always got His prayers answered, had to pray twice for a blind man's eyes to be opened:

They came to Bethsaida, and some people brought a blind man and begged Jesus to touch him. He took the blind man by the hand and led him outside the village. When he had spit on the man's eyes and put his hands on him, Jesus asked, "Do you see anything?" He looked up and said, "I see people; they look like trees walking around." Once more Jesus put his hands on the man's eyes. Then his eyes were opened, his sight was restored, and he saw everything clearly. (Mark 8:22–25 NIV)

Let this Scripture passage encourage you to never give up on receiving God's promises.

Confession: *God keeps His Word, and I will not give up until I experience His promises in my life.*

MAINTAIN YOUR FREEDOM IN CHRIST

It is for freedom that Christ has set us free. Stand firm, then, and do not let yourselves be burdened again by a yoke of slavery.

GALATIANS 5:1 NIV

Have you ever experienced freedom in a certain area of your life and later found yourself trapped in that same situation all over again? Perhaps you were once in bondage to debt, and you finally paid off all your bills, then a year later, the debt had piled up once more. Or maybe you spent years in bondage to emotional eating and ended up overweight. You worked hard to stop eating when you were fearful or upset, you lost weight, and you felt much better. But then something extremely stressful happened, and your emotions drove you to overeat again.

Freedom can be difficult to gain and sometimes even more difficult to maintain. Today's Scripture passage is meant to strengthen and encourage us to keep the freedom God gave us.

If we want to stay free after we are set free, we have to work at it. This is why Paul says to "stand firm." It means we will be tempted to let our freedom slip away, so we must intentionally guard against that. We are no longer under the law, but we have the great privilege of being invited to follow the Holy Spirit rather than doing as we please, according to our fleshly desires. Through the power of the Holy Spirit, we can live holy, righteous lives and glorify God. When we are free from bondage, we can live in peace and joy.

Confession: *I am free because Christ has set me free, and I will maintain the freedom He has given me.*

DON'T GIVE UP ON DOING GOOD

Let us not become weary in doing good, for at the proper time we will reap a harvest if we do not give up. Therefore, as we have opportunity, let us do good to all people, especially to those who belong to the family of believers.

GALATIANS 6:9–10 NIV

When we do what is right and good for a long time, and believe we are sowing good seed but not reaping a good harvest, we can become frustrated. But Paul urges us to not grow weary of doing good. We should not do good simply to receive a reward but because it is right. This may mean treating someone well for a long time before they begin to treat us well in return. They may never treat us well, but our reward comes from God, not from other human beings. When we look to people for appreciation or affirmation, we may be disappointed, but God never forgets what we have done, and He knows exactly how to bless us.

Part of verse 10 of today's scripture in the Amplified Bible, Classic Edition, offers an instruction that has changed my life. It reads, "Be mindful to be a blessing." To be mindful means to have your mind full of something or to purposefully think about it.

Developing the habit of thinking intentionally about ways to bless other people has greatly added to my joy. I encourage you to ask God to show you how you can bless specific people in your life. I believe He will. Learn to listen to people, because they often mention in conversation what they need, like, or want. If you are able, then try to do it for them.

Confession: *I do not give up on doing good, and I think of ways I can bless people.*

THE COMFORTER

And I will ask the Father, and He will give you another Comforter (Counselor, Helper, Intercessor, Advocate, Strengthener, and Standby), that He may remain with you forever.

JOHN 14:16

In today's scripture, Jesus is talking about the Holy Spirit, whom the Father would send once Jesus had ascended to heaven. The Holy Spirit was sent to take Jesus' place on earth. Jesus even told the disciples that they would be better off when He was gone because then the Holy Spirit would come (John 16:7). Why would they be better off?

Jesus could be in only one place at a time because He was limited by a human body, as we are. But the Holy Spirit can be everywhere at the same time, and Jesus promised that He would not only be with us who believe in Jesus, but He would be in us.

We never have to go far for help, comfort, guidance, or teaching, because the One who provides those things lives in us. The one who gives you strength lives in you. You can be encouraged today that you have all the help you need through the Holy Spirit, so lean on Him and draw on His provision at all times.

Confession: The Holy Spirit lives inside of me, and He helps me, strengthens me, guides and teaches me, helps me pray, and comforts me when I need comfort.

ASK FOR WISDOM

If any of you is deficient in wisdom, let him ask of the giving God [Who gives] to everyone liberally and ungrudgingly, without reproaching or faultfinding, and it will be given him.

JAMES 1:5

James 1 begins by talking about various trials we face. It seems to me that today's scripture, verse 5, indicates that even if our trial or trouble is our own fault, we can ask God for wisdom to fix the situation, and He will do it without finding fault or reproaching us. God is so good that He is even willing to help us when our own foolishness has gotten us into trouble.

I think we typically hesitate to ask God for help when we have misbehaved. But He invites us to draw near and receive the help we need. We should learn from our mistakes so we won't keep making them over and over, and we should also be repentant.

Just as we are always willing to help our children, God is always willing to help us. Even if He must discipline us in some way, it will be done out of love and with the intention of helping us learn an important lesson.

Always draw near to God, and never shrink back from Him.

Confession: *God helps me even when I don't deserve it.*

LEAVE THE PAST BEHIND

But one thing I do: Forgetting what is behind and straining toward what is ahead, I press on toward the goal to win the prize for which God has called me heavenward in Christ Jesus.

PHILIPPIANS 3:13–14 NIV

If we want to enjoy a bright and fulfilling future, we must leave the past behind us. Begin every day as though it is the first day of your life. We cannot see God's good plan for today or tomorrow if our focus is fixed on yesterday. We can learn from yesterday's mistakes, but we cannot go back and do things over.

When Abram and Lot went their separate ways, Lot chose the best land for himself, leaving Abram with the less desirable land and less property than he previously had (Genesis 13:1–12). Abram could have felt sorry for himself or resented Lot, but instead, he trusted God, who said, "Lift up now your eyes and look from the place where you are, northward and southward and eastward and westward; for all the land which you see I will give to you and to your posterity forever" (Genesis 13:14–15). God was telling Abram to look up and look around.

This is good advice for us. We need to look up and around instead of down and behind. Stop dwelling on what's behind you and start looking forward to what's ahead. God has a wonderful plan for your life, and you can trust Him to have good things in store for you. Don't spend your life mourning over what you have lost. Instead, take an inventory of what you have left, be thankful for it, and move forward, one step of faith at a time.

Confession: *I look ahead to the great future God has planned for me.*

LET GOD DEAL WITH OTHER PEOPLE

But in fact God has placed the parts in the body, every one of them, just as he wanted them to be.

1 CORINTHIANS 12:18 NIV

Trying to make other people into who we want them to be instead of letting them be themselves complicates relationships. We often like people initially because they bring newness and variety to our lives, but eventually the fact that they have flaws and are different than we are may bother us. Then we try to make them more like we are. This doesn't work, because God creates people differently on purpose. Just as every part of the human body can't be the head or the foot, in the body of Christ, every person has a different function and different traits—and we all need each other. Learn to love people the way they are, not the way you want them to be.

Many people are drawn to someone—perhaps a friend or even a spouse—who seems to be their complete opposite in many important ways. We tend to be attracted to people who complement (complete) us, not to people who copy us. They have what we lack. This can be wonderful until a problem arises in the relationship and we forget what drew us to the person to begin with. That's when we start to try to change them.

Only God can change people, and they change only when they are willing to be changed. If you want someone in your life to change, remember that you cannot do it. Pray about the situation, and trust God to do what needs to be done in that person's life, while letting Him work to make the changes He wants to make in you.

Confession: *I entrust the people in my life to God without trying to change them myself.*

GOD ALWAYS PROVIDES A WAY OUT

No temptation has overtaken you except what is common to mankind. And God is faithful; he will not let you be tempted beyond what you can bear. But when you are tempted, he will also provide a way out so that you can endure it.

1 CORINTHIANS 10:13 NIV

It is so comforting to know that God will never allow more to come on us than we can bear, and that no matter how bleak things look, He will always provide a way out. You may be going through something right now that seems impossible for you to endure, and you may be in despair. Let this scripture comfort you today, and know that God will not leave you stranded and helpless.

You may be tempted to give up, become angry, or feel sorry for yourself, but all these temptations are from Satan. God wants you to stay strong and keep your faith in Him. He may not be early, but He won't be late in bringing the help you need.

His timing in our lives is perfect.

Confession: *I believe that God is working in my life, and He will always provide a way out of any difficulty I find myself in.*

GOOD THINGS ARE COMING YOUR WAY

For the Lord God is a Sun and Shield; the Lord bestows [present] grace and favor and [future] glory (honor, splendor, and heavenly bliss)! No good thing will He withhold from those who walk uprightly.

PSALM 84:11

We know that we all make mistakes, but if we do our best to live a righteous life and repent when we sin, God will not withhold any good thing from us. I believe good things are coming your way and that your future is bright.

The prophet Jeremiah says in Jeremiah 29:11 that God has good plans for us: "'For I know the plans I have for you,' declares the Lord, 'plans to prosper you and not to harm you, plans to give you hope and a future'" (NIV). No matter what has happened in the past, God's mercy is new every day, and in Christ we can always have a new beginning. Don't let the devil convince you that it is too late for you, because it is never too late to begin again. God delights in people who won't give up, and He will be good to you not because you are good, but because He is good.

Confession: *I look forward to the future because I believe good things are coming my way.*

SEEDTIME AND HARVEST

Do not be deceived and deluded and misled; God will not allow Himself to be sneered at (scorned, disdained, or mocked by mere pretensions or professions, or by His precepts being set aside). [He inevitably deludes himself who attempts to delude God.] For whatever a man sows, that and that only is what he will reap.

GALATIANS 6:7

We are naturally born selfish, but we are born again generous. And we will stay selfish unless we work with the Holy Spirit as He helps us grow, mature spiritually, and learn to walk with Him. It is impossible to be happy and selfish, because God has created us to be givers, not takers.

I love the principle of sowing and reaping because I think it gives me a measure of control over my life. If I am lonely, I can sow seeds of friendliness and reap the harvest of more friends. If I am in financial need, I can sow financial seeds so someone can be blessed, and I will reap a harvest of abundance in my life.

The words we speak are seeds, as are our attitudes, thoughts, and actions. If you are not satisfied with the harvest in your life, take some time to examine your seed. For example, if someone is judging you critically, ask yourself if you have sown seeds of judgment. If you need mercy, do you sow seeds of mercy toward others? If you need forgiveness, do you sow seeds of forgiveness toward those who hurt you? Sow good seed, and you will reap a good harvest.

Confession: *I sow good seed, and I reap a harvest of good things in my life.*

BE MERCIFUL, KIND, AND GENEROUS

The merciful, kind, and generous man benefits himself [for his deeds return to bless him], but he who is cruel and callous [to the wants of others] brings on himself retribution.

PROVERBS 11:17

Generous people are happy people because God has created us to reach out to others rather than only think of ourselves. The deeds of those who are generous return to bless them. They will always have their needs met and an abundance to share with others.

If people are cruel and callous to the needs of others, they only bring misery on themselves. They are also sowing seed that will not bring a good harvest into their lives. They may well find themselves in need someday with no one to help them.

I encourage you to practice kindness and mercy toward the weak and fragile. Be extremely generous, and always go the extra mile. Do more than you have to and expect an overflow of joy, peace, power, and provision in your own life.

Confession: *I am a generous person. I am merciful and kind, and my deeds return to bless me.*

CHANGE YOUR ATTITUDE, CHANGE YOUR LIFE

Let this same attitude and purpose and [humble] mind be in you which was in Christ Jesus: [Let Him be your example in humility].

PHILIPPIANS 2:5

Your attitude is a product of your thought life. People can see how you think when they observe your attitude. If we have a positive attitude, we will have a good life regardless of our circumstances; if we have a negative attitude, we will not enjoy life, no matter how good it is.

Your attitude belongs to you, and nobody can make you have a bad one if you don't want to. Likewise, no one can make you have a good one if you don't want to. It is easy to have a good attitude when everything is going our way, but it is important to learn, as Paul did, how to be content, whether we are abased or abounding (Philippians 4:11–12). If the devil knows he can manipulate our attitude with circumstances, he will do so, and our emotions will always be up and down like a yo-yo.

The mental posture you take toward unpleasant circumstances determines whether or not you can enjoy your life while God is solving your problems. You don't have to be miserable because you have a problem. As a matter of fact, as Christians, we are privileged to have the joy of the Lord and the peace that passes understanding regardless of our circumstances. Decide right now that you will have an "up" attitude so you can have an above-average life.

Confession: *I have a positive attitude at all times. Being negative is useless, and I refuse to waste my time with a negative attitude. I believe God is good, and He will work good out of every difficulty I encounter.*

LIVE WITH A CLEAR CONSCIENCE

But if your eye is unsound, your whole body will be full of darkness. If then the very light in you [your conscience] is darkened, how dense is that darkness!

MATTHEW 6:23

Nothing complicates life like a guilty conscience. It pressures us and prevents us from being able to truly live. We may try to ignore it, but it constantly whispers to us, reminding us that we have not done right. We should always strive to keep our conscience free of offense toward God and toward other people.

There are only two ways to live with a clear conscience. The first is to do what is right. If we fail in that, we move to the second choice, which is to be quick to repent, admit our sins, and ask for God's forgiveness—and for other people's if necessary. A guilty conscience hinders our faith and worship, putting a stumbling block between us and God until we deal with our feelings of guilt in a godly way. When we sin against other people, we will feel guilty when we are with them until we resolve the situation by apologizing. There is no harder pillow than a guilty conscience. We will toss and turn at night if our conscience condemns us and we try to ignore it.

Take some time to examine your heart today. Are there people you aren't speaking to? Have you wronged anyone? Are there misunderstandings or hard feelings you need to put to rest with a friend? Work to remedy these broken relationships. Your conscience will be clear, and your free, easy fellowship with God will be restored.

Confession: *When I feel guilty, I quickly repent and ask forgiveness from God and other people.*

THE GOD OF RESTORATION

He restores my soul.

PSALM 23:3 NKJV

You can rejoice today that our God restores what has been lost or damaged in our lives. Many things damage our souls as we go through life, things like abuse, rejection, bullying, disrespect, criticism, and other negative experiences. I was sexually abused by my father for many years and abandoned to the abuse by my mother, who told me later in life that she just couldn't face the scandal that would have resulted had anyone found out what my father was doing. My soul was bruised and wounded by this and other things that happened to me. I saw myself as a victim and felt bitter and resentful. I thought these feelings represented my lot in life and saw no way out.

But God revealed to me through His Word that He wanted to restore my soul and make it like new. He wanted to set me free from all the effects of the abuse I had endured. As I trusted Him and worked with the Holy Spirit, over time that's exactly what He did. I want you to know without a doubt that He will do the same for you.

Any damaged area of your life will be restored and made brand-new as you study God's Word and trust Him to fulfill His promises in your life. He will give you beauty for ashes (Isaiah 61:3), and you won't be a victim, but a victor.

Confession: *God is restoring my soul and making me a new creature in Jesus.*

YOU ARE WHO YOU ARE

Only, let each one live the life which the Lord has assigned him, and to which God has called him [for each person is unique and is accountable for his choices and conduct, let him walk in this way].
1 CORINTHIANS 7:17 AMP

I hope you are accepting yourself as God designed you this moment and that you won't ever fight against yourself again. Instead of starting your day with negative thoughts and words about yourself, say, "I am what I am, and I cannot do anything God has not designed me to do—but I can do everything He has purposed for me. I accept myself as God's creation. He loves me and has a purpose for my life." Even if you aren't certain what that purpose is yet, this will help you move toward discovering it. We are always changing and improving, and we don't have to feel guilty and reject ourselves as this process of growth takes place.

Relax and know that because you're alive, you have a purpose. I believe God will use us daily if we ask Him to. There are many things God does through us without our realizing it. We may give a simple compliment without being aware of how much someone needs it. A smile may comfort someone going through a stressful ordeal. In such ways, we fulfill God's purpose for us in certain moments.

God uses small things as much as big things to fulfill His purpose for you. Remember that what may seem small and insignificant to you may be life-changing for someone else.

Confession: *I accept myself, and I believe God is using me to fulfill His purpose for my life and to bless other people.*

THE BE-ATTITUDES

Now when Jesus saw the crowds, he went up on a mountainside and sat down. His disciples came to him, and he began to teach them.

MATTHEW 5:1–2 NIV

I refer to the Beatitudes (Matthew 5:1–12) as the "Be-Attitudes" because I believe they teach us how we should live.

> Blessed are the poor in spirit, for theirs is the kingdom of heaven. Blessed are those who mourn, for they will be comforted. Blessed are the meek, for they will inherit the earth. Blessed are those who hunger and thirst for righteousness, for they will be filled. Blessed are the merciful, for they will be shown mercy. Blessed are the pure in heart, for they will see God. Blessed are the peacemakers, for they will be called children of God. Blessed are those who are persecuted because of righteousness, for theirs is the kingdom of heaven. Blessed are you when people insult you, persecute you and falsely say all kinds of evil against you because of me. Rejoice and be glad, because great is your reward in heaven. (vv. 3–12 NIV)

These are Christlike attitudes to which we should aspire. Study them, and ask the Holy Spirit to help you keep growing in them.

Confession: *The Holy Spirit helps me grow in Christlike attitudes.*

TRIALS AND TROUBLE ARE PART OF LIFE

I have told you these things, so that in Me you may have [perfect] peace and confidence. In the world you have tribulation and trials and distress and frustration; but be of good cheer [take courage; be confident, certain, undaunted]! For I have overcome the world. [I have deprived it of power to harm you and have conquered it for you.]

JOHN 16:33

In numerous places in God's Word, we read about how to behave during trials, but the Bible never tells us we can expect to live without them. We have faith for the times when life is difficult. Remaining steadfast during such times causes our faith to grow. The world needs to see the light of heaven in our faces if they are to believe our religion is real. How we behave during difficulty reveals who we are and how far we have progressed in our walk with God.

God promises us comfort and also encouragement in the amplification of 2 Corinthians 1:3–5. He promises us strength to endure (Romans 15:5), and He promises that He will never allow more to come on us than we can bear (1 Corinthians 10:13). Especially during times of trial and distress, the Comforter, the Holy Spirit, comforts us and pours out His love on us.

Know that you are loved, and God will always take care of you.

Confession: *I am not afraid of trials and difficulty, because I know that God will give me the strength to endure, and He will always take care of me.*

THE SPIRIT OF PEACE

You will guard him and keep him in perfect and constant peace whose mind [both its inclination and its character] is stayed on You, because he commits himself to You, leans on You, and hopes confidently in You.

ISAIAH 26:3

Peace is one of the most blessed things we can have. The scripture for today tells us we will be kept in peace if we keep our minds on the Lord. This is easy to do when all things are going well, but not so easy when we have trials and tribulations to deal with. We are tempted to think about our troubles and worry about how to solve them.

Instead of worrying, we should pray and thank God for His blessings in our lives, and His peace will be ours (Philippians 4:6–7). Ephesians 6 teaches us how to defeat the devil by wearing the spiritual armor God has given us, and one piece of that armor is the "shoes" of peace (Ephesians 6:15). We are told to put them on, which means we are to walk in peace. When the devil sees us at peace and realizes he cannot upset us, it aids in his defeat.

We are offered twofold peace: peace with God and the peace of God. Peace with God comes when our sins are forgiven, and the peace of God is ours when our will is surrendered to His will. Jesus says, "Do not let your hearts be troubled" (John 14:1). If we are assured that God loves us and will always take care of us, we can enjoy life in the midst of the storms we face at times.

Confession: *I enjoy peace at all times. During difficulties, I put on my shoes of peace, and I keep my mind stayed on the Lord.*

BELIEVING

Jesus answered, "The work of God is this: to believe in the one he has sent."

JOHN 6:29 NIV

Multiple times each day, we face the choice to either believe in the promises of God or to doubt them. Jesus says that the work He requires from us is that we believe in Jesus. I've recently been thinking about how peaceful and powerful it would be to continually live a life of believing God in every situation.

When I need to do something, I can believe God will help me. When I have trouble, I can believe that God will deliver me. When I have a need, I can believe God will meet that need. When I am sick, I can believe God will heal me. When I am tired, I can believe God will refresh and restore me.

There are hundreds, perhaps thousands, of opportunities for us to keep our peace by simply believing in the goodness of God each day. Of course, we can also doubt, but we don't have to. Instead, we can doubt our doubts, and when they try to steal our faith and confidence in God, we can chase them away by simply returning to believing.

Confession: I believe the promises of God, and that is the work He requires of me. I doubt my doubts and realize they are lies from Satan designed to steal my faith and peace.

TAKE CONTROL OF YOUR FEELINGS

Better a patient person than a warrior, one with self-control than one who takes a city.

PROVERBS 16:32 NIV

Our emotions ebb and flow like ocean waves. They do their own thing—and without any warning. Wishing our emotions were different won't change a thing, so we need to do more than wish. We need to do all we can about them and take proper action to manage them. If we make the effort to observe ourselves, we will easily perceive how quickly our feelings change.

A rebellious child does a lot of things without a parent's permission, and just wishing the child wouldn't do them won't make him or her stop. The parent must discipline the child to bring about the change. The same principle holds true with our emotions. They are often like rebellious children, and the longer they are allowed to do as they please, the more difficult it is to control them. We all have emotions, and they change often, but we can learn to manage them and live beyond them. I spent the first fifteen years of my life in a house where emotions were volatile, and it was normal to me to allow them to rule. Growing up, I learned that if you didn't get what you wanted, you yelled, argued, and stayed angry until you got your way. Thankfully, I now know better.

I encourage you to control yourself and teach your children at an early age how to do the same thing. Second Timothy 1:7 tells us that God has given us "power and love and self-control" (ESV), so in Him we do have the ability to control our emotions.

Confession: *I discipline my emotions and don't let them control me.*

COUNT THE COST BEFORE COMMITTING

Blessed is the man who walks not in the counsel of the ungodly, nor stands in the path of sinners, nor sits in the seat of the scornful.

PSALM 1:1 NKJV

Today's scripture says that we are not to take counsel from the ungodly. I believe that taking advice from our feelings fits into the category of "the ungodly" and is a big mistake. Feelings are simply fickle; they change frequently, and you just can't trust them.

We can hear a good speaker talk about the volunteers needed at church and be so inspired that we sign up to help. But that doesn't mean we'll feel like showing up when it's our turn to work. If we sign up and then don't show up because we don't feel like it, our actions don't have integrity or honor God. When we don't keep our word, we know it isn't right. And no matter how many excuses we make, the fact that we were not dependable sits on our conscience like a weight.

If we desire to follow the Holy Spirit, our actions must be governed by principles—a precise standard of right and wrong. How we feel does not alter that standard. We should always count the cost to see if we have what it takes to finish a thing before we begin it (Luke 14:28). If we begin and find we cannot finish, then we need to communicate openly and honestly with all parties involved. Our emotions will help us commit, but people who honor their commitments and finish the job must eventually press on without feelings to support them.

Confession: *I take the time to count the cost before making commitments, and I will finish what I start, no matter how I feel.*

THE SPIRIT OF LOVE

And this is his command: to believe in the name of his Son, Jesus Christ, and to love one another as he commanded us.

1 JOHN 3:23 NIV

God loves us, and He commands us to love one another. In "The Spirit of Love," A. B. Simpson shares the legend that when the apostle John was elderly and waiting for the Lord to call him home, he went to the church in Ephesus each Lord's Day. He walked up to the pulpit and simply said, "Little children, love one another," and sat down. When asked why he said nothing else, he answered, "There is nothing else to say; that is all there is, for, He that dwelleth in love dwelleth in God and God in Him."[5]

Jesus gave us one new commandment: that we love one another as He has loved us (John 13:34). It's important to understand that the type of love Jesus speaks of is not based on feelings. It is the same kind of love that God has for us. Romantic love may be based on feelings, but this love, to which we are called as believers, is not. It is seen in how we treat people—not merely our friends, but even our enemies.

Always remember to be quick to forgive, merciful, and ever ready to help those in need. Love is not a theory or a word; it is an action. "For God so loved the world that he gave his one and only Son" (John 3:16 NIV). Love gives and expects nothing in return. I encourage you to study love as often as possible.

Confession: *I am learning to love all people as Christ loves me.*

THE MIND OF CHRIST

*For, "Who has known the mind of the Lord so as to instruct him?"
But we have the mind of Christ.*

1 CORINTHIANS 2:16 NIV

The way we think is extremely important because our thoughts affect our words and actions. We should think thoughts that agree with God's Word and His will. To ensure that we are capable of doing this, God has given us the mind of Christ. We hold the thoughts, intents, and purposes of His heart.

"What would Jesus do in this situation?" is a good question to ask ourselves when we need to make a decision about an issue in our lives. When people mistreated Him, how did Jesus think? He maintained a peaceful spirit, so He must have kept His mind on things that promote peace. He trusted His Father at all times and in every situation. He believed the best of everyone, and His thoughts were always set on doing God's will.

As a believer, you have the mind of Christ in you because of the indwelling Holy Spirit. Think with the mind of Christ, and you will have a life you can enjoy and that pleases God.

Confession: I have the mind of Christ, and I think the same way He did.

GOD SUPPLIES MY NEEDS

He who has a bountiful eye shall be blessed, for he gives of his bread to the poor.

PROVERBS 22:9

Today's scripture is a wonderful and comforting verse. We don't have to worry if our needs will be met if we are generous to others; that's because God's Word tells us they will.

It is important to use wisdom with our finances—both in our giving and in our spending. If we foolishly get into debt by purchasing things we cannot afford and may not even need, we may find ourselves in want (Proverbs 22:7). But as believers, God gives us wisdom (James 1:5), so be sure to ask Him for it and to use it. His Word also instructs us to give to those who need help, so when you consider how you will use your financial resources, always keep in mind God's instruction to help the needy, and remember that doing so brings blessings.

Financial pressure is a terrible strain, and it steals our peace and joy. I encourage you to use wisdom and be prudent with your finances. Instead of going into debt to get what you want instantly, choose to wait and save so you can pay cash for it or cover its cost from your savings. Waiting may be hard, but it is easier than being pressured by debt. In addition, be sure to set aside money to use to help other people.

Confession: *I am a giver. I use wisdom with my finances, and God always meets all my needs.*

I AM AN AMBASSADOR FOR CHRIST

So we are Christ's ambassadors, God making His appeal as it were through us. We [as Christ's personal representatives] beg you for His sake to lay hold of the divine favor [now offered you] and be reconciled to God.

2 CORINTHIANS 5:20

As God's children, we represent Him everywhere we go, and it is important that we represent Him well. Jesus says we are lights in the world (Matthew 5:14). The only way some people will ever see Jesus is through people who are in relationship with Him. This is a huge responsibility—one we should work with the Holy Spirit to fulfill.

We can lead people into a relationship with Christ by behavior that glorifies God and shows people what He is like. For example, we can be patient with people, forgive them, be merciful, kind, love them unconditionally, and be full of joy and peace. These are qualities people in the world want and are looking for, and they can see them through us if we will follow the leadership of the Holy Spirit.

Just think how wonderful and amazing it is that we are Christ's personal representatives, and that He makes His personal appeal to other people through us. What an awesome privilege and responsibility.

Confession: I am an ambassador for Christ, so I represent Him, and I believe I have the great privilege and joy of leading people to follow Jesus.

MADE NEW IN CHRIST

Therefore, if anyone is in Christ, he is a new creation. The old has passed away; behold, the new has come.

2 CORINTHIANS 5:17 ESV

When we are born again, we are made new. Old things pass away, and all things become new. I like to think of it like this: We become new spiritual clay, and if we will work with Him, the Holy Spirit will mold us into the image of Jesus Christ.

As we allow the Holy Spirit to make us like Jesus, all things become possible (Matthew 19:26). We get a new beginning, a second chance to do things right, and we have a right relationship with Jesus. All our sins are forgiven, and God remembers them no more (Hebrews 8:12). We are justified in Christ, which means we are made just as though we had never sinned.

Everything doesn't change all at once. Change is a process, and it is necessary for us to study God's Word and learn to be obedient to His will. As we do, we will experience what I call the *law of gradual growth*. Little by little, God delivers us from bad habits and behaviors and replaces them with right habits and behaviors, which open the door for multiple blessings in our lives. We have peace with God, and the joy of the Lord becomes ours. We have hope, and we quickly learn that God never fails to keep His promises.

Confession: *I am a new creature in Christ. Old things have passed away, and all things are made new.*

NO OPPRESSION OR FEAR

You shall establish yourself in righteousness (rightness, in conformity with God's will and order): you shall be far from even the thought of oppression or destruction, for you shall not fear, and from terror, for it shall not come near you.

ISAIAH 54:14

Bad things do happen in life at times, but we don't have to spend our time worrying about them. We can trust God to be with us and see us through them. Walk in the righteousness that is in you through your faith in Christ, and oppression, destruction, fear, and terror shall not come near you.

Our enemy Satan may attack, but we can defeat his every fiery dart by lifting up the shield of faith (Ephesians 6:16).

When the devil comes against you, don't worry about what you need to do. Simply release your faith through prayer, asking God to fight the battle for you. Even when you *feel* fear, you don't have to be afraid. To be afraid means to run or take flight. As believers we are anointed by God to face any situation that comes our way, knowing that He is with us and will show us what to do. See yourself as a victor, not a victim. Remember, you are more than a conqueror through Christ who loves you (Romans 8:37).

Confession: *I will not worry and be afraid when trouble comes, because God is on my side, and He will fight for me.*

YOU ARE GOD'S WORKMANSHIP

For we are God's [own] handiwork (His workmanship), recreated in Christ Jesus, [born anew] that we may do those good works which God predestined (planned beforehand) for us [taking paths which He prepared ahead of time], that we should walk in them [living the good life which He prearranged and made ready for us to live].

EPHESIANS 2:10

We are created by God to do good works and live a good life. We are not saved by our good works. But because God lives in us, we want to do good works; it is part of our new nature. God has prepared a good path for us, and all we need to do is walk on it.

Each day we make dozens of decisions, and each decision brings a result. If we make good decisions, we will live a good life. But if we make bad decisions, we will not enjoy our life, even though a good life is available to us.

Doing good things for other people often requires sacrifice. This may not sound exciting, but our spirit rejoices when we do it. Acts 10:38 says that Jesus was anointed by the Holy Spirit, and "He went about doing good" and healing all who were oppressed of the devil. Notice that He "went about doing good." I love this thought, and I believe we can also go about doing good. Get up each day and think about what you can do to make someone else happy, and the happiness you give will come back to you multiplied many times over.

Confession: *I am God's workmanship, and I walk on the good path He has planned for me. I do the good works He has arranged for me to do.*

USE YOUR WILL TO CHOOSE GOD'S WILL

I call heaven and earth to witness this day against you that I have set before you life and death, the blessings and the curses; therefore choose life, that you and your descendants may live.

DEUTERONOMY 30:19

In order to live the life God wants us to live, it is vital that we understand our free will—our ability to make choices. God created us with free will, and His desire was (and still is) that we would use our free will to choose *His* will.

Free will is a huge responsibility as well as a privilege. It brings us freedom. God will always guide us to make the choices that will work best for us and lead us into His plan for us, but He will never force or manipulate us into those decisions.

Each day God gives us is a gift, and we have an opportunity to value it. One way to do this is to use each day purposefully, not wasting time or allowing ourselves to be manipulated by circumstances that we cannot control. Each day can count if we learn to live it on purpose rather than passively drifting through the day, allowing the wind of circumstances and distractions to make our choices for us. We can remember at all times that we are God's children, and He allows us to make our own decisions each day. Ask Him today to help you make choices that will direct you toward His purpose for your life.

Confession: I value the free will God has given me and ask Him to help me use it to make choices that will lead to fulfilling His purpose for my life.

YOU ARE THE HOME OF GOD

Do you not know that your body is the temple (the very sanctuary) of the Holy Spirit Who lives within you, Whom you have received [as a Gift] from God? You are not your own.

1 CORINTHIANS 6:19

You never have to look far for God; because you are a believer, He lives in you. According to today's scripture, the Holy Spirit lives in us. This is amazing to think about. God purchased us with the blood of Jesus, and we are not our own. We belong to Him.

Because our bodies are the home of God, it is important that we take care of them. Some people abuse their bodies by not getting enough sleep or exercise, by not drinking enough water, or by eating too much junk food. Since the world watches Christians, we should do our best to look our best at all times. We represent Jesus, and He is making His appeal to the world through us (2 Corinthians 5:20).

God cannot be any closer to you than inside of you, so when you feel lonely, remember that you are never alone. He is in you at all times.

Confession: *God lives in me, and I am His home.*

YOU HAVE RIGHT STANDING WITH GOD

For our sake He made Christ [virtually] to be sin Who knew no sin, so that in and through Him we might become [endued with, viewed as being in, and examples of] the righteousness of God [what we ought to be, approved and acceptable and in right relationship with Him, by His goodness].

2 CORINTHIANS 5:21

Today's scripture has been life-changing for me. For years, I had a vague feeling that God was mad at me for something I had not done right. I know I felt that way because my earthly father was almost always angry at me. Discovering that God had made me right with Him through Jesus changed everything. I had to meditate on this and study for a long, long time before it finally became revelation to me. But once it did, I no longer had to feel bad about myself or be concerned that God was angry with me.

See yourself as the righteousness of God. We sin and should repent and receive forgiveness, but what we do is different from who we are. We are God's children, and we are made right with Him. The more we understand that we have righteousness in us, the more we will make the right choices and do the right things. What is in us will be expressed through us in due time.

Confession: *I am the righteousness of God in Christ.*

YOUR WEAKNESSES ARE NOT A PROBLEM

But He said to me, My grace (My favor and loving-kindness and mercy) is enough for you [sufficient against any danger and enables you to bear the trouble manfully]; for My strength and power are made perfect (fulfilled and completed) and show themselves most effective in [your] weakness. Therefore, I will all the more gladly glory in my weaknesses and infirmities, that the strength and power of Christ (the Messiah) may rest (yes, may pitch a tent over and dwell) upon me!

2 CORINTHIANS 12:9

We don't have to worry about or struggle with our weaknesses, because God's strength and power show themselves most effectively through them. The apostle Paul worried about one of his weaknesses—a thorn in his flesh—until God spoke today's verse to Him. After that, he seems to have no longer been concerned about it. He even gloried in his weaknesses.

This doesn't mean that we don't make any effort to overcome our shortfalls with God's help, but if we are doing the best we can and trust God, He will use our weakness to show His strength. The apostles had weaknesses, and so do you and I.

Are you concerned that God won't be able to use you because of your weaknesses? Paul writes that God deliberately chooses the weak and foolish things of the world to confound the wise (1 Corinthians 1:27). Just imagine how amazed those who know you will be when they see God do mighty things through you. They will know it must be God, and this gives them hope for themselves.

Confession: *God's strength is made perfect in my weaknesses.*

RUN TO JESUS

*Come to Me, all you who labor and are heavy-laden and overbur-
dened, and I will cause you to rest. [I will ease and relieve and
refresh your souls.]*

MATTHEW 11:28

When we feel overburdened, as though everything in life is
caving in on us, there is a place we can go for help. Jesus invites
us to come to Him and let Him refresh us and relieve us of our
burdens. We don't have to carry them any longer; we can give
them to Him.

As we cast our care on Him, we find that He cares for us (1
Peter 5:7). If we insist on keeping our anxieties and burdens,
the Lord will let us hold on to them; but He is happy to take
them from us if we give them to Him. Sometimes we give them
to Him and then take them back, but we can give them to Him
again and again if necessary.

Jesus is waiting to help you. He already has a plan for your
deliverance. Although you may not see an answer, that doesn't
mean that one doesn't exist. What is impossible with man is
possible with God (Luke 18:27).

Confession: *I don't carry my burdens; I give them to Jesus, and
He refreshes my soul and does for me what I cannot do for
myself.*

GOD WILL GIVE YOU ALL YOU NEED

He who did not withhold or spare [even] His own Son but gave Him up for us all, will He not also with Him freely and graciously give us all [other] things?

ROMANS 8:32

Why do we worry that God won't meet our needs? Surely, since He has given us His only Son, He will also give us all other things. There is no greater gift than Jesus, so we need not worry about all the other less important things we need.

Some problems seem so big to us that we think they just cannot be solved. But all our problems are little to God, because there is nothing He cannot do. None of it is even an effort for Him.

Ask for the help you need. James 4:2 says, "You do not have because you do not ask" (NKJV). What we ask God for is never too much for Him to handle. If we don't get what we ask for, then either the timing isn't right for us to have it, or He has something better in mind for us. I don't want anything that is not right for me, and I often pray when asking for things, "God, if what I am asking isn't right for me, please don't give it to me, because I always want to be in Your will."

Confession: *I am not afraid to ask God for anything because He has already given me the best gift of all: Jesus.*

WALK IN THE SPIRIT

So I say, walk by the Spirit, and you will not gratify the desires of the flesh. For the flesh desires what is contrary to the Spirit, and the Spirit what is contrary to the flesh. They are in conflict with each other, so that you are not to do whatever you want.

GALATIANS 5:16–17 NIV

As believers, we are to focus on obeying and walking with the Holy Spirit, and then there will be no room for the works of the flesh. Normally, we do the opposite. We try hard to stop gratifying the flesh so we can walk in the Spirit; but we go about this backward. I wrote a book called *Making Good Habits, Breaking Bad Habits*, and the message of the book is that if we focus on developing good habits, we won't have to wrestle with bad habits.

Yesterday I said something that hurt a person I love very much. I quickly apologized and asked them to forgive me. I didn't make excuses. I simply owned the behavior. The person did forgive me, and today the situation is forgotten. Had I been too proud to take responsibility for my error and to ask for forgiveness, I would feel guilty, and our relationship would feel strained.

Nothing disarms the devil like simple obedience to God. When we don't obey, it is because of pride. We think we have a better idea or that what God is asking is too hard. But nothing God asks us to do is too hard, because He will always help us through the power of the Holy Spirit. I encourage you to focus on good things today and every day—and you will be amazed at how much better your life will be.

Confession: *I can do everything God asks me to do because the Holy Spirit helps me.*

ENDURE THE HARD TIMES FOR THE JOY AHEAD

Looking away [from all that will distract] to Jesus, Who is the Leader and the Source of our faith [giving the first incentive for our belief] and is also its Finisher [bringing it to maturity and perfection]. He, for the joy [of obtaining the prize] that was set before Him, endured the cross, despising and ignoring the shame, and is now seated at the right hand of the throne of God.

HEBREWS 12:2

When we face something difficult, it is easy to run away from it or just refuse to do it. But remembering that God is the Rewarder of those who diligently seek Him (Hebrews 11:6) encourages us to press on because we know something wonderful will be waiting for us once we get through the difficulty.

Good things don't come easily. They often require sacrifice, pressing through difficulty, and taking steps of faith that are hard. Running away is easy, but enduring brings us victory.

Are you facing something challenging right now and considering whether to give up or press on? I strongly encourage you to press on. Anything we run away from we will have to face sometime in the future. But once we go through what we are afraid of, it no longer has any power over us. When the time came for me to confront my father about the sexual abuse in my childhood, I was afraid and didn't want to do it, but with God's help I did. This helped break the power of the fear I had of him. When we have something to do, we can do it, even if we have to "do it afraid."

Confession: *I am obedient to God whether it is easy or hard. Even if I am afraid, I do it anyway.*

THE NARROW PATH

Enter through the narrow gate; for wide is the gate and spacious and broad is the way that leads away to destruction, and many are those who are entering through it. But the gate is narrow (contracted by pressure) and the way is straitened and compressed that leads away to life, and few are those who find it.

MATTHEW 7:13-14

Each day we face many responsibilities and choices. Matthew 22:14 states that "many are called, but few are chosen" (ESV). I heard someone say once that this scripture means that many are called, but few are willing to take the responsibility for their calling. God has many great opportunities for each of us, but they always involve responsibility.

Over the years, I have seen people doing things I felt God did not want me to do. He let me know that if I wanted the privilege of teaching His Word that He was offering me, I would have to live on the narrow path, not the broad path. On the narrow path, we don't get to take our fleshly baggage with us.

God is not partial to one person over another (Romans 2:11). The same guidelines apply to everyone. The promises of God are for "whosoever will" (Luke 9:24 KJV). God has done His part; now we must do ours. A relative may generously pay your tuition for four years of college, but that doesn't guarantee you will graduate. That part is up to you.

God loves you very much and has a great plan for your life, so I encourage you to stay on the narrow path of life.

Confession: *My goal is to live on the narrow path that will help me arrive at the destination God has for me.*

LEARNING OBEDIENCE

Although he was a son, he learned obedience through what he suffered.

HEBREWS 5:8 ESV

Today's scripture says that Jesus "learned obedience," but how could He learn obedience since He was never disobedient? He learned the cost of obedience by experience when He died on the cross. This experience gave Him the equipment He needed to be our High Priest (Hebrews 5:10).

I have been through very difficult things in my life, and perhaps you have too. Those difficulties have given me the experience I need to minister to other hurting people. I can truly say to them, "I know how you feel."

Experience is invaluable. It is impossible to put a price on it. Not only does it qualify us to help others, but it also enables us to put our trust in God. Each time we trust God in a situation and experience His faithfulness, it makes it easier to trust Him the next time we have trouble. Our pain is never wasted.

It is easy to talk about obeying God, but talking is different from doing. Jesus said if you love Him you will obey Him (John 14:15). He did not say, "If you obey me, I will love you." He loves us unconditionally, and our response to the amazing gift of His love should be joyful obedience.

Confession: *I learn from every experience God gives me, and I endeavor to be joyfully obedient to God because of His unconditional love.*

EMOTIONS AND SPIRITUAL MATURITY

For you are still [unspiritual, having the nature] of the flesh [under the control of ordinary impulses]. For as long as [there are] envying and jealousy and wrangling and factions among you, are you not unspiritual and of the flesh, behaving yourselves after a human standard and like mere (unchanged) men?

1 CORINTHIANS 3:3

Paul teaches in today's scripture that we are unspiritual if we are controlled by ordinary human impulses, such as emotions and feelings. Are you in control of your emotions, or do they control you? Feelings are fickle and ever-changing, and thus unreliable. I believe the number one way the enemy harasses and tries to hinder Christians is through our emotions.

We cannot always control how we feel, but we can control what we do. Mature Christians don't walk by feelings; they order their conduct according to God's Word. Emotions are fueled by our thoughts and words, so it is necessary to pay attention to what we think and say if we hope to walk by the Spirit instead of our emotions. What is right doesn't change just because we don't feel like doing it. People who are spiritually mature live beyond their feelings and do God's will no matter how they feel.

Paul specifically mentions jealousy and factions (dissension or strife) as indicators of a lack of spiritual maturity. Ask God to help you in these areas. Be content with what you have, not jealous of others, knowing that God will give you more when the time is right. Do your best to live in peace with all people.

Confession: *I do not live by emotion but by the Word of God.*

ZAPPED OR TRANSFORMED?

And all of us, as with unveiled face, [because we] continued to behold [in the Word of God] as in a mirror the glory of the Lord, are constantly being transfigured into His very own image in ever increasing splendor and from one degree of glory to another; [for this comes] from the Lord [Who is] the Spirit.

2 CORINTHIANS 3:18

As Christians, being transformed into the image of Jesus Christ should be our goal. Transformation is a process that takes time and is often painful. We cannot have "microwave maturity" and just be zapped and suddenly be mature. A process has a beginning, a middle, and an end. The beginning is easy, and the end is exciting—if we ever get there—but the middle is difficult. I can easily pray, "Lord, change me. I want to be just like You." But we cannot even know what it means to be like Him unless we understand God's Word—and this requires diligent study over a long period of time. First Peter 2:2 says that as newborn babies desire milk, we should desire the milk of God's Word so that we might be nurtured and grow.

Almost everything takes longer than we think it will. While you are growing in Christ, don't focus on how far you have to go; instead, celebrate your progress. Often the changes in us are so minute that we don't even see them right away. But if we look back two or three years, we will see how much we have changed.

God is working in you if you have asked Him to do so, and although your journey may not be like that of anyone else, it is a journey designed just for you. Relax and enjoy the trip.

Confession: *I am growing daily in Christ. He is working in me and changing me into His image.*

CHANGE YOUR MIND

So the great dragon was cast out, that serpent of old, called the Devil and Satan, who deceives the whole world.

REVELATION 12:9 NKJV

The only way we can see and experience the good plan God has for our lives is to have our minds totally renewed by God's Word (Romans 12:2). Before receiving Jesus as our Savior, we listened to the lies of the devil, which means that most of our thinking was wrong. As today's scripture reminds us, he is a deceiver, and John 8:44 clearly says "he is a liar." Because we have believed his lies, our minds need to be changed. If we want to be who God wants us to be and have what He wants us to have, we must learn to think as He thinks.

For example, I thought that because I had been sexually abused by my father, I would always have a second-rate life. But through studying God's Word, my mind was renewed, and I learned that "If anyone is in Christ, he is a new creation; old things have passed away; behold, all things have become new" (2 Corinthians 5:17 NKJV). Now that I know the truth and have cast down the lie, my life has improved and is getting better and better all the time. God promises us many wonderful things in His Word, but we receive them by faith. We must believe them in order to receive them.

Begin studying God's Word, determined to believe it no matter what you think, see, or feel, and soon you will see amazing and wonderful changes.

Confession: *I no longer believe the lies of Satan, because I am learning the truth of God's Word, and my mind is being renewed.*

THE TRUTH WILL SET YOU FREE

But when he, the Spirit of truth, comes, he will guide you into all the truth. He will not speak on his own; he will speak only what he hears, and he will tell you what is to come.

JOHN 16:13 NIV

The Holy Spirit reveals truth to us as we are able to receive it. This process continues throughout our lives. God's Word is truth, and anything that does not agree with His Word is a lie (a falsehood or deception). If God's Word tells me to forgive my enemies and I make an excuse for not doing it, I am operating in deception. God doesn't want our excuses; He wants our obedience.

Simply knowing the truth won't set us free, but as we apply the truth to our lives, we will experience freedom from the bondages of the past. Don't disobey and make the excuse that obeying what God asks is just too hard. Nothing God asks us to do is too hard because He is our Strength and our Helper. When we talk about "truth," it is often the truth about ourselves we must face in order to be set free. I prayed a long time for Dave to change until God showed me that I was the one who needed to change, not Dave. I had many problems that I was blaming on other people, including Dave.

Once I started taking responsibility for my behavior, God began changing me. It wasn't easy, but it was easier than remaining in bondage.

Confession: *I will study God's Word so I can learn the truth, and with God's help I will apply the truth to my life.*

DON'T BE IN A HURRY

I wait for the Lord, my soul waits, and in his word I hope.
PSALM 130:5 ESV

God operates more like a slow cooker than a microwave. Things that are very valuable take more time to develop than those that are less valuable. The longer meat cooks, the more tender it becomes. For years, I was hard-hearted because I had been mistreated and had become bitter. I needed a lot of tenderizing before God could use me. Hard-hearted, tough, mean, bitter, resentful, jealous, or selfish Christians are not vessels fit for the Master's use.

Our times are in God's hands (Psalm 31:15). We may think He is slow in doing certain things, but He will move in our lives at the right time. He acts at the appointed time—the time when He knows we are ready, not the time we think we are ready.

I started in ministry in 1976, and the ministry grew as I grew. I wanted a big ministry right away, but God knew I wasn't ready for it yet. He had a lot of work to do in me before He could do anything through me. The same goes for you. Let God take the lead, because He will never be content to follow you.

Surrender yourself and everything in your life to the Holy Spirit and let Him teach you. He will teach you all truth (John 16:13) and cause you to see clearly what needs to be done in you so He can do great things through you.

Confession: *I surrender myself and all I have to the Lord. I want Him to do with me as He pleases.*

GOING DEEPER IN GOD

When He had stopped speaking, He said to Simon (Peter), Put out into the deep [water], and lower your nets for a haul.

LUKE 5:4

Peter and the disciples had been fishing all night and caught nothing. They must have been weary and disappointed. When they obeyed Jesus' instruction to fish again, this time in the deep water, they caught so many fish that they needed other boats to help them haul in the catch.

We all need to go deeper in God. The apostle Paul understood this. He writes:

> [For my determined purpose is] that I may know Him [that I may progressively become more deeply and intimately acquainted with Him, perceiving and recognizing and understanding the wonders of His Person more strongly and more clearly], and that I may in that same way come to know the power outflowing from His resurrection [which it exerts over believers], and that I may so share His sufferings as to be continually transformed [in spirit into His likeness even] to His death, [in the hope] that if possible I may attain to the [spiritual and moral] resurrection [that lifts me] out from among the dead [even while in the body]. (Philippians 3:10–11)

If things are not working well in your life, perhaps you need less of yourself and more of God. Don't be a surface Christian, but one who has a deep relationship with the Lord.

Confession: *I am obedient to God and have a deep, personal relationship with Him.*

LIVING ACCORDING TO THE SPIRIT

For those who are living according to the flesh set their minds on the things of the flesh [which gratify the body], but those who are living according to the Spirit, [set their minds on] the things of the Spirit [His will and purpose].

ROMANS 8:5 AMP

If we want to live according to the Spirit, we must set our mind on the things of the Spirit. In practical terms, this means we should study God's Word and make sure our thoughts are in line with what He says. For example, we should speak God's Word aloud, spend time in prayer and fellowship with Him, and love Him with all our heart. We should also think about what we can do for others, what we can do for God, how we can give more, and how we can be more obedient to the Lord.

Our thoughts become words, and thoughts and words precede actions. I enjoy thinking about what I can do for others. What do I have that I could use to bless someone else? How many things do you own that you don't use, things that could be an answer to someone else's prayers?

God is a giver, and we should be generous givers, too. Be a blessing to as many people as you possibly can. Give them compliments, encouragement, help, and financial assistance if they need it and you can meet the need. I believe that generosity is the key to our personal happiness, and I encourage you to live according to the Spirit and be as generous as you possibly can.

Confession: I keep my mind on spiritual things, not on things of the flesh. I live according to the Spirit, and I am generous with all God has given me.

GOD WILL GIVE YOU PEACE

Now may the Lord of peace himself give you peace at all times in every way. The Lord be with you all.

2 THESSALONIANS 3:16 ESV

God offers us the peace that passes all of our understanding (Philippians 4:7). He is talking about having peace in the midst of problems. Thankfully, we don't have to worry and be afraid because if we pray and give our problems to Him, He will give us peace.

Jesus said that He left us His peace, not the same peace the world has, but His own special peace, and that we should stop allowing ourselves to be upset and disturbed, fearful and intimidated (John 14:27).

None of us knows what a day may bring. We always hope for good things, but unexpected storms can arise. When those sudden storms of life come, just remember that God's peace is available to you if you will pray instead of being anxious. We may not know the way, but Jesus *is* the way, and He will lead and guide you to a place of safety.

Confession: *Even when unexpected storms arise in my life, I remain peaceful.*

BE DEEPLY ROOTED
IN GOD'S LOVE

So that Christ may dwell in your hearts through faith—that you, being rooted and grounded in love, may have strength to comprehend with all the saints what is the breadth and length and height and depth.

EPHESIANS 3:17–18 ESV

A tree that has deep roots will not be uprooted in storms. Likewise, if we are deeply rooted in God's love and are fully assured of His love for us, we won't be moved by the storms of life.

Sometimes when people are having trouble or something painful happens to them, they begin to think that God doesn't love them. This couldn't be further from the truth. God loves us unconditionally at all times, and He will not allow anything to separate us from that love (Romans 8:38–39). God's love is a gift that is ours if we will receive it. The more you meditate on the fact that God loves you, the more secure you will be, and the less fear you will have. "Perfect love casts out fear" (1 John 4:18 ESV).

I encourage you to think often about what the Bible says about God's love for you. Meditate on it and say aloud "God loves me." The amplification of 1 John 4:16 says we should be conscious of and recognize God's love. God shows us His love in a variety of ways, but if we are not looking for it, we will miss it. Watch for God's love, and it will add an enthusiasm to your life that you did not previously have.

Confession: *God loves me at all times, and He loves me unconditionally.*

DECLARE WAR ON SELFISHNESS

People will be lovers of themselves, lovers of money, boastful, proud, abusive, disobedient to their parents, ungrateful, unholy, without love, unforgiving, slanderous, without self-control, brutal, not lovers of the good, treacherous, rash, conceited, lovers of pleasure rather than lovers of God.

2 TIMOTHY 3:2–4 NIV

Today's scripture describes the world today very well. Jesus says that to be His disciples, we are to forget ourselves, lose sight of ourselves and our own interests, take up our cross, and follow Him (Mark 8:34). I believe the cross we carry is to live an unselfish life. We are born selfish, but when we are born again, God empowers us to be generous. However, generosity doesn't happen automatically; we must choose generosity and express it again and again.

True joy comes from giving, not getting. It is more blessed to give than to receive (Acts 20:35). Prepare yourself each morning by asking God what you can do for other people that day. Then wait in His presence to see what ideas come to your heart.

Yesterday morning, I kept thinking about a woman I know. Her husband died a few months ago, and I felt I should send her a simple text telling her that many people love her and that I was thinking of her. This was an easy thing to do, and it meant a great deal to her.

Be sure to follow the whispers you sense from God because you never know how important they may be to someone else.

Confession: *I declare war on selfishness, and I pray that God will show me when I am being selfish and help me refuse it and choose generosity instead.*

TAKE ACTION

And one of you says to him, Good-bye! Keep [yourself] warm and well fed, without giving him the necessities for the body, what good does that do?

JAMES 2:16

When we hear of someone struggling or in need, it's easy to say "I'll pray for you." But if we have the ability to meet their need in a tangible way, that is what we should do. Prayer is good, but several years ago, God led me to stop asking Him to do things I could easily do myself but didn't do because I didn't want to make the sacrifice they required.

Love is not just words or theory; it is action. When someone tells you they love you, the words are meaningful, but you still may not feel loved. However, if someone does something for you to meet a practical need, like help you with a project, baby-sit your children, or give you a ride because your car is being worked on, you feel loved.

People don't always remember what you say to them, but they do remember how you make them feel. Let's do our best to help everyone feel valuable and important. What if we were to get really bold, and instead of simply saying "I'll pray for you," ask "Is there anything I can do to help?" Often, we are afraid to ask because the response may involve something we don't want to do. Be a blessing to people each day, and your days will be filled with joy.

Confession: *I do my best to help everyone I encounter feel valuable and important, and I will do all I can to meet people's needs in tangible ways.*

THE POWER OF ONE

For just as by one man's disobedience (failing to hear, heedless-ness, and carelessness) the many were constituted sinners, so by one Man's obedience the many will be constituted righteous (made acceptable to God, brought into right standing with Him).

ROMANS 5:19

Adam's disobedience brought sin to all humanity, and Christ's obedience brought righteousness to all who believe in Him. Adolf Hitler was committed to a cause that brought unbeliev-able destruction. William Wilberforce was committed to a cause that brought slavery to an end in England and greater equality to all.

One committed person can do amazing things with God on their side. History is filled with stories of the changes just one person has made. Will you be one of them? You may think that you have no special talent and that you could not possibly do anything that would make much difference, but you could be wrong.

I was—and am—the least likely person to lead a ministry that covers the globe with God's Word. But I said yes to God when He called me to ministry, and His power added to my commitment has brought change to many lives. We can all do something, but the one thing we should never do is nothing.

__Confession:__ I will be obedient to God and step out in faith to do whatever He asks me to do. I want to help people, and I refuse to do nothing.

NO CONFUSION

And you will seek Me and find Me, when you search for Me with all your heart.

JEREMIAH 29:13 NKJV

Seeking God seems to be the prerequisite to enjoying a good life. *Seek* is a strong word that means to go after something with all your strength and to keep searching until you find what you're looking for. There are things we can do without, and then there are vital things we cannot do without. We are to seek God as a vital necessity in life.

When people are taken to a hospital, the first thing the medical professionals do is check their vital signs. This gives them a good idea of how serious the situation is. I have learned that it is vital for me to seek God each morning before I even try to do anything else. We need Him, and seeking Him early is wise.

Those who seek God with diligence will have guidance and clarity from Him and will not live in confusion about decisions they need to make. Seeking God simply means spending time with Him, talking with Him (praying), and studying His Word. Set aside time to do this regularly, and you will realize it is time well spent.

Confession: *God is a vital necessity in my life, and I take time to seek Him on a regular basis.*

WHY DO YOU DO WHAT YOU DO?

Take care not to do your good deeds publicly or before men, in order to be seen by them; otherwise you will have no reward [reserved for and awaiting you] with and from your Father Who is in heaven.

MATTHEW 6:1

God is more interested in why we do things than in what we do. It is very important to Him that our motives are right. In 1 Corinthians 3:13–15 Paul said that when the day of Christ's return comes, we will all stand before the judgment seat of God, and our works will be judged to see if they were pure or not. Those not done with right motives will be burned up and all of our reward for them lost—although we ourselves will be saved.

We are not saved by our works, but our works done with right motives will receive a reward. Take time to ask yourself why you do the things you do. We should not do something simply to please people, especially if we resent doing it. We should not do things to be seen or noticed or thought well of. When we do something good, it should be because we love God and are being obedient to Him.

I am looking forward to my rewards, and I hope you're looking forward to yours also. Take time occasionally to do a motive check and remove anything from your life that you are not doing with pure motives. You might find that you will have more time and less stress.

Confession: *I do what I do with pure motives and because I love God and want to be obedient to Him.*

TRUST GOD IN EVERYTHING

When He was reviled and insulted, He did not revile or offer insult in return; [when] He was abused and suffered, He made no threats [of vengeance]; but he trusted [Himself and everything] to Him Who judges fairly.

1 PETER 2:23

We only have two options in life: trust God or be miserable. No one was more mistreated than Jesus, yet today's scripture tells us that when He was abused and suffered, He entrusted Himself and everything to God. Can you trust God with what happens to you and in all your circumstances?

It is more important that we represent Jesus well in the world around us than that we get what we want all the time. Anyone can be happy when they are not hurting and everything is going the way they want it to go. But God wants us to have joy all the time, even when our circumstances do not seem right or fair and we are waiting on Him to deliver us from them.

What is going on in your life? How do you need to trust God in the midst of it? If you are not trusting Him, you are probably worried, anxious, negative, and joyless. But you can make a decision right now to trust God. Isaiah 12:2 says, "Behold, God is my salvation; *I will trust*, and will not be afraid; for the Lord God is my strength and my song, and he has become my salvation" (ESV, italics mine). Trusting God brings peace and joy into our lives even in the midst of difficult circumstances. Stop trying to control everything, striving to solve problems on your own, and being frustrated because nothing you do seems to work. Put your trust in God.

Confession: *I daily make the decision to put my trust in God.*

HOW TO GET WHAT YOU WANT

Delight yourself in the Lord, and he will give you the desires of your heart.

PSALM 37:4 ESV

We all have things that we want, and we usually try to get them. We struggle, think of how we can obtain them, become angry, and get jealous of others who have what we want—all to no avail. We only end up frustrated and often confused.

God wants us to seek Him, not things. Matthew 6:33 tells us to seek first God's kingdom and His righteousness, and He will give us all other things. It is best to ask God for what you want and trust Him to give it to you if it is right for you—and to do it in His way and timing. Sometimes the things we think we want would not be good for us if we got them.

Ask God for what you want, and then spend your time being a blessing to other people, praying for them, and studying God's Word. Be content with what you have now, and be thankful for all your current blessings. Trust God to know what is best for you.

If you are frustrated and unhappy now, it is probably because you want something you are struggling to get, and nothing you do is working. Release the situation to God, and ask Him to give you what He knows is best.

Confession: *I want God's will, not my own. I will seek God, not things, and He will give me what is best for me.*

SEEK THE MOST EXCELLENT THING

Now about the spiritual gifts (the special endowments of supernatural energy), brethren, I do not want you to be misinformed.

1 CORINTHIANS 12:1

In today's verse, Paul writes about the importance of the gifts of the Holy Spirit. He explains this in verses 4–10. At the end of his lesson, he writes, "And I will show you a still more excellent way" (1 Corinthians 12:31 ESV). In the next verse, which begins 1 Corinthians 13, he begins his instruction on love and its characteristics. I want us to focus on one sentence in 1 Corinthians 13:5, which says that love "does not insist on its own way." Love is not selfish.

Love gives and focuses on making others happy; it is not self-seeking. As I have mentioned, it is impossible to be happy and selfish at the same time, so if you are unhappy, you might want to do a heart check to see if the problem is selfishness.

God has created us to reach out to others and work for what will benefit them, not to focus on ourselves and only think of what will benefit us. Love is something that can be seen and felt, and it is what every person in the world needs. If we give it away, we will find it coming back to us (Galatians 6:7).

Each day, take some time to think about what you can do for someone. If you can't think of anything, ask God to show you something. He may not answer immediately, but He will in due time. Decide to be ready whenever He calls, and be assured that your happiness will increase.

Confession: *I look for ways to be a blessing and help other people, and God takes care of me.*

BREAK FREE FROM ENTANGLEMENTS

No soldier gets entangled in civilian pursuits, since his aim is to please the one who enlisted him.

2 TIMOTHY 2:4 ESV

We all have a purpose in life, and we should know what it is and focus on it. Beware of getting entangled in things that will take you away from your purpose or even away from being able to spend time with God.

We can become entangled in other people's problems and spend a great deal of time trying to help them. But if they don't want to help themselves, we waste our time. My brother was addicted to drugs and alcohol, and Dave and I tried to help him. He lived with us for four years, and during that time, we did everything possible to help him. But he was still doing the same things, and he was hiding it and lying to us about it. I realized that if we had not been able to help him in four years, it was because he didn't really want help, and we asked him to move to his own apartment. To some, this could sound unloving. But actually, we were applying some tough love. We gave him all the tools he needed to build a good life for himself, but only he could take advantage of the help we offered. I had become entangled in his problems, and it was preventing me from fulfilling what God had called me to do.

If you are entangled in anything that does not bear good fruit, I encourage you to get untangled and get back to fulfilling your purpose.

Confession: *I will not allow myself to become entangled in things that take me away from God and His purpose for me.*

KEEP YOURSELF CALM

Blessed (happy, fortunate, to be envied) is the man whom You discipline and instruct, O Lord, and teach out of Your law, that You may give him power to keep himself calm in the days of adversity, until the [inevitable] pit of corruption is dug for the wicked.

PSALM 94:12–13

God disciplines those He loves (Proverbs 3:12 NIV), and we should appreciate and submit to His discipline. Discipline is not a bad thing; it is our friend because it teaches us the right way to live so we can enjoy the blessings Jesus died to give us.

Our scripture for today says that God will keep working with us through discipline and instruction until we learn to stay calm in adversity, while we wait for God to deal with our enemies.

For years I was up and down emotionally. If my circumstances were good, I was up, and if they were bad, I was down. This was very tiring, and it was not a good example to anyone around me. I finally learned that being discouraged or depressed when facing trouble and difficulty doesn't do any good. It never solves the problem. But if we put our trust in God and continue enjoying life in the midst of our problems, we defeat the devil and our breakthrough comes. Instead of feeling guilty or angry when God disciplines and instructs you, be thankful that He loves you enough to take the time to do it.

Confession: I am thankful when God disciplines and instructs me because He is helping me learn to be calm in adversity.

OFFER ALL OF YOURSELF TO GOD

Therefore, I urge you, brothers and sisters, in view of God's mercy, to offer your bodies as a living sacrifice, holy and pleasing to God— this is your true and proper worship. Do not conform to the pattern of this world, but be transformed by the renewing of your mind.

ROMANS 12:1–2 NIV

Offer yourself each day to God for His use. Give Him all your faculties, meaning your mind, mouth, will, emotions, desires, hands, feet, eyes, and everything about you. According to today's scripture, "this is your true and proper worship." Live wholly for God because you are important to His plan, and He needs you.

People who belong to the world live for themselves. They are selfish and self-centered. When they do pray, their prayers are usually requests, asking God to give them something they want. Instead of doing this, ask God what you can do for Him and who you can be a blessing to each day. As you delight yourself in the Lord, He will give you things you desire (Psalm 37:4).

God loves you very much, and He has a good plan for your life, one that is productive for His kingdom and gives you great joy and peace.

Confession: *I offer myself to You, Lord, for Your use. I hold nothing back, and all that I am and everything I have belongs to You.*

AGGRESSIVE ACTS OF KINDNESS

A new command I give you: Love one another. As I have loved you, so you must love one another. By this everyone will know that you are my disciples, if you love one another.

JOHN 13:34–35 NIV

Many people in the world don't know what real love is. When I married Dave, I was one of those people. All the people who said they loved me had hurt or abused me, and the words "I love you" meant nothing to me. Love is more than a theory, a sermon, or mere words; it is action. Aggressive acts of kindness communicate more than words of love without action to back them up.

Do things to show people you love them. Use your time, money, and energy to bless them. In doing so, you are blessing God. Jesus says that whatever we do for "one of the least [in the estimation of men] of these My brethren," we do for Him (Matthew 25:40). Serving others is the best way to serve God. He loves His people, and He rejoices when we do things that bless others. Random acts of kindness—doing things for people you may not even know for no reason except to show them God's love—are powerful.

When I have done this, I have often been told "No one has ever done anything like this for me." I usually respond with "God has been good to me, and I just wanted to bless someone." These opportunities allow me to bless people while also being an example of the goodness of God. In blessing others your joy will increase.

Confession: *I love to do things for other people and to help them feel loved.*

BE KIND AND GENEROUS

Do not forget or neglect to do kindness and good, to be generous and distribute and contribute to the needy [of the church as embodiment and proof of fellowship], for such sacrifices are pleasing to God.

HEBREWS 13:16

The New Testament contains more than fifty references to the fact that faith and love must work together. What have you asked God—in faith—to do for you? My next question is: Are you intentionally walking in love? Colossians 3:14 tells us that above all else, we are to "[put on] love." The words *put on* are intentional words that require purposeful action. I have never gone into my closet and had my clothes jump on my body. I pick them out carefully to make sure they are comfortable and look good on me.

We not only wear physical clothes; we also wear spiritual clothes. We wear our attitudes and other spiritual qualities, such as kindness, mercy, forgiveness, patience, and gentleness (Colossians 3:12–13). We would not go out of the house physically naked, and we should make sure we don't go out spiritually naked, either. Each morning, decide that you will show kindness, be merciful, walk in love, forgive anyone who might hurt or offend you, and be joyful. Instead of waiting to see how you feel, make up your mind about how you will behave, and your feelings will follow.

You have the power to change someone's day and help them be happy. Live to give, not to get, and God will give you more than you can imagine.

Confession: *I will not forget or neglect to be kind to people and to show them mercy and love.*

HELP THOSE WHO CANNOT HELP THEMSELVES

Religion that God our Father accepts as pure and faultless is this: to look after orphans and widows in their distress and to keep oneself from being polluted by the world.

JAMES 1:27 NIV

Take time today to think about all the people in the world who are either too young or too old to take care of themselves. Pray about what God would have you do to help them. You may know a widow you could invite to your home for dinner. Or perhaps she needs financial help, and you could occasionally pay a bill for her or give her a gift certificate for food or clothing.

You could contact orphanages in your city about fostering or adopting a child or being part of a big brother or sister program. You could send gifts at Christmas to the children in the program, or perhaps just go and visit them.

Our ministry supports and contributes to many different orphanages, and we feed hungry children all over the world. I want my religion to be real and not just a routine that includes going to church regularly but not really doing anything to help anyone. You may feel the same way.

If you don't know what to do to help someone, ask God to show you. Expect Him to give you an assignment that will help someone else and also increase your joy.

Confession: *I help the helpless and it is my joy to do so.*

WHEN LIFE GETS DIFFICULT

It is [only] eleven days' journey from Horeb by the way of Mount Seir to Kadesh-barnea [on Canaan's border; yet Israel took forty years to get beyond it].

DEUTERONOMY 1:2

Sometimes life is hard when we wish it were easy. God sometimes leads us the long, hard way, as He did the Israelites after they left Egypt and headed to the Promised Land. He took them through the wilderness, and although a shorter route would have taken only eleven days, their travels took them forty years. Why? Because their attitude was bad, and they were not ready for the warfare they would face when they entered the Promised Land. In addition, they were not willing to trust God to help them defeat their enemies when they entered the Promised Land. They faced difficulties in the wilderness, but I believe those challenges were designed to prepare them for the battles they would fight in the Promised Land.

It is important to trust God, no matter how He leads you. Whether your way is easy or difficult, trust Him. After the Israelites crossed the Jordan River and went into the Promised Land, they fought one battle after another as they took the territory that God had promised them. They learned to fight in God's strength. If you know God has asked you to do something, don't back down just because it is hard. He is with you and will help you win every battle.

Confession: I trust God whether He leads me the hard way or the easy way, because I know that however He leads me will be best for me.

GIVE GOD THE GLORY

But by the grace of God I am what I am, and his grace to me was not without effect. No, I worked harder than all of them—yet not I, but the grace of God that was with me.

1 CORINTHIANS 15:10 NIV

Do you want to be closer to God? One way to do it is to make sure that you give Him the credit and glory for anything good you do. Paul worked hard in ministry, but he did so by God's grace. He said that by the grace of God "I am what I am." One thing we must not do is try to take God's glory for ourselves, because Isaiah 42:8 says that He will not share it with anyone.

The English evangelist Henry Varley said to D. L. Moody, "The world has yet to see what God can do through a man who is totally yielded to Him."[6] I believe it's equally true that the world has yet to see what God could do through a man or woman who will give Him all the credit and glory. The more we rely and depend on God, the closer we feel to Him. Know without a doubt that you need Him in everything you do, even things you have done many times before.

God is our strength and ability. Jesus says, "Apart from me you can do nothing" (John 15:5 NIV). And Paul writes, "For I know that nothing good dwells within me, that is, in my flesh" (Romans 7:18). God's Spirit is in us as believers in Jesus. Because of this, we can do anything we need to do. Before each thing you do, ask Him to help you, and thank Him when it is done.

Confession: *I lean and rely on God all the time. I can do nothing without Him, and I give Him the glory for anything good I do.*

DON'T LET YOUR EMOTIONS VOTE

For this very reason, make every effort to add to your faith good-ness; and to goodness, knowledge; and to knowledge, self-control; and to self-control, perseverance; and to perseverance, godliness.

2 PETER 1:5–6 NIV

Learn not to ask yourself how you feel about things, but instead if doing or not doing something is right for you. In the United States, we don't allow people to vote until they are eighteen because we assume they would be too immature to know what they are doing. Why not look at your emotions the same way? They have always been a part of you, but they are very imma-ture. They are without wisdom and cannot be trusted to do the right thing, so just don't let them vote. Sometimes, people grow up physically, but their emotions don't. If their emotions are left unchecked, their lives will be a series of unfinished and dis-appointing ventures.

People frequently ask me how I feel about traveling so much in my ministry. I have simply learned to say "I don't ask myself how I feel about it." If I asked myself too often, I would find that I don't like it much and might be tempted to stop doing something I believe God wants me to do. Someone asked me if I was excited about an upcoming conference, and I said, "I have something better than excitement: I am committed." So, I am led not by excitement or the lack of it—I just go where I believe God calls me to go. Then, I am fulfilled and satisfied in know-ing I have obeyed God and helped other people. The loss of the feeling of excitement does not mean we are not supposed to do certain things anymore. Emotions don't get a vote.

Confession: *When I need to make a decision, I don't let my emotions vote.*

RESPOND WITH LOVE

But love your enemies, do good to them, and lend to them without expecting to get anything back. Then your reward will be great, and you will be children of the Most High, because he is kind to the ungrateful and wicked.

LUKE 6:35 NIV

How do you react to people who are rude? Do you respond in love as God's Word says we should, or do you join them in their ungodly behavior? When a clerk in a store is rude to me, I can instantly feel my emotions start to rise up. When I feel that happening, I know I need to take action. I have to reason with myself and remember that the person being rude probably has a lot of problems and may not even realize how they sound.

I am very thankful that I know the Word of God and have His Spirit in my life to help and comfort me. I always want my behavior to be an example to others for Christ and not something that would make Him ashamed of me. Since that is the case, I have to work with the Holy Spirit to develop the ability to act on God's Word when people are rude instead of merely reacting to them with behavior that matches or tops theirs.

Jesus says we have done nothing special if we treat people well when they treat us well, but if we are kind to someone who would qualify as an enemy, then we are doing well (John 6:32–34 NIV). Will you act on the Word of God and love people who are unkind or rude to you for His sake?

Confession: *I pray for people who treat me rudely and display God's love toward them.*

SELF-CONFIDENCE

For we [Christians] are the true circumcision, who worship God in spirit and by the Spirit of God and exult and glory and pride ourselves in Jesus Christ, and put no confidence or dependence [on what we are] in the flesh and on outward privileges and physical advantages and external appearances.

PHILIPPIANS 3:3

God wants us to be confident, but not self-confident. If we put our confidence in other people, they will often disappoint us. And if we put our confidence in ourselves, we will definitely disappoint ourselves. But if we put our confidence in God, we will never be disappointed (Psalm 22:5).

I am not suggesting that we don't trust people at all, but there is a part of us that belongs only to God, and He wants us to realize that no matter who else is in our lives, He is the One who provides all strength. I have learned that even when people do help me, it is God working through them to do it. He works through people, and often, when we ask Him for something, He uses a person to get it to us. We should thank the person, but we should also thank God for using them.

In the Amplified Bible, Classic Edition, Proverbs repeatedly says that a fool is a "[self-confident] fool." Just remember: We need confidence in God, not self-confidence. We can only be self-confident in His confidence.

Confession: *All good things come from God, so my confidence is in Him and no one else.*

DON'T OVERESTIMATE YOURSELF AND UNDERESTIMATE OTHERS

For by the grace (unmerited favor of God) given to me I warn everyone among you not to estimate and think of himself more highly than he ought [not to have an exaggerated opinion of his own importance], but to rate his ability with sober judgment, each according to the degree of faith apportioned by God to him.

ROMANS 12:3

Overestimating ourselves (thinking more highly than we should of ourselves and our abilities) sets off a chain reaction of problems. If we are haughty and arrogant, we will tend to exclude others and be unwilling to associate with people we feel are beneath us. We will have no ability to adjust and adapt to others because we will feel we are always right.

Getting along with other people requires humility. The humble receive God's help, but He resists the proud and haughty (James 4:6). According to the Amplified Bible, Classic Edition, we should not rely on our own understanding; when we trust in the Lord with all our heart and all our mind, He will direct our paths (Proverbs 3:5–6).

At times, God allows just enough trouble in our lives to force us to trust Him. Paul writes in 2 Corinthians 12:2–20 that God refused to remove the thorn in his flesh to keep him from being puffed up with pride because of the greatness of the revelations he had been given (2 Corinthians 12:7). Stay safe by staying humble.

Confession: *I will humble myself under God's mighty hand because I know I am nothing without Him.*

SYMPTOMS OF CONFIDENCE IN GOD

And many people shall come and say, Come, let us go up to the mountain of the Lord, to the house of the God of Jacob, that He may teach us His ways and that we may walk in His paths. For out of Zion shall go forth the law and instruction, and the word of the Lord from Jerusalem.

ISAIAH 2:3

If we have confidence in God, our minds will be focused on Him much of the time. We will pray our way through each day knowing that we need His help with everything we do. We won't be worried or anxious because we trust that the Lord has a plan for our life and will always take care of us. We will be thankful because we know that every tiny blessing and every big blessing is a gift from God.

If our trust is in God, we will verbalize our dependence on Him to Him and to others. When we are successful at all we attempt to do, we will not boast or brag. True faith leans on, relies on, trusts in, and rests in God.

Nothing relieves stress like trusting God in every situation. We can exhaust ourselves trying to solve our own problems and take care of ourselves, or we can trust God. I've tried both, and I can assure you that trusting God is the better choice.

Confession: *I put my trust in God, and He never fails me.*

ARE YOU OPTIMISTIC OR PESSIMISTIC?

[What, what would have become of me] had I not believed that I would see the Lord's goodness in the land of the living!

PSALM 27:13

Today I want to tell you a story about two twins:

Two twins were alike in every way, except one was an optimist and one was a pessimist. The parents were concerned and took them to the doctor, who suggested a test: "For their birthday this year, give the pessimist the best racing bicycle money can buy but give the optimist a box of manure."

When the day came, the pessimist was led to his bike. He said, "I will probably crash and break my leg." The optimist opened his box of manure and, after a momentary shock, ran outside looking all around. He said, "You can't fool me; where there is this much manure, there has to be a pony somewhere."

Which twin would you have been? Being pessimistic is not pleasing to God. It does not represent a faith-filled attitude, and it gives you no benefits. When you get up every day, start by saying "This is a good day, and something good is going to happen to me and through me." Positive thinking is godly thinking, because there is nothing negative about God.

Confession: *I am a positive and optimistic person. I see good things in my life, and I do good things for other people.*

INJUSTICE COLLECTORS

Declare His glory among the nations, His marvelous works among all peoples.

1 CHRONICLES 16:24

Those who feel sorry for themselves collect every memory they can about how mistreated they have been and what people have not done for them. They think of all the hardships and difficulties they have experienced. They look for others who will sympathize with them, and if they can find no one, they are happy to feel sorry for themselves.

What if we decided to be "blessing collectors"? We could make ourselves happy no matter what's going on in our lives. Our perspective on any situation is what makes us happy or sad. Some people find a problem with everything, and others may see the problem but know that God is good and loves them. They trust Him to solve the problem at the right time and in the right way. Try being happy; you have nothing to lose except a bad attitude.

Confession: *I refuse to feel sorry for myself, and I will believe the best of everyone.*

KNOW YOUR ENEMY'S NATURE

*You are of your father, the devil, and it is your will to practice the
lusts and gratify the desires [which are characteristic] of your father.
He was a murderer from the beginning and does not stand in the
truth, because there is no truth in him. When he speaks a false-
hood, he speaks what is natural to him, for he is a liar [himself] and
the father of lies and of all that is false.*

JOHN 8:44

We all have an enemy, the devil (Satan). He is not only our
enemy but also God's. He comes only to steal, kill, and destroy
(John 10:10). He has been a liar from the beginning, and his
goal is to keep us from knowing the truth of God's Word.

We blame people for many things when actually the devil
is behind them. The good news is that we have authority over
Him in Jesus' name (Luke 10:19). James 4:7 tells us to submit
to God and resist the devil, and he will flee. Our power to resist
him is found in submitting to God.

Satan deceived Eve in the Garden of Eden, and she did what
God had told Adam they should not do (Genesis 2:16–17; 3:1–
6). She was tempted by the devil, and through her persuasion,
Adam was also tempted. They both sinned by disobeying God,
and through them sin entered the world. Thankfully, God sent
His only Son, Jesus, to undo what the devil had done, and we
no longer have to live in bondage to sin. Be sure to educate
yourself about your enemy by reading and studying God's
Word. Watch and pray that he does not deceive you.

Confession: *Through the Holy Spirit, I have power and authority
over the devil. I submit myself to God; I resist the devil, and he
must flee.*

CONVICTION IS NOT CONDEMNATION

Therefore, there is now no condemnation for those who are in Christ Jesus, because through Christ Jesus the law of the Spirit who gives life has set you free from the law of sin and death.

ROMANS 8:1–2 NIV

There's a difference between condemnation and conviction. Condemnation is a guilty feeling that presses us down and says we must pay for what we have done wrong. Conviction is the work of the Holy Spirit, showing us that we have sinned and inviting us to confess our sins so we can receive God's forgiveness and help to improve our behavior in the future. Condemnation makes a problem worse, but conviction is intended to lift us out of it.

When you feel condemned, ask yourself if you are guilty according to God's Word. If so, confess your sin to God, turn away from it, and don't repeat it. Apologize to anyone you may have wronged. Then forgive yourself and let the matter go. Jesus purchased all the forgiveness we will ever need on the cross, so receive it and experience the joy of redemption.

You may find that you are not guilty according to God's Word. For example, for many years I drove myself to work incessantly because I felt good when I was accomplishing something, and I felt guilty if I enjoyed myself. This kind of thinking doesn't agree with God's Word. When I stopped believing my feelings and started examining them in light of God's Word, I realized I had been deceived—and I finally learned to rest and enjoy it.

Confession: *I do not waste my life feeling guilty. I receive the conviction of the Holy Spirit, but I do not receive condemnation.*

DON'T BE AFRAID TO HOPE

Then Jesus said to the centurion, "Go your way; and as you have believed, so let it be done for you." And his servant was healed that same hour.

MATTHEW 8:13 NKJV

Hope is the expectation that something good is going to happen, and we all need hope. But some people are afraid to hope because they have been hurt so much in life. They have had so many disappointments they don't think they can face the pain of another one. Therefore, they refuse to hope so they won't be disappointed. This way of thinking leads to a negative lifestyle.

Many years ago, I was extremely negative. My philosophy was this: "If you don't expect anything good to happen, then you won't be disappointed when it doesn't." I had encountered so many disappointments in life and so many devastating things had happened to me that I was afraid to believe that anything good might take place. When I really began to study the Word and to trust God to restore me, one of the first things I realized was that my negativism had to go, and I had to believe God's Word.

God has a perfect plan for each of us, but we must think and speak in agreement with His will and plan for us. We certainly can't control Him with our thoughts and words, but we can think and speak what His Word says.

Practice being positive in each situation that arises and expect God to bring good out of it, as He promises in His Word (Romans 8:28).

Confession: I am not afraid to hope, because I believe God has good plans for me.

BELIEVE GOD'S PROMISES

For as many as are the promises of God, they all find their Yes [answer] in Him [Christ].

2 CORINTHIANS 1:20

Today's scripture teaches us that all of God's many promises are ours in Christ. They are given by His goodness and grace and received through our faith. Faith is the evidence of things we do not see, and it gives us hope that what we believe will actually happen (Hebrews 11:1). There is always a waiting period between asking God for something and receiving it. The waiting requires patience and is often a test of our faith.

We can say that we have faith, but we don't really know we have it—or how much we have—until we have to use it. Faith pleases God (Hebrews 11:6). It means that we trust Him, and our trust in Him glorifies Him.

Abraham wanted a child, but both he and his wife were beyond childbearing years. What he wanted was impossible in the natural realm. But what is impossible to human beings is possible with God (Luke 18:27). When Abraham had no reason to hope based on human reason, he hoped in faith—and God's promise to give him a biological heir came true. Don't be afraid to believe God for things that seem impossible because there is nothing God cannot do.

Confession: I trust God, and I believe He can do anything. All things are possible with Him.

THE JOY OF THE LORD IS YOUR STRENGTH

Do not sorrow, for the joy of the Lord is your strength.

NEHEMIAH 8:10 NKJV

Even though Satan comes only to bring destruction, Jesus came so we might have and enjoy our lives (John 10:10). I was at least forty-five years old before I ever let myself enjoy my life. Because of growing up in incest and a joyless atmosphere, I developed the habit of merely trying to survive each day. It never occurred to me that one of the reasons Jesus died and rose from the dead was so we could all enjoy our lives. Due to sexual abuse, I never really got to experience being a child. God actually had to teach me how to enjoy life.

I felt guilty most of the time. If it wasn't one thing, it was another; but it was all a result of my childhood. I had a wounded soul and needed Jesus to heal it, and He did. He gave me beauty for ashes and the oil of joy for mourning (Isaiah 61:3).

God's will is for us to enjoy every day of our lives. I have good news for you: Even while you are having trials and problems, you can cast the care of them onto God (1 Peter 5:7) and still enjoy your life. The joy of the Lord is your strength (Nehemiah 8:10). Satan does all he possibly can to steal your joy because he wants us to be weak and powerless. Don't let him win. Enjoy life and laugh as often as you can. I'm sure the devil hates to hear us laugh.

Confession: *I will enjoy my life and not let the devil steal my joy. He may come against me, but he will not win in the end, because God is on my side.*

BE YOURSELF

For You formed my innermost parts; You knit me [together] in my mother's womb. I will give thanks and praise to You, for I am fearfully and wonderfully made; wonderful are Your works, and my soul knows it very well.

PSALM 139:13–14 AMP

God will never help you be anyone other than yourself. He won't help you be someone else, and you don't have to compare yourself to others or compete with them. Just be yourself. You may not be able to do what someone else can do, but you can do things they can't. I tried for a long time to be like Dave, my pastor's wife, my neighbor, and others, but I didn't succeed. I only grew more and more frustrated. I tried so hard to be like other people that I lost myself and didn't know who I was.

God showed me that I didn't like who I was and that it was wrong for me to feel that way. He created each of us to be unique and different than everyone else. You may know someone who is a good example for you, but you still can't be exactly like that person. Embrace yourself and your strengths and weaknesses. Trust God to show His strength through your weaknesses.

God chooses the weak and foolish things of this world to confound those who think they are wise (1 Corinthians 1:27). He is not looking for ability, but for availability. Make yourself available for God's use, and I assure you that you will be amazed at the great things He will do through you, just the way you are.

Confession: *I only want to be the best version of me that I can be.*

LEARN TO CONTROL YOUR ANGER WITH GOD'S HELP

When angry, do not sin; do not ever let your wrath (your exasperation, your fury or indignation) last until the sun goes down.

EPHESIANS 4:26

Have you recently struggled with the fact that you are a Christian who is trying to live a godly life, yet you still feel angry? Many Christians are confused about anger and think that as people who want to be Christlike, they should never get angry. They wonder why they keep having to deal with anger when it's something they don't want to feel.

We need to understand that not all anger is a sin, but some of it is. The Bible speaks of a righteous anger that even God Himself displayed at times in Scripture (Psalm 7:11 NIV).

What's the difference between apparently innocent emotions that are simply part of life and emotions that are sinful? Unacceptable and sinful anger is that which fills us with bitterness, resentment, and unforgiveness and/or motivates us to hurt a fellow human being. When we want to lash out vengefully and inflict pain on others, we are definitely out of God's will. God says that vengeance is His (Deuteronomy 32:35), and our position is to be one of faith in Him, waiting patiently and lovingly as He works justice in our lives. Controlling the passion of anger, especially if you have an aggressive and outspoken nature, can be one of the more challenging things you will face in life, but controlling it is certainly possible with God's help.

Confession: *With God's help, I do not allow anger to control me; I trust God to bring justice.*

WHAT DO YOU EXPECT TO HAPPEN?

All the days of the desponding and afflicted are made evil [by anxious thoughts and forebodings], but he who has a glad heart has a continual feast [regardless of circumstances].

PROVERBS 15:15

Shortly after I began to study God's Word, I was combing my hair one morning in the bathroom when I sensed that something bad was going to happen. It wasn't a strong feeling, just a vague impression, but enough that I was aware of it. I soon realized that I had actually had that feeling with me most of my life. When I asked God about this, the words that came to mind were *evil forebodings.*

I did not know what those words meant, nor had I ever heard of evil forebodings. Shortly after this happened, I found the phrase in the amplification of today's scripture. I realized at that time that most of my life had been made miserable by evil thoughts and forebodings. Yes, I had circumstances that were very difficult, but even when I didn't, I was still miserable because my thoughts were poisoning my outlook and robbing me of my ability to enjoy life and see good days. Even if nothing bad was happening at the time, I vaguely sensed that something bad was about to happen. Because of that, I was unable to really enjoy my life.

Today's scripture teaches us how to overcome evil forebodings, and that is to have a glad heart regardless of our circumstances. The next time you feel something bad is going to happen, start thanking and praising God for all the good He has done and will do in your life.

Confession: *I do not allow evil forebodings to take away my joy.*

PEACE THAT PASSES UNDERSTANDING

The Lord will give strength to His people; the Lord will bless His people with peace.

PSALM 29:11 NKJV

When Jesus went to heaven, He left us His peace (John 14:27)—His own special peace—not peace as the world knows, but the peace that passes understanding. We can have peace regarding the past, the present, and the future. We can enjoy peace regarding ourselves and everything and everyone that concerns us. We can face big problems or challenges in life and still have peace, as long as we put our trust in God.

A simple, childlike faith is all we need. God is a loving Father, and His will for us is righteousness, peace, and joy in the Holy Spirit (Romans 14:17). Faith is not the price that buys God's blessings; it is merely the hand that expectantly and thankfully receives them. When we realize how much God has done for us through Jesus, how could we not be thankful?

Peace has a lot to do with how we think. We can worry, or we can think, *I believe God is working on this problem, and I will see my breakthrough at just the right time.* One piece of spiritual armor we have as believers is the helmet of salvation, and we are told to put it on (Ephesians 6:11, 17). To me, this means we are to think like a follower of Christ—according to God's Word. Trust God and hope in Him, receiving His peace and expecting good things to happen to you and through you.

Confession: *I trust God and receive His peace. I look forward to all the good things He has planned for my future.*

HAVE YOUR MIND RENEWED

Do not be conformed to this world (this age), [fashioned after and adapted to its external, superficial customs], but be transformed (changed) by the [entire] renewal of your mind [by its new ideals and its new attitude], so that you may prove [for yourselves] what is the good and acceptable and perfect will of God, even the thing which is good and acceptable and perfect [in His sight for you].

ROMANS 12:2

The renewing of the mind is life-changing because our thoughts lead to our words, attitudes, and actions. We should keep our minds in a positive condition and think about and meditate on God's Word. The more we study it, hear it, think about it, and read books about it, the more it becomes part of who we are. As we grow in knowing and understanding God's Word, we are dramatically changed.

According to Ephesians 4:23, our mind should be constantly renewed. We are to set our minds and keep them set on things above (God's things), not things on the earth (Colossians 3:2).

I can say without hesitation that learning God's Word has completely changed me and my life. It is full of power. It is the truth—the only real truth that exists. Anything that doesn't agree with God's Word is false. Believe God's Word no matter what you see, how you feel, or what you think, and confess (speak aloud) God's Word daily. As your mind is renewed by God's Word, you will come to know through experience what God's good and pleasing will is.

Confession: *I believe God's Word is full of power. It is the truth, and it is life-changing. I will believe God's Word above all else and base my life on it.*

BEWARE OF FORBIDDEN FRUIT

When the woman saw that the fruit of the tree was good for food and pleasing to the eye, and also desirable for gaining wisdom, she took some and ate it. She also gave some to her husband, who was with her, and he ate it. Then the eyes of both of them were opened, and they realized they were naked; so they sewed fig leaves together and made coverings for themselves. Then the man and his wife heard the sound of the Lord God as he was walking in the garden in the cool of the day, and they hid from the Lord God among the trees of the garden.

GENESIS 3:6–8 NIV

A woman once told me that she loved another man and did not love her husband anymore. She *feels* she can never be happy without the other man, but I know from God's Word and life's experiences that she will never be happy with him, either. Once the excitement of having the forbidden fruit wears off, the misery will begin.

In the Garden of Eden, Satan made the fruit look like something Eve could not pass up. But the moment Eve ate the fruit and gave a piece to Adam and he ate, they both lost something they never got back. They were ashamed and felt guilty, and they hid from God. Disobeying God, even if it seems appealing, absolutely cannot produce lasting joy.

The nature of the flesh is to want what it thinks it cannot have. But once the flesh attains what it thought it wanted, the craving starts all over again. No matter how much it has, it is still never satisfied. It is vital for us to obey God's Word instead of being led by our emotions.

Confession: *I obey the Word of God, not my feelings.*

FOCUS ON PAST VICTORIES

For the Lord your God is He Who goes with you to fight for you against your enemies to save you.

DEUTERONOMY 20:4

We all face problems in life, and when we do, a very helpful way I have found to deal with them is to think about troubles I have dealt with in the past that God has resolved. There are times when He shows us something to do about a situation, and if He does, we should do it. But if He doesn't show us anything, we should take a stand of faith and trust Him to do what we cannot do.

For a long time, I tried to change myself into the person I thought God wanted me to be, but all I got was frustrated. I was afraid that God was not pleased with me, and I felt guilty most of the time because I didn't measure up to what I thought the Bible said I should be.

I finally gave up, told God I could not change myself and asked Him to change me if He wanted to. How do we change? Certainly not through worry or fear that God will reject us if we don't change, but by studying His Word and letting its power transform us (Romans 12:2). We should pay close attention to the fact that God changes us "from glory to glory" (2 Corinthians 3:18 NKJV). This means the changes we need don't all come at once but in small degrees, so that we can maintain the changes God brings in our lives.

When you face a problem, remember how He has helped you in the past and trust that He will help you again.

Confession: *I remember my past victories and trust God to do what I cannot.*

PRAY AT ALL TIMES

Pray at all times (on every occasion, in every season) in the Spirit, with all [manner of] prayer and entreaty. To that end keep alert and watch with strong purpose and perseverance, interceding in behalf of all the saints (God's consecrated people).

EPHESIANS 6:18

Prayer is a privilege, not an obligation. It is not something we have to do, but it is something we get to do. James 4:2 teaches us that there are certain things we do not have because we do not ask God for them. How many things do we do without simply because we don't ask?

Do you ever feel you don't deserve to ask God for much? I think we all do at times, but Hebrews 4:15–16 tells us that Jesus is our High Priest who understands our weaknesses because He has been tempted just as we have, yet without sinning. Therefore, we can go boldly to the throne of grace and receive the help we need. We are to approach God boldly, not in weakness, asking for barely enough to get by. We pray in Jesus' name, which means we present to God all that Jesus is, not all that we are.

I encourage you to begin asking God for bigger and better things than you ever have before. He wants to hear your bold prayers, and He is waiting to answer them.

Confession: *I have the privilege of prayer, and I approach God's throne boldly and ask for all that I need, because God hears and answers my prayers.*

THE DIVINE EXCHANGE

Therefore if any person is [ingrafted] in Christ (the Messiah) he is a new creation (a new creature altogether); the old [previous moral and spiritual condition] has passed away. Behold, the fresh and new has come!

2 CORINTHIANS 5:17

To summarize today's scripture in simple terms, God takes all the bad in our lives and gives us all His good. He takes our sin and gives us His righteousness. He takes our past and gives us a good future. He takes our anxiety and worry and gives us His peace. He takes our pain and the wounds we have in our soul and gives us His healing. He takes our insecurity and gives us His confidence.

I can't understand why anyone would not want to surrender their life to God if they understand how good He is. Receive Jesus as your Lord and let Him be the center of your life. Based on Acts 17:28 (NIV), let's say with the apostle Paul, "In Him we live and move and have our being."

It is easy to be obedient to God when you understand that what He asks you to do or not do is only for your benefit. Let yourself be guided and led by the Holy Spirit. He is your Comforter, Helper, Strengthener, Advocate, and Teacher. He guides us into all truth. A Spirit-led life is a successful, powerful, and enjoyable life.

Confession: *God is good, and He is my life. I am led by the Holy Spirit, who teaches me truth and helps me with everything I need to do.*

BE CONFIDENT

For we [Christians] are the true circumcision, who worship God in spirit and by the Spirit of God and exult and glory and pride ourselves in Jesus Christ, and put no confidence or dependence [on what we are] in the flesh and on outward privileges and physical advantages and external appearances.

PHILIPPIANS 3:3

Without confidence, we are like a jet sitting on the runway with no fuel in it. Confidence in God is the fuel we need to do the things He wants us to do. Don't seek self-confidence, but seek to have your confidence firmly planted in Christ alone. We can only be self-confident in His confidence.

God will give you many opportunities in life, but you will need confidence to take steps of faith to act on them. Paul said a wide door of opportunity opened to him, but that many adversaries came with it (1 Corinthians 16:9). When we step into a God-given opportunity, we need confidence not only that with God's help we can do what lies before us, but that we can also defeat the opposition the devil uses trying to get us to give up.

If you are facing a new challenge or a new opportunity right now, don't let fear stop you. Keep putting one foot in front of the other. No matter how long it takes, don't ever give up.

Confession: *I have confidence in God, and I believe He will help me do all He asks me to do. I will not live in fear, and I will never give up.*

ALL HAVE SINNED AND
ALL ARE JUSTIFIED

Since all have sinned and are falling short of the honor and glory which God bestows and receives. [All] are justified and made upright and in right standing with God, freely and gratuitously by His grace (His unmerited favor and mercy), through the redemption which is [provided] in Christ Jesus.

ROMANS 3:23–24

Today's scripture gives us such good news. Jesus has provided the answer to sin. To be justified by Christ means to be made just as though you never sinned. I don't know about you, but I would probably need to think about this a long time to even begin to know how wonderful it is. The Bible says that where sin abounds, grace abounds much more (Romans 5:20).

We do not need to live under condemnation (feeling guilty about our sin). The price for our sin has been paid. All sin—past, present, and future—has already been forgiven. All we need to do when we sin is admit it, repent (turn away from it), and freely receive God's gift of forgiveness.

We receive right standing with God through faith in Jesus; it can never be earned through keeping rules and regulations. In fact, it cannot be earned in any way. It is a gift and must be accepted as such. Righteousness with God brings peace with God, and both are wonderful gifts. Be thankful for all that Jesus has done for you and show your gratitude by being joyfully obedient to Him.

Confession: *All my sins are forgiven, and I am justified through Jesus Christ. I am made right with God, and I have peace with Him.*

GOD BEGAN A GOOD WORK IN YOU, AND HE WILL FINISH IT

And I am convinced and sure of this very thing, that He Who began a good work in you will continue until the day of Jesus Christ [right up to the time of His return], developing [that good work] and perfecting and bringing it to full completion in you.

PHILIPPIANS 1:6

Have you received Christ as your Savior but don't feel that you are making any progress in changing into the person He wants you to become? We all feel that way at times. Sometimes we grow frustrated and try to change ourselves. Always remember during those times that God began a good work in you, and He certainly will finish it. It might not be on your expected time-table, but it will happen at the right time.

Jesus is the author and the finisher of our faith (Hebrews 12:2 NKJV). Trying to finish what God started is a mistake. We should do anything He shows us to do to make progress, but we should not just try one thing after another in our own strength. It will only frustrate us because it will not work.

God changes us as we study His Word and lean on the Holy Spirit to teach us to apply it to our lives. The Bible says we are constantly being transformed into Christ's image (2 Corinthians 3:18). Don't just look at how far you still have to go; look at how far you have come.

Confession: *God is changing me little by little, and He will finish the work He has begun.*

IF GOD DOESN'T DO IT, IT WON'T GET DONE

For while the Law was given through Moses, grace (unearned, undeserved favor and spiritual blessing) and truth came through Jesus Christ.

JOHN 1:17

God wants us to do His works but to avoid "works of the flesh," meaning using our human energy to try to do God's job. I like to say that the works of the flesh are "works that don't work." Have you ever tried to change another person—one of your children, or perhaps a spouse? I have, and I can tell you that it did not work. Only God can truly change people, because it is a work that must be done from the inside out.

My husband loves sports, and I don't care for any of them. In the early years of our marriage, I tried to get him to do what I wanted him to do instead of what he wanted to do. This was selfish on my part, but at that time I was so busy thinking he was wrong that I couldn't see my own faults. Instead of making him dislike sports, I think he began to like them more. I always say, "If it bounces or rolls, Dave likes it." Dave and I have been married over fifty-seven years, and he still enjoys most sports.

Instead of God changing Dave, He changed me. Now I like for him to watch sports, because that means I can have the other television and watch whatever I want. When he plays golf, I have about six hours by myself, and I have learned to enjoy my time alone. One of the best things in our marriage is that we give each other freedom to be ourselves.

Confession: *Only God can change people. I will pray for people to be what God wants them to be, but I won't try to change them. I will let God work on me and trust Him with other people.*

DON'T BE EASILY OFFENDED

It is not conceited (arrogant and inflated with pride); it is not rude (unmannerly) and does not act unbecomingly. Love (God's love in us) does not insist on its own rights or its own way, for it is not self-seeking; it is not touchy or fretful or resentful; it takes no account of the evil done to it [it pays no attention to a suffered wrong].

1 CORINTHIANS 13:5

As it says in today's verse, love is not touchy or easily offended, and it always believes the best of everyone. In practical terms, to walk in love means that when someone hurts your feelings, instead of thinking they did it on purpose, you give them the benefit of the doubt and believe they didn't even realize they hurt you. You will also forgive them because that is what love does.

It is easy to forgive people when we remember how often we need forgiveness. We always have a choice, and we can choose whether to get hurt, offended, and angry or to believe the best and stay happy. Choosing to be happy is one of the best things you can do for yourself.

I doubt many people get up each day and plan on hurting people. They may be hurting, and often people who are hurting in turn hurt others. If you hurt or offend someone, apologize right away and ask them to forgive you. I recently hurt one of my children's feelings and didn't mean to at all. I asked for forgiveness right away, and our peace was immediately restored.

Confession: *I believe the best of every person, and if I hurt or offend someone, I ask them to forgive me right away.*

STRIFE IS CAUSED BY TRYING INSTEAD OF TRUSTING

What leads to strife (discord and feuds) and how do conflicts (quarrels and fightings) originate among you? Do they not arise from your sensual desires that are ever warring in your bodily members? You are jealous and covet [what others have] and your desires go unfulfilled; [so] you become murderers. [To hate is to murder as far as your hearts are concerned.] You burn with envy and anger and are not able to obtain [the gratification, the contentment, and the happiness that you seek], so you fight and war. You do not have, because you do not ask.

JAMES 4:1–2

Strife happens when people bicker, argue, or engage in heated disagreement. It is an angry undercurrent that runs through relationships and situations, and our world is filled with it. Strife ultimately causes the destruction of many relationships.

In our ministry, we have a staff pastor who handles conflict resolution. If strife exists in any of our departments or between any of our employees, he works with them to resolve it. If it is not resolved, eventually they won't be able to work for us because we know that God's anointing (presence and power) abides where there is peace.

Instead of getting angry when you don't get what you want, pray. I love the part of today's scripture that simply says "You do not have, because you do not ask." This is so simple yet so powerful. God can do in a moment what we could not do in a lifetime.

Confession: *I do all I can to avoid strife, and when I need something, I trust God instead of trying to make it happen.*

DO YOU PRAY AND PLAN? OR DO YOU PLAN AND PRAY?

I have glorified You down here on the earth by completing the work that You gave Me to do.

JOHN 17:4

As you glance at the title of today's devotion, you may not see the difference right away, but it's big. We should not make plans and then pray that God will make them work. We should pray that He will show us His plan before we plan anything for ourselves.

We must diligently avoid works of the flesh (trying in our own strength), because they only make us miserable. We end up disappointed because they don't work. When we are working with God to carry out His plans, things are usually smooth and easy. This doesn't mean the devil won't try to get involved and make things difficult, but God's plans ultimately work out, whereas ours rarely do. If they do, we labor trying to make them work, and in the end they fail anyway.

Let me encourage you to pray before you do anything major. You may not hear God give you specific instructions, but your prayer will honor Him, and He will direct your path.

Confession: *I want God's plan, not mine, so I pray before taking any major action.*

CHOOSE YOUR FRIENDS CAREFULLY

Blessed (happy, fortunate, prosperous, and enviable) is the man who walks and lives not in the counsel of the ungodly [following their advice, their plans and purposes], nor stands [submissive and inactive] in the path where sinners walk, nor sits down [to relax and rest] where the scornful [and the mockers] gather.

PSALM 1:1

We should choose our close companions—those we spend a lot of time with—carefully and not take advice from ungodly people. If you need advice, ask someone who is wise and spiritually mature and who will give you an answer based on Scripture.

We tend to take on the traits of the people we spend a lot of time with, so choose to be around people you would want to be like. For example, I like to be with people who are generous because I want to be generous. I don't want to spend my time with people who gossip or who are critical and negative.

There are enough unpleasant situations and things that drag us down emotionally in the world, so we should spend time with happy, uplifting people, not with those who will pull us down further. Be kind to everyone. Don't shut out of your life people who don't know God. They need your influence. Just make sure you are affecting them and they are not infecting you.

Confession: *I choose my friends and associates carefully, and I pray that God will surround me with people who can add to my life.*

HELP THE POOR

Whoever stops his ears at the cry of the poor will cry out himself and not be heard.

PROVERBS 21:13

When you help the poor, you are giving to God, and He repays you (Proverbs 19:17). I often think about the people who are homeless and what it must be like to live on the streets in winter, perhaps covered with only a cardboard box. I think of hungry children and people who are always under financial strain. I not only pray for them, but I pray for God to send someone in need across my path so I can help them.

Make sure the church or ministry organizations you donate to financially use a portion of the money they receive to help the poor. Our religion is in vain if all we do is sit in church each week and then do nothing to help anyone. James 1:27 says that religion that is pure and undefiled is to visit, help, and care for orphans and widows in their affliction.

Simply feeling sorry for the poor is not enough. We need to be "moved with compassion," as Jesus was (Matthew 14:14 NKJV). The more you help others, the happier you will be.

Confession: I love to help people who need help. I love to relieve human suffering, and I pray that God will put opportunities in my path to be able to help people.

DON'T WORRY

Do not let your hearts be troubled (distressed, agitated). You believe in and adhere to and trust in and rely on God; believe in and adhere to and trust in and rely also on Me.

JOHN 14:1

Are you worried about anything or anyone today? If so, you can lighten your load by praying instead of worrying and casting the care of your concerns on God (1 Peter 5:7). Worry has never solved a problem, nor has it helped or made anyone feel better. Excessive worry can actually cause you to develop physical problems—headaches, digestive problems, aches and pains, and other conditions.

Worry is our way of trying to solve our own problems, and it simply doesn't work. Worry is like rocking in a rocking chair all day long; it keeps you busy but gets you nowhere. God promises to meet all our needs, but we need to trust Him and ask Him to help us. James 4:2 says that we do not have because we do not ask.

Jesus invites us to come to Him if we are overburdened. The amplification of Matthew 11:28 says He will give us rest and refreshment for our soul. No matter how many problems we have, if we are peaceful inside, we can still enjoy life.

Confession: *I refuse to worry about anything. God cares for me, and He will meet my needs as I put my trust in Him.*

GOD'S WORD IS TRUTH

Sanctify them in the truth; your word is truth.

JOHN 17:17 ESV

Many people today don't want to take direction from anyone or be told what to do. And they don't want to read words of truth in a book called the Bible. This kind of independence is responsible for many unpleasant results and even tragedies. I am sure, if you stop and consider it, you know of situations in which people have been determined to go their own way and ended up with terrible problems. This does not have to happen. God has given us instructions for life in His Word. They are true—and they work.

To be able to enjoy life and avoid unnecessary problems, we must live according to the truth found in God's Word and not according to the lies we hear from other people, the world, or the enemy. The enemy is always out to deceive us by tempting us to believe things that are not true, but these lies can become personal realities for us if we believe what the enemy says to us. When we are deceived, we don't know, enjoy, or live by the truth. But when we live according to the truth, we reap great benefits.

We must know how to separate what is true from what is not. We can do this, but the battle for truth takes place in our minds, and we have to fight for it. We must examine what we believe and why we believe it and be firmly convinced of God's Word so that when the devil challenges us concerning it, we can stand firm on the truth.

Confession: *I believe the truth of God's Word, and I refuse to allow the enemy to deceive me.*

GOD IS WITH YOU

Yes, though I walk through the [deep, sunless] valley of the shadow of death, I will fear or dread no evil, for You are with me; Your rod [to protect] and Your staff [to guide], they comfort me.

PSALM 23:4

At some point in our lives, all of us will walk through the valley of the shadow of death—facing our own death, the death of a loved one, or some other extraordinarily difficult time. Are you walking through that valley right now, or are you still wounded from a time in the past when you have walked through something similar? Remember that where there is a shadow, there must be light. And the Light of the World, Jesus, has promised to be with you always. Ask Him right now to comfort, restore, and guide you. And know that He will never leave you or forsake you.

God never promised that life would be easy. In fact, Jesus said that in this world we would have tribulation (great trouble or suffering). But Jesus also said, "Be of good cheer [take courage; be confident, certain, undaunted]! For I have overcome the world. [I have deprived it of power to harm you and have conquered it for you]" (John 16:33). This does not mean that we will never have to go through anything difficult, but that we are more than conquerors (Romans 8:37). We know we have the victory even before the trouble begins. Just imagine how much easier a difficult season will be if you know from the beginning that you will have the victory.

Confession: *Even though I go through the valley of the shadow of death, God is always with me and I have the victory.*

LOVE GOD MORE THAN ANYONE OR ANYTHING

And He replied to him, You shall love the Lord your God with all your heart and with all your soul and with all your mind (intellect).
MATTHEW 22:37

We can only love God because He loved us first (1 John 4:19). And we can only love because He has put His love in us (Romans 5:5). Let that love flow through you back to God, and love others as you love yourself (Mark 12:31). Who do you love most? When we make sure it is God, and He is first, we will enjoy our life much more than if He's not our priority.

Seeking God first is something we have to do on purpose, because the devil uses the distractions and worries of this world to push us away from Him. "Delight yourself in the Lord, and he will give you the desires of your heart" (Psalm 37:4 ESV). The easiest way to live is to keep God first in your thoughts, conversations, finances, relationships, and every other area of your life.

God's presence brings you joy (Psalm 16:11). All you have to do is think of Him, and you can sense His presence with you. Think of Him throughout the day, ask for His help, and thank Him for all He does in your life. Tell Him multiple times each day that you love Him. He wants your love more than anything else.

Confession: I love God more than anything or anyone, and He is always first in my life.

THE DOUBLE-PORTION BLESSING

Instead of your shame you will receive a double portion, and instead of disgrace you will rejoice in your inheritance. And so you will inherit a double portion in your land, and everlasting joy will be yours.

ISAIAH 61:7 NIV

When people mistreat us, we often feel that someone should pay us back for the pain we have endured. When people are abused, abandoned, or rejected, they experience shame because they often feel that what happened to them was their fault, but that is usually not true. I was sexually abused by my father. I felt for years that the abuse was my fault, and I experienced a lot of shame. But God is our Restorer, and if you have been unjustly hurt, He will pay you back.

God promises to give us a double blessing for our former shame and disgrace and to give us everlasting joy. I have received this in my life, and I know that you can experience it also. I encourage you to stop trying to get revenge. Let God be your Vindicator. Forgive those who hurt you so your prayers will be effective (Mark 11:23–25), and ask God to give you the double-portion blessing.

Confession: *As I release those who have hurt me, and I forgive them completely, I will experience the double-portion blessing from God.*

GOD WILL MEET YOUR NEEDS

Consider the ravens: They do not sow or reap, they have no store-room or barn; yet God feeds them. And how much more valuable you are than birds!

LUKE 12:24 NIV

You are valuable to God. You belong to Him, and He always takes care of His own. Your part is to trust Him, and His part is to provide. You can sow a seed and aim it by faith directly at your need; birds cannot do that, yet God provides for them. Surely you believe you are more valuable than a bird. If God takes care of them, how much more will He take care of you?

We don't always know how or when God will meet our need, but we can be assured that He will at just the right time. I urge you to enter the rest of God and enjoy your life while you are waiting for Him to meet your need. God is still doing miracles, and yours may come today. Look for it expectantly.

Confession: I am valuable to God, and He will meet my need. I put my trust in Him and continue to enjoy my life while He works on my problem.

KEEP WALKING ON THE WATER

Then Peter got down out of the boat, walked on the water and came toward Jesus. But when he saw the wind, he was afraid and, beginning to sink, cried out, "Lord, save me!" Immediately Jesus reached out his hand and caught him. "You of little faith," he said, "why did you doubt?" And when they climbed into the boat, the wind died down.

MATTHEW 14:29-32 NIV

Faith is a spiritual force. The enemy knows that if God places faith in us to do something, and we develop a positive attitude toward it and consistently believe we can actually do it, then we will do considerable damage to his kingdom of darkness.

Today's scripture tells us that Peter stepped out of the boat at Jesus' command to do something he had never done before. It required faith. But Peter made a mistake: He spent too much time looking at the storm. When he became frightened, he began to sink. He cried out to Jesus to save him, and He did. But notice that the storm ceased as soon as Peter got back into the boat.

The devil brings storms into your life to intimidate you. During a storm, be determined to go through it with the Holy Spirit's help instead of getting back in the boat. I like to say, "*Step* out and *stay* out, and you'll *find* out that God is faithful."

Confession: *I step out and stay out when storms come into my life.*

MAKE SURE YOU'RE REALLY HELPING PEOPLE

But let every person carefully scrutinize and examine and test his own conduct and his own work.

GALATIANS 6:4

Some people find their self-worth in taking care of others. Yet too many of them act like martyrs, constantly complaining about having to do so much for the people they care for. But you can't stop these caretakers. I know a woman who talks about the unfairness of having to sacrifice her life for others, yet she still looks for people to help and latches on to anyone she can find to care for.

If you feel trapped in this behavior and really want to get out of it, I suggest you locate your true responsibility and give up the rest. Some people will become angry that you're no longer helping them, but at least you'll regain your life and your peace. For four years, Dave and I spent time, money, and effort trying to help a wounded person from a dysfunctional home, wanting to see him have a chance at a good life. While we did everything for him, things went well, but when it came time for him to take care of himself, he went back to his old ways.

If you've tried to help someone for years, and they are still not helped, consider whether they really want help. You may want to see change in their life, but they have to want it, too. Make your life simpler. Help all the people you can, but don't become a professional caretaker who feels used up and burned out.

Confession: *As God gives me strength, I let go of trying to help people who don't really want to be helped.*

NO FEAR

For God did not give us a spirit of timidity (of cowardice, of craven and cringing and fawning fear), but [He has given us a spirit] of power and of love and of calm and well-balanced mind and discipline and self-control.

2 TIMOTHY 1:7

If you experience fear in your life, it is not from God, because He never gives us a spirit of fear. God gives us courage, boldness, power, love, discipline, and self-control. It is the devil who tries to rule us with fear. We receive from God through faith, and we receive from the devil through fear. As the old saying goes, "When fear knocks on your door, send faith to answer."

Courage is not the absence of fear; it is going forward in the presence of fear. We must often "do it afraid." We cannot run from our problems and overcome them. We can face them, knowing that God is always with us and will provide everything we need to be more than a conqueror (Romans 8:37). Don't let fear steal your destiny.

Fear is the number one emotion that Satan uses to prevent us from making progress in life. Resist it when you first recognize it and don't let it take root in your life.

Confession: *God is on my side, and I will not fear.*

TRUST GOD AND DO GOOD

*Trust (lean on, rely on, and be confident) in the Lord and do good;
so shall you dwell in the land and feed surely on His faithfulness,
and truly you shall be fed.*

PSALM 37:3

When we have a need, as believers, we are taught to trust God,
and that's exactly what we should do. But we learn from today's
scripture that there is something else we should also do, and
that is to "do good." This scripture has helped me a lot because
I have learned that when I cannot help myself and am waiting
for God to take care of my problem, I can help others. I can do
good while I wait, and by doing so, I am sowing seed for my
harvest.

When we are hurting, we often withdraw and isolate our-
selves. We don't feel like keeping our commitments, and we
may even become trapped in self-pity. But we have a much
better option. We can cast our care on God (1 Peter 5:7) and
continue doing good things for others. Not only does being a
blessing give us joy, but it is also a powerful tool against the
enemy. Romans 12:21 says that we overcome evil with good.
Start practicing this principle today, and you will see amazing
results.

Confession: *While I wait for God to take care of my problem, I
continue trusting Him and being good to other people and doing
what is right.*

GOD WILL GUIDE YOU

Let the morning bring me word of your unfailing love, for I have put my trust in you. Show me the way I should go, for to you I entrust my life.

PSALM 143:8 NIV

God's mercies are new every morning, and His loving compassion is never failing (Lamentations 3:22–23 ESV). Each morning when you wake up, remind yourself that God loves you and tell Him that you love Him. Trust God to take care of your problems and to guide you in what you should do while you wait for the solutions. If there is something you can do to help your situation, trust God to show you what it is.

God doesn't always solve our problems miraculously. Many times, He shows us what to do. I had been having trouble with my stomach for a couple of years. I was often nauseated in the morning and had frequent intestinal problems. I had been to the doctor and was even given nausea medicine, but nothing helped. I continued to pray about it, and God showed me that some mints I ate daily had an ingredient in them that irritated my stomach. I stopped eating them, and my stomach improved 95 percent. Ask the Lord for wisdom to know if there is anything you can do to help solve your problem.

Confession: *God is my Helper, and He gives me insight into how to solve my problems.*

I WILL NOT FEAR
OTHER PEOPLE

When I am afraid, I put my trust in you. In God, whose word I praise—in God I trust and am not afraid. What can mere mortals do to me?

PSALM 56:3–4 NIV

The fear of others is a huge fear in a lot of people's lives, but if we truly understand how much God loves us, it will cast out fear (1 John 4:18). We all have times when we feel fear, but we can decide how we want to handle it. Will we give in to it, or will we resist it? One of the wisest things to do is to remind yourself of how mighty God is and to remember that He is with you all the time. He is on your side and always fights for you if you put your trust in Him.

If you really think about it, what can mere mortals do to you? They can reject you or talk bad about you. They might be able to take something away from you, but I believe Proverbs 6:31 teaches that anything they take God will restore seven times more. Don't let the fear of other people control your life. People who try to control you with fear don't really care anything about you and will abandon you when you need them most.

Confession: *I will not let the fear of other people control me. God is for me, and there is nothing a mere mortal can do to me.*

BLESSED ARE THOSE WHO TRUST IN THE LORD

But blessed is the one who trusts in the Lord, whose confidence is in him. They will be like a tree planted by the water that sends out its roots by the stream. It does not fear when heat comes; its leaves are always green. It has no worries in a year of drought and never fails to bear fruit.

JEREMIAH 17:7–8 NIV

We are blessed when we put our confidence in the Lord. One of His major blessings is peace, because when we trust God, we don't need to worry. We are like deeply rooted trees drawing on the strength of God in times of trouble.

Today's scripture says that even in an entire year of drought (time of trouble), we will never need to worry, and we will continue to bear good fruit. Producing this good fruit means displaying the fruit of the Spirit (Galatians 5:22–23), even though we are hurting personally, and continuing to do good while we are still in pain. Many people find it difficult to trust God, but it is much easier than worrying, fretting, and being upset all the time. Why not try trusting God? I can promise you that you can never solve even one of your problems through worry.

Confession: *I put my trust in the Lord, and even in a time of continuous trouble, I still bear good fruit.*

GOD'S WORD HAS SELF-FULFILLING POWER

For as [surely as] the earth brings forth its shoots, and as a garden causes what is sown in it to spring forth, so [surely] the Lord God will cause rightness and justice and praise to spring forth before all the nations [through the self-fulfilling power of His word].

ISAIAH 61:11

When a farmer plants a seed in the ground, that seed contains everything needed to reproduce a plant just like the one the seed came from. The seed has self-fulfilling power. All the farmer needs to do is water the seed and keep the weeds from choking the life out of it, and the seed does the rest.

The Word of God functions the same way. It has self-fulfilling power. When it is planted in our hearts and we water it with our faith and keep the weeds (sin) out of our lives, we will see amazing things develop simply from believing God's Word.

Faith is amazing. It is "the substance of things hoped for, the evidence of things not seen" (Hebrews 11:1 NKJV). God created everything we see in the world from nothing, and He will do the same for us as we believe and trust in His Word.

When we put a tomato seed in the ground, we will get tomatoes, and likewise, when we put our faith in God's Word, we will get what it promises.

Confession: *I continue to believe God's Word even when I don't see immediate results.*

YOU CAN CHOOSE
YOUR ATTITUDE

Be happy [in your faith] and rejoice and be glad-hearted continually (always); be unceasing in prayer [praying perseveringly]; thank [God] in everything [no matter what the circumstances may be, be thankful and give thanks], for this is the will of God for you [who are] in Christ Jesus [the Revealer and Mediator of that will].

1 THESSALONIANS 5:16–18

All of us have the privilege and responsibility of choosing our attitudes, no matter what circumstances or situations we find ourselves in. The key word here is *choosing*. Attitudes don't just happen; they are the products of our choices. Over time, the thought patterns established in our minds can put us on "autopilot," which means that when certain types of situations occur, we are programmed to think about them in certain ways.

Just as airplane pilots must maintain contact with air traffic control towers, you and I must stay in touch with God—the One who sees the big picture of our lives and orchestrates everything that involves us so that everything in our lives happens at the right time, moves at the appropriate speed, and causes us to arrive safely at the "destinations" He has planned for us. If we want to stay on track with God, we have to make communication with Him a priority. He will help us navigate the ups and downs of life and find our way through days when we can't seem to see the next step we need to take. Communicate with God frequently through prayer, reading His Word, worship, and acknowledgment of His presence and guidance throughout every day.

Confession: *I choose to have a good attitude and to stay in regular contact with God each day.*

DON'T FEAR BAD NEWS

They will have no fear of bad news; their hearts are steadfast, trusting in the Lord.

PSALM 112:7 NIV

I lived a life full of trouble, negativity, and bad things until I was twenty-three years old, and I developed the habit of expecting bad news. I thought if I expected it, it would hurt less when it came. I had a vaguely threatening feeling all the time, as though something bad would happen at any moment. I was afraid to believe good could happen to me, because I didn't want to be disappointed.

God taught me that my anxious thoughts and evil forebodings were making me miserable and opening a door for the devil to bring bad things into my life. He wanted me to be positive and believe for good things. This was very difficult in the beginning, but as I kept pressing forward, I started to see evidence of things changing. Now I expect good news and good things to happen in my life. I still have trouble occasionally, but not nearly as often as I once did, and God always helps me solve the problem.

Confession: *I am a positive person, and I expect good news and good things daily.*

WAIT ON GOD

But they who wait for the Lord shall renew their strength; they shall mount up with wings like eagles; they shall run and not be weary; they shall walk and not faint.

ISAIAH 40:31 ESV

Waiting on God doesn't mean we sit idly by and do nothing. We may not take physical action, but we are very active spiritually, in our hearts. I was surprised and delighted when I learned that to wait, in the context of today's scripture, means to expect something good. What we expect is what we draw to ourselves.

Our faith or lack of faith is like a magnet drawing good or bad into our lives, depending on what we believe. God wants us to believe that He is always good and that He loves us and will always do good things for us. We may have to wait longer than we would like for them, but His timing is always perfect. When we wait, even if God is not doing anything in our circumstances yet, He is doing something inside us. He is teaching us patience and to trust Him. Often, He is also testing our faith. We are strengthened as we wait on the Lord— strengthened physically, mentally, and emotionally. Our faith is also strengthened. Learn to enjoy waiting, because you will spend more time waiting than you do receiving..

We wait for one thing, and when we finally get it, then before long we are waiting for something else.

Confession: As I wait on God and expect Him to do amazing things in my life, I am strengthened, and I wait with joy.

JESUS HAS OVERCOME THE WORLD

I have told you these things, so that in Me you may have [perfect] peace and confidence. In the world you have tribulation and trials and distress and frustration; but be of good cheer [take courage; be confident, certain, undaunted]! For I have overcome the world. [I have deprived it of power to harm you and have conquered it for you.]

JOHN 16:33

Jesus tells us that in the world we will have tribulation. He doesn't want us to be surprised by our troubles, but to hold our peace and remain confident in Him in the midst of them. He actually says that when trouble comes, we should cheer up, because He has overcome the world and deprived it of power to harm us.

This is such good news. Satan may come against us, but he will never win. We might lose a battle now and then, but we have already won the war. I used to think that life would be so good if only I didn't have trouble stalking me all the time. I kept waiting for my trouble to go away, but I discovered that God wanted me to learn how to face it with confidence, knowing that He would always take care of me. He wants to do the same for you. Are you worried about something right now? If so, read today's scripture over and over, and let the reality of what it says sink into your heart.

Confession: *I know that life is not perfect and that at times I will experience trials and difficulty. But Jesus has conquered the world and deprived it of the power to harm me.*

ENTERING GOD'S REST

For he who has once entered [God's] rest also has ceased from [the weariness and pain] of human labors, just as God rested from those labors peculiarly His own.

HEBREWS 4:10

We can labor mentally and emotionally, trying to solve our own problems, or we can put our trust in God and enter His rest. His rest is a supernatural rest that enables us to do what we need to do in life—and to do it in total peace. I labored with my problems and with myself until I completely wore myself out and finally decided to believe God's Word. When I did, I started to learn the joy of entering God's rest.

We cannot solve our own problems unless God specifically shows us what to do, so we might as well believe His Word. If you have never done this, you can give it a try, and you will find out that it works.

The Israelites could not enter God's rest because of their unbelief (Hebrews 3:19). But you and I still have an opportunity to enter His rest (Hebrews 4:1); and according to Hebrews 4:11, we should be diligent in not letting the opportunity pass us by. Today you can enter God's rest, so don't wait any longer.

Confession: I refuse to live in worry and anxiety. I will not labor with my problems, but instead, I believe God's Word and enter His rest.

BE SUSPICIOUS OF SUSPICION

Love bears up under anything and everything that comes, is ever ready to believe the best of every person, its hopes are fadeless under all circumstances, and it endures everything [without weakening].

1 CORINTHIANS 13:7

I can honestly say that obedience to today's scripture was a challenge for me. I was brought up to be suspicious. I was actually taught to distrust everyone, especially if they pretended to be nice, because they must want something from me. In addition to being taught to be suspicious of others and their motives, I had several very disappointing experiences with people, not only before I became an active Christian but afterward as well. Meditating on the components of love and realizing that love always believes the best has helped me greatly to develop a new mindset.

When your mind has been poisoned, or when Satan has gained strongholds in your mind, it needs to be renewed according to God's Word. We have the wonderful Holy Spirit in us to remind us when our thoughts are going in the wrong direction. God does this for me when I am having suspicious thoughts instead of loving thoughts. Trust and faith bring joy to life and help relationships grow to their maximum potential. Suspicion cripples an entire relationship and usually destroys it. The bottom line is this: God's ways work; our natural, human ways don't. God condemns judgment, criticism, and suspicion, and so should we.

Next time you are tempted to be suspicious, choose to believe the best instead.

Confession: *I believe the best about people.*

PURPOSE AND SELF-ACCEPTANCE

But who are you, a human being, to talk back to God? "Shall what is formed say to the one who formed it, 'Why did you make me like this?'"

ROMANS 9:20 NIV

God gives us free will (the ability to make our own choices), but if we are wise, we will use our free will to choose God's will for our lives. Part of His desire for us is that we live *on* purpose *for* a purpose, yet many people feel useless and waste their time wondering why they are alive. "Who am I? What am I here on earth to do?" is the cry of many hearts. You are here because God enjoys you and wants you alive in this moment. You are important to Him, and you fit into His purposes. You are not an accident. You are personally designed by the hand of God, and He has given you abilities you are to use to serve Him and other people.

Many of us compare ourselves—and our strengths and weaknesses—to other people. This is a huge mistake. God will never help you be anyone other than yourself. I believe self-acceptance is vital if we intend to find and fulfill God's purpose for our lives. Unless we accept who we are and what we are good at—or not so good at—we will struggle in whatever we try to do. I like to say, "Give God everything you are and give Him everything you are not." When we accept ourselves, we can thrive in our areas of strength and either work to improve our weaknesses or find ways to compensate for them.

I encourage you to get to know yourself, accept yourself, learn to appreciate yourself and your strengths—and fulfill God's purpose for your life.

Confession: *I accept myself and intentionally pursue God's purpose for my life.*

SPEND YOUR DAYS WISELY

So teach us to number our days, that we may get us a heart of wisdom.

PSALM 90:12

When we ask God for direction each morning, He probably won't give us a specific outline of what the day should look like, but we can depend on Him to guide us as we schedule and plan our day. God has given us common sense and wisdom as gifts, and as a part of our free will, He expects us to use them as we decide how to spend our time and energy. Perhaps you haven't thought about needing wisdom as you think about how to spend your time, but we can seek wisdom in every area of life—big or small.

As you seek wisdom about this day, consider these questions: *How much can I realistically accomplish today? What can I achieve without frustration and stress? What is most pressing and must be done today? What could I roll over to tomorrow if needed? Am I planning to do anything that will accomplish nothing except to waste my time?*

As you think about your day today, I believe wisdom would also leave room to live a balanced life that includes time with God, rest, laughter, and investing in certain relationships, in addition to achieving your goals.

For years, I did not always apply the principles I am encouraging you to apply today. I learned by my mistakes, and I hope you can learn without making the same ones I made.

Confession: *I use wisdom as I spend my time each day.*

NO MORE REPROACH

And the Lord said to Joshua, This day have I rolled away the reproach of Egypt from you. So the name of the place is called Gilgal [rolling] to this day.

JOSHUA 5:9

The word *reproach* means to blame, disgrace, or shame. Just as God "rolled away" the reproach of Egypt from the Israelites, He rolls shame and reproach away from us.

There was a time in my life when I realized I had a shame-based nature because of things I had done and things that had been done to me. Shame had poisoned my inner being, and deep down inside, I did not like myself. I now know that when we receive for ourselves the forgiveness God offers us for our past sins and the cleansing He makes available for things that have been done to us, the reproach is rolled away. We are free from shame and disgrace.

We can never deserve or work to earn God's blessings. We can only humbly accept them, appreciate them, and be in awe of God's goodness and love for us. Self-hatred, self-rejection, refusal to accept God's forgiveness, not understanding righteousness through the blood of Jesus, and all related problems will keep us bound in shame and disgrace. But because of Jesus, we have hope for freedom from shame.

Today, remember that you are in right standing with God through Jesus—not through your own works—and thank Him for forgiving you, setting you free, healing you, and rolling all shame and reproach off of your life.

Confession: *I live in the righteousness Jesus accomplished on my behalf, and I reject shame, disgrace, and reproach.*

GOD'S COMMANDS
ARE NOT TOO DIFFICULT

*For this commandment which I command you this day is not too
difficult for you, nor is it far off.*

DEUTERONOMY 30:11

Often, when someone comes to me for advice and prayer, when
I tell them what the Word of God says or what I think the Holy
Spirit is saying, their response is "I know that's right; God has
been showing me the same thing. But *it's just too hard.*" I believe
God showed me that the enemy tries to inject this phrase into
people's minds to get them to give up, and He instructed me to
stop saying how hard everything was, assuring me that if I did,
things would get easier.

Even when we are determined to press through and do
something, we spend so much time thinking and talking about
how hard it is that the project ends up being much more dif-
ficult than it would have been had we been positive instead of
negative. When we think things will be hard, they are.

When I initially began to see from the Word of God how
I was supposed to live and behave, and compared it to where I
was, I was always saying, "I want to do things Your way, God,
but it is so hard." The Lord led me to today's scripture in which
He says that His commandments are not too difficult or too far
away.

The reason our Lord's commands are not too difficult for us
is that He gives us His Spirit to work in us powerfully and to
help us in all He asks of us.

Confession: *I believe I can do all things through Christ, and that,
as I trust Him, hard things become easier.*

GOD IS YOUR REWARDER

And without faith it is impossible to please Him, for the one who comes to God must believe that He exists, and that He proves to be One who rewards those who seek Him.

HEBREWS 11:6 NASB

We cannot please God without faith. None of our works please Him if they are not done in faith. We receive from God only through faith, not in any other way. In John 6:28, we read that some people asked what they must do to please God, and He said that the work that God requires is "that you believe in the One Whom He has sent" (John 6:29).

Today's scripture says that we are to believe that He exists and rewards those who diligently seek Him (NKJV). I was in church for many years without ever hearing that God wanted to reward me. Do you see God as your Rewarder, and are you expecting a reward if you have diligently sought Him?

We might think it would be wrong to expect a reward from God. After all, He has already given us Jesus—the best gift of all. But He wants us to believe because He wants to do many wonderful things for us, and we can't receive them if we don't believe. We don't expect rewards because we think we deserve them, but because God tells us that faith pleases Him, He does reward those who diligently seek Him.

Confession: *I have faith in God and I believe He exists. He is my Rewarder, and I diligently seek Him.*

DON'T BE MOVED BY BAD REPORTS

Overhearing but ignoring what they said, Jesus said to the ruler of the synagogue, Do not be seized with alarm and struck with fear; only keep on believing.

MARK 5:36

Jesus was on His way to heal the synagogue ruler's daughter when servants came from the ruler's house and told Him not to bother because the girl was dead. Today's scripture says that Jesus overheard them but ignored what they said. This is a good way for us to respond to certain situations in our lives. When we are trusting God to do amazing things, or things that may seem impossible to others, people will often speak discouraging words. The best thing we can do is ignore their negativity and keep believing.

God often gives us a gift of faith concerning something He wants to do in our life, and it does sound impossible to those without the gift of faith. Dave and I had a gift of faith when we began our ministry, while most of our extended family and friends thought we were making a very big mistake. I am so glad we listened to God and not to people.

In the story in Mark 5, Jesus did reach the girl and raised her from the dead. If He can do that, He can certainly do whatever you need Him to do in your life today.

Confession: *I am not moved by negative reports about things God has given me faith to believe for.*

WALK IN LOVE

You, my brothers and sisters, were called to be free. But do not use your freedom to indulge the flesh; rather, serve one another humbly in love. For the entire law is fulfilled in keeping this one command: "Love your neighbor as yourself."

GALATIANS 5:13–14 NIV

If I were allowed to teach only three messages for the rest of my life, the first would be that we are saved by grace through our faith in Jesus, and by faith we are justified and made right with God. The second would be the importance of spending regular quality time with God. The third would be receiving God's love, loving Him in return, and walking in love with others.

People who walk in love cannot be unhappy, because their minds are not on themselves but on what they can do for God and others. We cannot be both selfish and happy at the same time, and love is the polar opposite of selfishness. The love I am referring to is not a carnal (human) love. It is not a feeling, although it may include feelings. It is the same kind of love God gives to us. It is unconditional, everlasting, and powerful. Love is a decision about how we will treat people. It is something that can be seen and felt, and it is displayed in a variety of ways.

When I teach about love, I offer this summary of 1 Corinthians 13:4–8: Love is patient with people, it is humble, it is never jealous, and it always believes the best about them. Love helps others, it gives, and it is quick to forgive. Ask God to help you love others and treat them the way you want to be treated.

Confession: *I receive God's love, I love Him in return, and I walk in love toward others.*

THIS WILL END WELL

And we know that in all things God works for the good of those who love him, who have been called according to his purpose.

ROMANS 8:28 NIV

Today's scripture is one of the most comforting in the Bible to me. What a thrill to know that all things work together for good for those who love God and want His will. When we are going through very difficult times, this is very important to remember. We see a similar scripture in Genesis 50:20, where Joseph told his brothers who had hated him and treated him cruelly that what they meant to harm him God intended for good.

Joseph's brothers sold him into slavery and told their father he had been killed by a wild animal. But God had his eye on Joseph and kept moving him from place to place until he finally ended up in Pharaoh's palace as his number one assistant. Not all of Joseph's journey was pleasant. He spent years in prison for a crime he did not commit, but God used that to get him into Pharaoh's presence, and God gave him favor (Genesis 41).

No matter what you are going through, believe that God will work it out for good and that you will be amazed at the end result.

Confession: *I trust God, and I believe that all things in my life work together for good.*

GOD WILL NOT LEAVE YOU WITHOUT SUPPORT

For He [God] Himself has said, I will not in any way fail you nor give you up nor leave you without support. [I will] not, [I will] not, [I will] not in any degree leave you helpless nor forsake nor let [you] down (relax My hold on you)! [Assuredly not!] So we take comfort and are encouraged and confidently and boldly say, The Lord is my Helper; I will not be seized with alarm [I will not fear or dread or be terrified]. What can man do to me?

HEBREWS 13:5–6

Even if you feel very much alone, I can assure you that you are not. God is with you and has promised to never leave you without support. If you read today's Scripture verses carefully, you'll see "I will not" four times in the words God has spoken. If the Lord says something once, we should believe it, but if He repeats it three more times, I think He is definitely trying to assure us that we will be taken care of. This passage assures us that beyond any doubt or question that God will not leave us helpless or without support.

God's got you! He is holding you in the palm of His hand (Isaiah 49:16), and He will not let you go. You may be facing situations you have never faced before and have no idea what to do. If so, I encourage you to not let fear take over, because when you have to have an answer, God will give you one. You don't have to fear; there is nothing anyone can do to you that God cannot fix and turn around for good (Romans 8:28).

Confession: *God will never leave me without support. He will never let me go or relax His hold on me.*

GOD ALWAYS DOES
WHAT HE PROMISES

God is not human, that he should lie, not a human being, that he should change his mind. Does he speak and then not act? Does he promise and not fulfill?

NUMBERS 23:19 NIV

It is good to know that it is impossible for God to lie. He is not like humans, who may not always do what they say they will do. God always does what He says He will do. He doesn't speak and then not act. He promises and then fulfills.

Our obvious problem is that God doesn't give us a schedule for how long we will need to wait to see a promise fulfilled. Our dealings with God involve an element of faith. We must trust that His timing is always exactly right. Our timing is always "now," but God knows many things we do not know. If He brings certain things into our lives before the time is right for us to have them, they can actually hurt us instead of help us.

With God all things are possible (Matthew 19:26), but it is impossible for Him to lie!

Confession: I know that God always keeps His word. It is impossible for Him to lie, and I put my trust in Him at all times in all things.

BE AN OPTIMIST

[What, what would have become of me] had I not believed that I would see the Lord's goodness in the land of the living! Wait and hope for and expect the Lord; be brave and of good courage and let your heart be stout and enduring. Yes, wait for and hope for and expect the Lord.

PSALM 27:13-14

God wants us to be positive and optimistic, always expecting something good to happen. We draw to us what we expect and believe, so a wise person will not be pessimistic and negative. I used to be very negative, and I had a lot of negative things happen in my life. But God has changed me, and now I have a hard time being around negative people.

There is nothing negative about God and nothing negative about faith. We will see the Lord's goodness in the land of the living, not just when we go to heaven.

You can form the habit of being positive at all times. There will be times when you will have to stick with your positive faith even though things look bleak, but what do you have to lose?

Even if you believe for something good and don't get it, you will be happier than if you have a negative attitude all the time. However, good things will happen to you if you put your trust in God and maintain a right attitude.

Confession: *I believe that good things are coming my way. I am always positive because being negative is not God's will, and it does no good.*

PUT YOUR TREASURE IN HEAVEN

Do not store up for yourselves treasures on earth, where moths and vermin destroy, and where thieves break in and steal. But store up for yourselves treasures in heaven, where moths and vermin do not destroy, and where thieves do not break in and steal.

MATTHEW 6:19-20 NIV

Money alone won't provide a satisfying, fulfilling life. Wisdom is found in knowing that we aren't working merely for earthly things but that we are storing up treasure in heaven. Wisdom teaches us to live carefully, remembering that this earthly life is short. Now is the time to follow God, to adjust our priorities, and to focus on the things that truly matter most. When we pray for wisdom, we are praying for God to show us the best choice—His best—for our lives.

Money and possessions are fleeting. The world's financial structure can collapse in a day. In 1929, the United States stock market crashed, and suddenly America was in a depression. In 2008, the stock market fell almost seven thousand points in one day, and people's investments suddenly lost almost half their worth. If we live primarily for money and possessions and seek our security in them, situations like these are threatening. But when we find our security in God, we are safe, settled, and secure.

Enjoy the money you have and use it to help others, but don't make it the source of your confidence, your security, or your hope. Put your hope in Christ alone (Psalm 62:5–7).

Confession: *I use my money wisely, and I help others with it. But I do not trust in any earthly thing, but instead, I put my hope in the Lord.*

RECEIVING MERCY

Have mercy on me, O God, according to your unfailing love; according to your great compassion blot out my transgressions. Wash away all my iniquity and cleanse me from my sin.

PSALM 51:1–2 NIV

Today's scripture is very comforting and encouraging, and it is a great one to turn into a prayer each morning. After asking for mercy, take time to be quiet before God and purposefully receive the mercy and forgiveness you have asked for. The Bible says, "Ask, and you will receive, that your joy may be full" (John 16:24 NKJV). I think a lot of people ask, but they don't receive.

God's mercies are new every morning, so we can have a fresh start each day (Lamentations 3:22–23). Thankfully, we don't have to drag yesterday's mistakes into today. Don't ever live in the fear that if you sin, you will not be forgiven. God took care of the sin problem when Jesus paid for our sins on the cross. If you are feeling guilty today because of something you did in the past, pray this scripture and let go of the past.

Today is a new day, and God wants you to be free to enjoy the day He has made and given you.

Confession: *Each day I receive mercy and forgiveness for my past sins, and I get a fresh start every day.*

DON'T TRY TO HIDE FROM GOD

Whoever conceals their sins does not prosper, but the one who confesses and renounces them finds mercy.

PROVERBS 28:13 NIV

Don't ever try to hide your sins from God. It is useless because He already knew the sins you would commit before you committed them. God is not surprised by your behavior, and He loves you anyway. Repent and be willing to turn completely away from sin. Receive a fresh start, and from this day forward, talk with God about everything. When you talk about it, you release it instead of trying to hide it in your soul, where it can eat away at your confidence.

According to Romans 3:23–24, we have all sinned, and we all fall short of the glory of God. At the same time, we are all justified freely by His grace through the redemption Jesus offers us. The devil will try to tell you that you are worse than anybody else, but this is not true. We all sin, but thankfully God has provided an answer for all of us. Believe it and receive it by faith.

Believe God's Word more than you believe your feelings. Just because you feel guilty doesn't mean you are. If you have repented, you are forgiven.

Confession: *I will not try to hide my sin from God, instead I will tell Him everything. He knows anyway, so I am wasting time trying to hide anything from Him.*

FORGIVE QUICKLY

For if you forgive other people when they sin against you, your heavenly Father will also forgive you. But if you do not forgive others their sins, your Father will not forgive your sins.

MATTHEW 6:14–15 NIV

I believe Satan gains more ground in a believer's life through unforgiveness than through anything else. We tend to think it is too hard to forgive someone who has hurt us, but hanging on to unforgiveness is actually much harder than letting it go. Always remember that you can do anything God has told you to do. If He tells us to forgive, we can forgive.

Forgiveness is not a feeling; it is how we treat people and how we talk about them. Pray for those who have hurt and even abused you. It is difficult to stay angry with someone when you are praying for them.

We are good at remembering what others have done to us, but we easily forget what we have done to hurt others. We all need forgiveness, but we won't get it if we are not willing to forgive people. If you are angry with anyone, I strongly encourage you to let it go today. Don't waste any more of your time being angry. Turn the situation over to God and let Him be your Vindicator (Romans 12:19).

Confession: *I will not hold unforgiveness, but I forgive quickly as God forgives me.*

ANSWERED PRAYER

*Two men went up into the temple [enclosure] to pray, the one a
Pharisee and the other a tax collector. The Pharisee took his stand
ostentatiously and began to pray thus before and with himself:
God, I thank You that I am not like the rest of men—extortioners
(robbers), swindlers [unrighteous in heart and life], adulterers—or
even like this tax collector here. I fast twice a week; I give tithes of
all that I gain. But the tax collector, [merely] standing at a distance,
would not even lift up his eyes to heaven, but kept striking his
breast, saying, O God, be favorable (be gracious, be merciful) to
me, the especially wicked sinner that I am!*

LUKE 18:10–13

God doesn't answer our prayers because we are good, but
because He is good. Be like the tax collector mentioned in
today's scripture and ask God to have mercy on you because
of your sin. Be thankful for all the grace God gives you, and
don't keep a record of your good works. Remember every good
thing anyone does for you, but quickly forget the good you do
for others.

Don't compare yourself with other people, especially not in
a way that makes you feel you are better than they are. Paul
teaches that we are not to think more highly of ourselves than
we ought to, but to think according to the degree of faith that
is given to us (Romans 12:3). If we are good at anything, it is
because God has given us a gift. We should be humbly grate-
ful, not proud, which always causes us to think more highly of
ourselves than we should.

Confession: *I know I don't deserve anything from God, but I am
very thankful for everything He does for me.*

JUDGE NOT

*Do not judge, and you will not be judged. Do not condemn, and
you will not be condemned. Forgive, and you will be forgiven.*

LUKE 6:37 NIV

The devil loves to fill our minds with thoughts of judgment
about other people, but God's Word warns us against doing
this. People tend to be quick to give their opinion about things
that they have no real knowledge about. I have been judged
falsely many times, and it always hurts. When it happens, the
first thing I want to do is defend myself, but God tells us to
leave that to Him.

If you have ever been judged falsely, remembering how it
felt should help you not to judge others. We recognize sin, and
we can judge something as sin, but our response should be to
pray for the person, not judge them. We never know what a
person is going through or has gone through in their life. We
don't know what has caused them to act the way they do. I
know that after being sexually abused by my father for almost
fifteen years, I had some problems in my personality, and peo-
ple usually didn't like me unless they took the time to really get
to know me.

Today, because of the internet, judgment and gossip quickly
spread far and wide. We should be careful not to sow seeds of
judgment unless we want to reap them.

Confession: I will not judge or criticize people, but I will pray for
them and leave them in God's capable hands.

SEASONS OF LIFE

To everything there is a season, and a time for every matter or purpose under heaven.

ECCLESIASTES 3:1

When we seek God for a better understanding of His will for us, most of us would like a clear blueprint for the rest of our lives. But if we truly want to do God's will, we can trust Him to guide us into it one day at a time without showing us everything at once. I worked at many jobs before I had the idea to teach God's Word. Each of these jobs was right at the time I had it, because the time had not yet come for me to do what God ultimately had in mind for me. God sometimes has to spend the first half of our lives getting us into position for the second half.

In the Old Testament, Moses was called to lead the Israelites out of bondage and slavery in Egypt, but prior to that, he had been raised in Pharaoh's palace and lived there for forty years, and for forty years after that, he lived in the wilderness as a shepherd. *Then* God appeared to him and gave him specific instructions. The first eighty years of his life helped prepare him for the remainder of it. We can see the seasons of Moses' life and realize that some of them may have seemed useless but, in reality, were not. During the time Moses spent in Egypt and the wilderness, he was becoming the man God needed him to be.

God works the same way with you and me. He leads us through the seasons of life and uses each one to prepare us for the next.

Confession: *I embrace every season of life, trusting that God is doing in me exactly what He needs to do to prepare me for the next season.*

BE READY FOR CHANGE

As Jesus walked beside the Sea of Galilee, he saw Simon and his brother Andrew casting a net into the lake, for they were fishermen. "Come, follow me," Jesus said, "and I will send you out to fish for people." At once they left their nets and followed him.

MARK 1:16-18 NIV

The men who became Jesus' disciples had careers as fishermen and were busy. But when Jesus said, "Follow Me," they immediately left what they were doing and followed Him. They didn't ask what the pay and benefits would be, where they would sleep, or what the workday would look like. Jesus' disciples took a risk to follow Him.

If we are not willing to risk what we have now, we will never find out what we could have in the future. I don't advise being foolish, but I think the disciples must have appeared foolish as they left all to follow Jesus. Faith will take us places reason would not allow us to go. Living by faith requires us to take certain steps without always knowing what will happen.

Many people are fearful of giving up what they feel is safe, but with God, we can be safe in the midst of a risk. As long as He is guiding our steps, we are not in danger.

What if the early disciples had not followed their hearts but leaned on their own reasoning? They could have missed being part of the greatest miracle in the world. I encourage you today not to miss your moment or your miracle. When God calls you, say yes to Him and step out in faith.

Confession: *When I hear God asking me to do something, I say yes immediately.*

GOD WILL MEET ALL YOUR NEEDS

And God is able to make all grace (every favor and earthly blessing) come to you in abundance, so that you may always and under all circumstances and whatever the need be self-sufficient [possessing enough to require no aid or support and furnished in abundance for every good work and charitable donation].

2 CORINTHIANS 9:8

We all have needs, and they are different at different times in our lives. The good news is that no matter what kind of need we have—physical, emotional, spiritual, financial—God can meet it. Jesus can heal you anywhere you hurt. One of the great fears we face in life is not having our needs met, but God has not given us a spirit of fear (2 Timothy 1:7). Fear is a tool Satan uses to make us miserable. The Bible says that God's perfect love casts out fear (1 John 4:18). However, we need to believe that God loves us with a perfect love and receive it continually in our lives. He loves us on our ugly days as well as on our pretty ones.

Just about the time we think we have conquered a sin, it slips up on us, and we feel ashamed. If we are not careful, the devil will try to make us think God is angry with us and perhaps doesn't love us anymore. But he is a liar! Even when you have made mistakes, you can still go boldly to the throne of God's grace and ask for whatever you need, and God will provide. Ask and receive that your joy may be full (John 16:24).

Confession: *God will meet all my needs, and I don't worry about anything.*

DON'T TAKE ON OTHER
PEOPLE'S RESPONSIBILITIES

So then, each of us will give an account of ourselves to God.
ROMANS 14:12 NIV

I have always been a responsible person, so irresponsible peo-
ple tend to irritate me. I used to resent being responsible for
what others neglected to do until God showed me that I had
a false sense of responsibility and that a lot of what I did was
unnecessary.

Do you automatically step up and do whatever needs to be
done, and then feel sorry for yourself? If people disappoint you
by ignoring their responsibilities, you may feel the only way to
avoid more pain is to do everything yourself. But experience
has taught me that such reasoning only amplifies the problem.
You could be feeding irresponsibility in someone else by doing
what they need to do themselves.

We love people and want to help them, but sometimes
tough love helps them more than emotional love. Tough love
isn't being mean; it simply allows people to experience the
consequences of their actions instead of rescuing them. Doing
someone else's job for them feeds a lazy, immature, irresponsi-
ble attitude in them. Try doing only the things you are respon-
sible for, not what someone else is responsible for—unless it's
an emergency. Examine whether you really need to do every-
thing you're doing. Ask God to help you do what you truly
need to do and release what you don't.

Confession: *I focus on my own responsibilities and don't take on
things others should do for themselves.*

INNER STRENGTH

I pray that out of his glorious riches he may strengthen you with power through his Spirit in your inner being, so that Christ may dwell in your hearts through faith.

EPHESIANS 3:16–17 NIV

Inner strength is much more important than external strength. Muscles help you pick up heavy items, but they won't help you get through a difficult or challenging time without giving up or being discouraged or in despair. When God strengthens us in our inner being, we can go through long periods of difficulty and remain as stable as we would if all our circumstances were good. Paul knew how to be abased and how to abound and be content in all things (Philippians 4:11–12).

Stop asking God to remove life's difficulties. Instead, ask Him to help you face them and remain stable. Paul never prayed for people's problems to go away; instead, he prayed for their ability to deal with them and maintain a good attitude and keep a good temper. When something happens that hurts us or is hard for us, we should never simply *try* to not let it bother us. We need God's help to deal with it, and we should begin to pray right away for His help in handling the situation according to His Word.

Confession: *When I face difficulties in life, I immediately pray for God to help me deal with them according to His Word and His will.*

HOW TO DEAL WITH YOUR ENEMIES

Rejoice not when your enemy falls, and let not your heart be glad when he stumbles or is overthrown, lest the Lord see it and it be evil in His eyes and displease Him, and He turn away His wrath from him [to expend it upon you, the worse offender].

PROVERBS 24:17-18

When someone has hurt or mistreated you and you later discover that something bad or difficult has happened to them, are you happy and think they deserved it? I admit that I have done this. But after studying today's scripture, I realized this is not the way God wants us to be. Not only are we told to love our enemies and pray for and bless them (Luke 6:27–28), but we are warned not to desire revenge.

We should never think, *I will pay you back for hurting me* (Proverbs 24:29). Remember, God says that vengeance belongs to Him and that He is our Vindicator (Romans 12:19). We are to walk in love and pray for people to be forgiven for their sins against us, as Jesus did when He was being crucified (Luke 23:34), or as Stephen did when he was being stoned (Acts 7:60).

It requires real spiritual maturity to understand that when people hurt you, they are actually hurting themselves more, and to be willing to forgive and pray for them.

Confession: *If anyone hurts me, I will not have an attitude of revenge, but I will trust God to make the situation right.*

BE FINISHED WITH EVIL

So be done with every trace of wickedness (depravity, malignity) and all deceit and insincerity (pretense, hypocrisy) and grudges (envy, jealousy) and slander and evil speaking of every kind.

1 PETER 2:1

Based on today's scripture, we have decisions to make—decisions to be the kind of people God wants us to be. This doesn't happen without a decision and the application of self-control. God wants us to be done with all hypocrisy and pretense. He wants us to be genuine, to be truthful with ourselves and others, and not to pretend to be something other than what and who we are. He doesn't want us to hold grudges but to offer forgiveness instead, just as He forgives us. One of the best things we can do for ourselves is to daily let go of what is behind and enjoy the day the Lord gives us.

Be done with jealousy and trust that God has a plan for your life and that He will give you what is right for you at the right time. Being jealous of someone will never get you what you want; it even may delay it. Don't say evil things about others. If you think you see a fault in someone, pray about it instead of talking about it. Evil speaking of any kind is not pleasing to God, and when we do it, we end up feeling bad. We are created to love one another, not to be critical toward one another. If you need to adjust the way you feel and act, there is no better time than the present. God will help you follow through if you are willing to do your part.

Confession: I will not slander, be jealous, hold grudges, or speak evil about or toward anyone. I will pray and let God be the judge.

THE INNER LIFE

Do not let your adornment be merely outward—arranging the hair, wearing gold, or putting on fine apparel—rather let it be the hidden person of the heart, with the incorruptible beauty of a gentle and quiet spirit, which is very precious in the sight of God.

1 PETER 3:3–4 NKJV

We actually live two lives—the outer life (the one we show to the world) and the inner life (the one filled with the secrets that only we and God know). The inner life or "the hidden person of the heart" is the most important to God because it is the real us. We can pretend and show others anything we choose to, but our thoughts, attitudes, and intentions reside in our inner person—and these are the most important parts of us.

Our attitude has a lot to do with the kind of life we will have. Zig Ziglar said that "Your attitude, not your aptitude, will determine your altitude."[7] A good attitude can take you a long way, but no matter how talented or intelligent you are, if you have a bad attitude, eventually people will not want to work with you. Another important part of having a good attitude is to be thoughtful toward other people and take an interest in their dreams and goals instead of only expecting them to sacrifice their life to serve you.

God delights in a beautiful mind and attitude. Do your best to keep yours in line with His Word, and ask Him to help you in your weaknesses.

Confession: *I will do my best to keep my inner life in line with God's Word. I know my attitude is very important, and I choose to have a good one in all situations.*

PASSIONATE PURSUITS

So I commend the enjoyment of life, because there is nothing better for a person under the sun than to eat and drink and be glad. Then joy will accompany them in their toil all the days of the life God has given them under the sun.

ECCLESIASTES 8:15 NIV

To be passionate means to be compelled to do something by strong, intense feelings. But in order to have passion, we must enjoy what we do. I want to do what I am doing; I love it and cannot imagine doing anything else. I suggest that you ask yourself what you love, what you enjoy, and what makes you feel alive, because it is difficult to give your life to anything and pour your heart into it unless you are passionate about it.

I don't believe a loving God would have us do something for a prolonged period of time if we despise doing it. Some people may pursue careers simply because they pay big money, yet they are miserable all of their lives. May I suggest that money isn't as important as joy and enjoyment? Do something you enjoy! This doesn't mean to live selfishly. True joy is not to be confused with entertainment. Entertainment is temporary and gives us a fun experience on the surface, but true joy is deep and lasting.

It makes me sad to watch people go through life miserable because they deeply dislike what they are doing each day. I urge you: Don't be afraid to make a change or take a risk. You never know what you may find on the other side of what you think is safe. Find something that you can be committed to, and do it with all your heart.

Confession: *I pursue the passions God has put in my heart.*

BE ALERT AND ACTIVE

Then said the Lord to me, You have seen well, for I am alert and active, watching over My word to perform it.

JEREMIAH 1:12

In today's scripture, God describes Himself as "alert and active." This is wonderful news because it teaches us that He is always watching over us and working on our behalf. Because we are created in God's image (Genesis 1:27) and told to imitate Him (Ephesians 5:1), it is reasonable to assume that we can also be alert and active as we go through our lives.

Being active and alert is the opposite of being passive. Adam was passive in the Garden of Eden when Eve gave him the forbidden fruit. Without any opposition to her suggestion, he ate it (Genesis 3:1–6). God had specifically instructed Adam not to eat fruit from that particular tree, and He had also told him that if he did eat of it, the result of his disobedience would be severe (Genesis 2:16–17). Adam had the God-given opportunity to choose to obey God or to yield to temptation, which he did.

Passivity is non-action or non-resistance. People who are passive are led by their feelings or lack of feelings, instead of following the leading of the Holy Spirit. They have free will, or the power of choice, but they don't use it. Passivity does not lead to desirable results. It affects passive people in negative ways and can have negative consequences for others, too.

God has prearranged a wonderful life for each of us. Let's be active and alert, so we can make choices according to His will in order to enjoy it.

Confession: *I am active and alert, and I choose to do God's will.*

THE DEVIL IS A LIAR

You are of your father, the devil, and it is your will to practice the lusts and gratify the desires [which are characteristic] of your father. He was a murderer from the beginning and does not stand in the truth, because there is no truth in him. When he speaks a falsehood, he speaks what is natural to him, for he is a liar [himself] and the father of lies and of all that is false.

JOHN 8:44

One of the devil's favorite lies is to tell us we have no value and are worthless. He loves to make us feel guilty, condemned, insecure, and unconfident. But the truth is in God's Word.

What we do is not who we are. Dave and I have four adult children. When they do something we don't like, they don't stop being our children, nor do we stop loving them. Similarly, God is our Father, and He never stops loving us. He sees us through our faith in Jesus. If you have received Jesus as your Savior, then you are considered to be "in Christ," and He is in you. In Christ, we become new creatures; old things pass away, all things are made new, and we are made right with God (2 Corinthians 5:17, 21). The thief (the enemy) comes only to steal and kill and destroy, but Jesus came that we might have and enjoy our lives to the full (John 10:10).

One of the most life-changing lessons I have learned is that you cannot enjoy your life if you don't enjoy yourself. You are with yourself all the time, and if you don't like, love, and enjoy yourself, you will be miserable. Today, start loving the creation God made you to be with His own hand while you were in your mother's womb (Psalm 139:13).

Confession: *I have worth and value to God, so I can enjoy myself and my life.*

STAY STRONG BY RESISTING WORRY

Who of you by worrying can add a single hour to your life?

LUKE 12:25 NIV

Only a deep trust in God can help us avoid the useless emotion called worry. Our trust in God increases as we have experience with Him and see His faithfulness in our lives. God is good, and He always takes care of us. He may not do exactly as we would prefer, and we may not always understand why He acts as He does, but He is good and He is faithful.

So then, why do we worry? It may be a difficult thing to face, but I think we worry simply because we are afraid we won't get what we want. If we can say "Your will be done, Lord, and not mine," and mean it, it will eliminate most of our worry. All fear is a result of not fully understanding the unconditional love of God and then not trusting that, because He loves us, He will always do what is best for us. "Perfect love casts out fear," and God's love is the only love that is truly perfect (1 John 4:18 NKJV).

I once read that a day of worry is more exhausting than a week of work. This is another good reason not to worry. Most of us don't have much excess energy to spare, so the next time you are tempted to worry, just remember that if you do, it will be a waste of time. Corrie ten Boom said, "Worry does not empty tomorrow of its sorrow. It empties today of its strength."[8] Stay strong today by resisting the temptation to worry.

Confession: *I remain strong by refusing to worry when I am tempted to do so.*

DON'T BE DECEIVED

Jesus answered them, Be careful that no one misleads you [deceiving you and leading you into error].

MATTHEW 24:4

To be deceived means to believe a lie. We should pray that we are not deceived and that the Holy Spirit will continually guide us into truth. The problem with believing lies is that if we believe something, even if it isn't true, it becomes true for us. It affects us as though it is true. For example, if I believe I have no value and am a failure, then I will fail, be depressed, and have no confidence. The only way to know the truth is to know God's Word. The Holy Spirit is the Spirit of Truth, and He will guide us into all truth if we will listen to Him (John 16:13).

If you are just beginning to study God's Word, you may feel overwhelmed and hopeless. But if you stick with studying, reading, and listening to the Word, as you are learning what it says, you will gradually overcome fear and despair—and be filled with hope. Learning the truth is a lot of fun, and it fills us with joy. If you simply study God's Word thirty minutes each day for thirty days, you will be amazed at what you will learn— that God loves you (1 John 4:16), that your sins are forgiven and God has forgotten them (Hebrews 8:12), and that God has a good plan for your life (Jeremiah 29:11). You will also learn that He rewards those who diligently seek Him (Hebrews 11:6 NKJV), that He is always with you (Joshua 1:9), that He will provide what you need (Philippians 4:19), and thousands of other wonderful truths.

Confession: *The devil is a liar, but God's Word is truth. I will study God's Word, listen to it, read it, and meditate on it until I have it in my heart all the time.*

YOU MAY HAVE THE ANSWER YOU NEED

The plans of the mind and orderly thinking belong to man, but from the Lord comes the [wise] answer of the tongue.

PROVERBS 16:1

Sometimes, God speaks to us out of our own mouths. I learned this years ago when I was in a challenging situation and didn't know what to do. My own thoughts left me confused and conflicted, and even though I was praying diligently about the circumstances, I didn't make progress until I took a walk with a friend one day.

This friend and I discussed the issue for about an hour as we enjoyed the nice day and each other's company. We talked about several options and explored what the outcomes of each one might be. Suddenly, a specific resolution to the problem settled in my heart. As I was talking about the situation, a wise answer suddenly came out of my mouth, and I knew in my heart it was from the Lord.

What God was leading me to do about the situation wasn't something I was naturally inclined to do. I struggled with His guidance because I wanted to convince God that my situation should be dealt with differently from the way He was leading me. I realized that I'd had trouble hearing His voice because my mind had been set against the plan He revealed to me. In the end, though, I obeyed, and God's plan proved to be the best solution.

Confession: *I trust God to give me the answers to my problems, and I know He will sometimes send them through the words of my own mouth.*

WHAT ARE YOUR PRIORITIES?

For where your treasure is, there will your heart be also.

LUKE 12:34

What today's scripture means is that we invest ourselves in what we value or see as a priority. A priority is something we regard as more important than another thing. When we say, "I don't have time," what we are really saying is "It's not my priority." Hopefully, most of us believe that what we do is important, or we would not spend time doing it, but certain things must always be more important than others. We have to have the ability to know which things in our lives are most important to us and then be sure that we make time for them. If we don't, we will spend our lives doing what is urgent rather than what is important.

We usually do what we truly want to do, but rarely do we admit this. If we are not doing what we know in our heart we should be doing, we often excuse our behavior by saying that we didn't have time. I have only heard one person say "I don't exercise because I don't want to," but I have heard hundreds say they don't have time to take a walk or go to the gym. Our time belongs to us, and we can prioritize it wisely if we truly want to.

The apostle Paul prayed for the early followers of Jesus to learn to sense what was vital and approve what was excellent and of real value (Philippians 1:9–10). Even though what we are doing might be good, it may not be the best way for us to spend our time. If we ask God to help and guide us as we set our priorities, He will.

Confession: With God's help, I set clear priorities and live my life according to them.

THE ARMOR OF GOD

Put on God's whole armor [the armor of a heavy-armed soldier which God supplies], that you may be able successfully to stand up against [all] the strategies and the deceits of the devil.

EPHESIANS 6:11

Satan has studied us all our lives, so he knows what bothers us. I like to say "He sets us up to get us upset." He tempts us at the point of our greatest weakness, but we can ask God to strengthen us in those weaknesses and help us stand against the enemy.

God has given us spiritual armor to protect ourselves, but we have to put it on, meaning that we believe that it has spiritual power, and we apply it to our lives. Ephesians 6:12–18 teaches that our armor includes the breastplate of righteousness, the belt of truth, the shoes of peace, the shield of faith, the sword of the Spirit, and the helmet of salvation. In addition, we learn that we are to cover everything with prayer. In practical terms, putting on our spiritual armor means that we should know we have been made right with God through Jesus (Romans 3:22), we should know the truth and always cling to it, and we should lift up the shield of faith with which we can quench all the fiery darts of the enemy. Make sure your thoughts line up with God's Word, and always walk in peace.

Pray about everything. You can pray anywhere, anytime, about anything. You can pray short prayers or long prayers; they simply need to be sincere.

Confession: *God has given me armor to protect myself from the devil's attacks. I put it on daily, and I pray about everything.*

PRAY BOLDLY

For we do not have a High Priest who cannot sympathize with our weaknesses, but was in all points tempted as we are, yet without sin. Let us therefore come boldly to the throne of grace, that we may obtain mercy and find grace to help in time of need.

HEBREWS 4:15–16 NKJV

When we know we have sinned, we often feel we don't have the right to ask God for anything. If we do ask Him for something, we ask sheepishly or we don't ask for much. It is wonderful to know that Jesus understands us and our weaknesses, and He doesn't reject us because of them. It is hard for us to imagine Jesus being tempted in all the same ways we are, but He was, although He never sinned.

According to today's Scripture verses, we are to go boldly to God's throne and ask for what we want and need, and He will hear and answer our prayer. He doesn't answer us because we are good, but because He is good. When we pray in Jesus' name, we are presenting to God all that Jesus is, not all that we are. I urge you to start praying more boldly than ever before because God "is able to do exceedingly abundantly above all that we ask or think" (Ephesians 3:20 NKJV).

Confession: *I will pray boldly because God is good, and He understands my weaknesses. He answers my prayers even when I don't deserve it.*

DON'T COMPARE YOURSELF TO OTHERS

Let us not become vainglorious and self-conceited, competitive and challenging and provoking and irritating to one another, envying and being jealous of one another . . . But let every person carefully scrutinize and examine and test his own conduct and his own work. He can then have the personal satisfaction and joy of doing something commendable [in itself alone] without [resorting to] boastful comparison with his neighbor.

GALATIANS 5:26; 6:4

We are all different, and God has a different plan for each of us. Even if we do the same things, we will usually not do them the same way. At some point in our lives, many of us get trapped in comparing ourselves to other people. I tried to be meek and sweet like my pastor's wife. I tried to make my family's clothes like my neighbor did. I tried to play a guitar because I thought it would be great to sing and preach. I tried to be more easygoing like my husband, Dave, but none of it worked.

We are all born with a temperament that includes both strengths and weaknesses. God can help us strengthen our weaknesses, but we must be who we are. God will never help us be somebody else. I tried to pray like other people I knew; I tried to change myself; I tried and tried and tried. But it was all useless and not God's will. Thank God, I finally accepted myself, and since then, I have just tried to be the best me that I can be.

Confession: *I will not compare myself to other people, because God has created me uniquely, and He doesn't want me to try to be like someone else.*

THE SEED OF GOD IS IN YOU

No one who is born of God will continue to sin, because God's seed remains in them; they cannot go on sinning, because they have been born of God.

1 JOHN 3:9 NIV

Our scripture for today tells us something wonderful. If we are born again, we cannot deliberately, knowingly, habitually sin. We will sin at times, but we don't live constantly in sin, because we have God's nature in us. We are new creations (2 Corinthians 5:17), and the new part of us does not want to sin.

A seed has an embryo in it. When it is first planted, we don't see any evidence that it is doing anything. But when we water it with God's Word, give it sunshine (time spent with God), and wait patiently, it grows into what the seed is designed to produce. As we grow, we become more and more like Jesus, and we sin less and less. We will never be completely free from sin as long as we are in our flesh and bone bodies. But, praise God, we can improve. I say "I'm not where I need to be, but thank God I'm not where I used to be. I'm okay and I'm on my way."

Confession: *I cannot continually practice sinning because I am born of God. His seed is in me, and I am changing daily.*

LEARNING TO RULE OVER NEGATIVE EMOTIONS

He who has no rule over his own spirit is like a city that is broken down and without walls.

PROVERBS 25:28

None of us can successfully live intentionally and stop wasting time unless we face the truth about how much time we waste on feelings such as guilt, fear, worry, anxiety, jealousy, envy, greed, resentment, hatred, bitterness, unforgiveness, self-pity, and other negative emotions. If we want today to go well, we need to be prepared to deal with any negative emotions that may try to steal our peace, joy, focus, and productivity.

Emotions we don't want may visit us quite suddenly, without an invitation from us. All it takes is for someone to swoop in front of us and grab the parking place we have been waiting for, and we get a visit from anger. Or someone we work with gets the promotion we believe we deserve more than they do, and we get a visit from jealousy and resentment.

Because we never know on any given day what our circumstances may be, and because we cannot control other people's actions, we are in danger every day of wasting time on negative, useless emotions.

For too long, we have allowed ourselves to be victims of energy-draining, time-wasting emotions, thinking we can't help the way we feel. But the truth is that we can manage our emotions and not allow them to manage us. This may not be easy, especially if you are someone who has lived by emotions for a long time, but it is possible with God's help.

Confession: *I manage my emotions instead of allowing them to manage me.*

TAKING CARE OF GOD'S TEMPLE

You were bought with a price [purchased with a preciousness and paid for, made His own]. So then, honor God and bring glory to Him in your body.

1 CORINTHIANS 6:20

If you are a believer in Jesus and have received Him as your Savior, you are God's home (1 Corinthians 6:19), and according to today's scripture, you are to use your body to glorify Him. The Holy Spirit lives in you, and He wants to work through you to help other people, so it is important for you to take care of yourself. You only have one body, and if you wear it out, you cannot go to a store and buy another one.

Many people abuse their bodies by not getting enough sleep, not drinking enough water, eating too much junk food, or not exercising. These are four simple things each of us can do to help keep ourselves healthier so we can serve God as long as possible.

We need balance in our lives. We need to work, but we also need to play and rest. We need to be able to eat a dessert now and then, but not daily. We need to serve and do things for others, but we also need to do something for ourselves once in a while. According to 1 Peter 5:8 in the Amplified Bible, Classic Edition, living in an unbalanced way can open a door for the devil to bring trouble into your life. As God's home, you are very valuable. Don't ever forget this.

Confession: I am God's home, and I glorify Him by taking good care of myself and living a balanced life.

BE ROOTED IN FAITH

Withstand him; be firm in faith [against his onset—rooted, established, strong, immovable, and determined], knowing that the same (identical) sufferings are appointed to your brotherhood (the whole body of Christians) throughout the world.

1 PETER 5:9

Satan is determined to make us miserable and to steal everything Jesus died to give us. But if we are rooted in our faith in God, we will be immovable. We should always resist the devil at his onset. The minute you realize he is attacking or lying to you, resist him immediately. Tell him that he is a liar and that you will not be moved.

At times, we all go through difficulties, trials, and tribulations, but they don't last forever. God works them for our good if we will trust Him (Romans 8:28). We also go through dark times, but Isaiah says we will receive the secret riches of dark places (Isaiah 45:3).

Trials make us use our faith, and each time we use it, it grows stronger. Things that upset you now will not bother you at all later on. When you are rooted in faith, you will grow spiritually and be strong in God and the power of His might.

Confession: *I resist the devil at his onset, and I always win because I am more than a conqueror through Jesus Christ (Romans 8:37).*

THOSE WITHOUT ROOTS FALL AWAY

Have the roots [of your being] firmly and deeply planted [in Him, fixed and founded in Him], being continually built up in Him, becoming increasingly more confirmed and established in the faith, just as you were taught, and abounding and overflowing in it with thanksgiving.

COLOSSIANS 2:7

Dave and I have a huge oak tree in our backyard. It was there when we built our home and has probably been there many, many years. Its roots go deep into the ground and wind themselves around some of the roots of other trees and under rocks and boulders buried in the ground. When storms come, that oak tree never budges. The branches sway in the wind, but the trunk never moves.

As believers in Christ, we should be like that oak tree. Isaiah 61:3 says that we will "be called oaks of righteousness, the planting of the Lord, that he may be glorified" (ESV). Those who have no roots will fall away from their faith when the storms of life come. They lose hope; they are tempted to give up on God; they worry and are depressed.

Spiritual roots develop over time and with experience. The longer you walk with God and study His Word, the deeper your roots will be. As you experience His goodness and faithfulness, you will gain experience—no storm will move you.

__Confession:__ I am rooted deep in God, and when the storms of life come, I am not moved.

FORGIVE YOURSELF AND DON'T LOOK BACK

As far as the east is from the west, so far has he removed our trans-gressions from us.

PSALM 103:12 NIV

God has a good plan for you and your life. No matter what is behind you, it is important to let it go and look forward. If you have made mistakes in the past, as most of us have, you can learn from them, but living in regret does no good.

To live under the burden of regret is to dwell on the past. When you struggle with regret, learn to remind yourself that the past is over and done and you cannot change it. Instead, you can receive God's total forgiveness when you repent of your mistakes or failures. His forgiveness is immeasurable, as we learn from today's scripture.

Once you've received God's forgiveness, it is *vital* for you to forgive yourself. You may have to say many times a day "I forgive myself." You may have to look in the mirror and say to yourself "[Your name], you are forgiven." You may have to write yourself a letter and remind yourself of scriptures that assure your forgiveness. Whatever it takes to forgive yourself, make the effort and do it. God is doing something new in your life, and you can only embrace it fully if you are free from the regrets of the past.

Confession: *I do not dwell on the past, because God is doing a new thing in my life, and I will embrace it.*

GOD CAN DO WHAT
WE CANNOT DO

*Then he said to me, This [addition of the bowl to the candlestick,
causing it to yield a ceaseless supply of oil from the olive trees] is
the word of the Lord to Zerubbabel, saying, Not by might, nor by
power, but by My Spirit [of Whom the oil is a symbol], says the Lord
of hosts.*

ZECHARIAH 4:6

God can do with ease what we cannot do with any amount of
struggle and effort. He changes us by His grace as we study His
Word and spend time developing an intimate relationship with
Him. I tried for years to change myself, and it does not work.
I felt I had more things wrong with me than anyone else. You,
too, may feel that way at times, but it is a lie from the devil. We
all have things wrong with us, but God knew that when He
accepted us as His children. He knows everything we will do
wrong before we even do it and has already provided forgive-
ness through the blood of Jesus. All we have to do is repent and
receive His grace.

We can see our lives change, but never through our works of
the flesh, our own efforts. We must work the works of God; our
own works (our efforts and bright ideas of what we can do to
change ourselves) never work. "Help me Jesus" is probably the
most powerful prayer you can pray, and if you are anything like
I am, you will have to pray it many times each day. But, don't
be discouraged or feel guilty. God loves you just as much while
you are changing as He will once you have changed.

Confession: *Only God can change me, and I am going to trust
Him to do it. He knows me and isn't surprised by anything I do;
and He loves me through it all.*

WORKS OF THE FLESH

Those who live according to the flesh have their minds set on what the flesh desires; but those who live in accordance with the Spirit have their minds set on what the Spirit desires. The mind governed by the flesh is death, but the mind governed by the Spirit is life and peace. The mind governed by the flesh is hostile to God; it does not submit to God's law, nor can it do so. Those who are in the realm of the flesh cannot please God.

ROMANS 8:5–8 NIV

God's Word teaches us that He is not pleased with our works of the flesh. These works are the results of our trying, through our own energy, to do what only God can do. With man, many things are impossible, but with God all things are possible (Matthew 19:26). God can accomplish more in a few seconds than we can in a lifetime. He wants us to ask Him for what we want and need and trust Him to do it in His way and on His schedule. We are partners with God, and we do have a part to play, which is to obey what He shows us to do. Our part is not to come up with our own plan and then pray that God will make it work.

Works of the flesh are works that don't work. They exhaust, disappoint, and frustrate us, because we try and try and always fail. Have you ever said, "I've tried everything I know to do, and nothing is working?" It isn't working because it is your plan, not God's. Pray this instead: "If you don't do it, Lord, it won't get done! Apart from You, I can do nothing" (see John 15:5).

Confession: *I turn myself and everything I want over to God. I want His plan, not mine. Apart from You, Jesus, I can do nothing.*

STARTING SOMETHING NEW

For the dream comes through much effort, and the voice of the fool through many words.

ECCLESIASTES 5:3 AMP

God is the author and the finisher of our faith (Hebrews 12:2), but He is not obligated to finish anything He didn't start. I am an aggressive person and can easily come up with ideas of things to do. These ideas may be good things, yet not be "God things." Starting new things is exciting, and many of them are God's will, but we should do all we can to make sure they are God's will. Otherwise, we will be frustrated and worn out from trying to make something work when it is never going to work.

King Solomon writes in today's scripture that a dream comes to pass "through much effort," and this is true. It is easy to look at something someone else has done and wish you had what they have or were doing what they are doing. But you may have no idea what it took for them to get to where they are.

Jesus teaches that we should make sure we can finish before we start (Luke 14:28–30). If you do all you can to hear from God and make an honest mistake, don't worry; God will help you get back on the right track. But don't proudly think you can do something just because you get a bright idea. This caution is not meant to make you afraid to venture out into new things, but to encourage you to pray first and take baby steps to see if God's hand is on your idea.

Confession: *I will pray before starting anything new in my life, and I will humble myself under God's mighty hand that in due time He may exalt me (1 Peter 5:6).*

BEAR ONE ANOTHER'S BURDENS

Bear (endure, carry) one another's burdens and troublesome moral faults, and in this way fulfill and observe perfectly the law of Christ (the Messiah) and complete what is lacking [in your obedience to it].

GALATIANS 6:2

We are not to be impatient with other people when they have a troublesome moral fault but to bear with them, pray for them, and encourage them. Tell them to repent, receive God's forgiveness, and not to feel guilty, because we all have weaknesses, and we all need compassion and people who will be patient with us.

If we are going to please God, then we will have to put up with some things people do that irritate us—annoying little habits. Perhaps they talk too much, they don't return your things when they borrow them until you ask for them back, they are chronically late, they are emotionally needy or clingy, or they have other habits or tendencies that bother you. One of the best ways to bear with people is to remember that we also have annoying habits, but we don't usually see ours. One reason we don't see our faults is because we are too busy judging others.

Don't focus only on the shortcomings of other people; focus on their strong points. The person who is always late may also be very generous to you. The person who talks too much may be the first one to offer to help when you have a need. Always look for the good in people, and you won't notice the irritating things as much.

Confession: *I focus on the good things in people, and I always believe the best. I will love people and bear with them in obedience to God's Word.*

THE PAST HAS NO POWER

God is faithful (reliable, trustworthy, and therefore ever true to His promise, and He can be depended on); by Him you were called into companionship and participation with His Son, Jesus Christ our Lord.

1 CORINTHIANS 1:9

Everyone who is born again is a new creation, and nothing from the past has any power over them unless they allow it to. Second Corinthians 5:17 (NIV) says, "Therefore, if anyone is in Christ, the new creation has come: The old has gone, the new is here!" We will not be victorious in our new life with God until we understand this Scripture verse. Without it, we will always see ourselves the way we once were. We tend to remember all our failures and keep detailed records of everything anyone has ever told us we could not do. But we don't see what God sees. He believes in us, but we don't always believe in ourselves. We either don't know or we don't believe that God lives in us through the Holy Spirit, and we don't see what we are capable of through Him.

A time came in my life when I began to study God's Word seriously and made the decision to take the promises I found in it and apply them to my life. Once I believed them for myself, I was unstoppable. My journey has been long and at times very difficult, but the rewards have been far greater. When we have faith, it motivates us to keep going. Faith sees in the spiritual realm what the eye cannot see in the natural realm. Faith does not rely on feeling or emotion, but it relies on God, who is faithful and true.

Confession: *I live by faith and rely on God, who is faithful and true.*

THE TRUTH WILL MAKE YOU FREE

So Jesus said to those Jews who had believed in Him, If you abide in My word [hold fast to My teachings and live in accordance with them], you are truly My disciples. And you will know the Truth, and the Truth will set you free.

JOHN 8:31–32

To abide in Christ means to live in, remain, and stay in Christ. It does not mean a Sunday morning visit to church. It is realizing that Christ lives in you and that your life is in Him. Jesus says, "Apart from me you can do nothing" (John 15:5 NIV). One of the greatest thrills of my spiritual life was when I discovered that God wanted to be involved in everything I did, not just the spiritual things.

When we do abide in Christ, we will know the truth, and if we apply it to our lives, it will make us free. The truth is in God's Word. Jesus is the Word made flesh who came to dwell among us (John 1:14). He said, "I am the way, the truth, and the life" (John 14:6 NKJV). The Holy Spirit is the Spirit of Truth who guides us into all truth (John 16:13). He teaches us the truth of God's Word, and He also teaches us the truth about ourselves, which is not always easy to look at honestly.

The truth does make us free, but it must be received. Ask God to teach you truth about your motives, your behaviors, and all other areas of life.

Confession: *I abide in Christ and want Him involved in everything I do. He teaches me truth and I am always glad to receive it.*

SEEK GOD IN THE MORNING

Satisfy us in the morning with your unfailing love, that we may sing for joy and be glad all our days.

PSALM 90:14 NIV

It is wise to begin every morning reminding ourselves of God's unfailing love and asking Him to show us how He wants us to live each day—and asking Him to help us do it. I like to say "Pray and then plan." If we acknowledge God in all our ways, He will direct our paths (Proverbs 3:5–6). God simply wants to be asked if He approves of our plan and told that if He doesn't, we are happy to change it. Proverbs 16:3 says, "Commit to the Lord whatever you do, and he will establish your plans" (NIV). Our plans won't work well unless God blesses them, and if they agree with His will, then He does. Most of the details of daily living God leaves to our choice, but He does want to be acknowledged.

Scheduling is the art of planning your activities so you can achieve your goals in the time you have available. Effective scheduling can maximize your effectiveness and reduce your stress level. Lack of scheduling, on the other hand, reduces productivity and results in wasting time instead of enjoying the rewards of a fruitful life and the best God has for you.

Don't try to make plans and set goals on your own, but first commit yourself and your day to the Lord. You may know what you need to do, but ask Him to guide you in setting your priorities. Offer all you are and have, including your time, to Him, and ask for His guidance as you plan your day.

Confession: *I pray and then plan.*

CALLED TO FREEDOM

For you, brethren, were [indeed] called to freedom; only [do not let your] freedom be an incentive to your flesh and an opportunity or excuse [for selfishness], but through love you should serve one another.

GALATIANS 5:13

Under the Old Covenant, God's people had to obey countless laws in order to please Him. But when Jesus came, He did away with the written law of the Old Testament and said now the law of God is written on our hearts (Hebrews 8:10 NIV). We know right from wrong if we are in relationship with God. It is up to us to choose to do the right thing, and Paul teaches us that we should not use our freedom as an opportunity or excuse to operate in the flesh and do things we know are wrong. Neither should we use it as an excuse to be selfish.

For example, a person may be tempted to go to a movie that bothers their conscience, but they say, "I'm free to watch it anyway." They won't lose their salvation because they went against their conscience, but they have displeased God and not done what is best for them. We are free to make choices, but we are not free from God's moral standard, which is holiness and righteousness.

Your conscience is a great friend, and if you listen to it, you will avoid a lot of trouble.

Confession: I am free from the Law, but I won't use my freedom as an excuse to sin. I am thankful for a healthy conscience, and I pray I will always pay attention to it.

NO CONDEMNATION

There is therefore now no condemnation for those who are in Christ Jesus. For the law of the Spirit of life has set you free in Christ Jesus from the law of sin and death.

ROMANS 8:1–2 ESV

I suffered with guilt and condemnation for many years even after I received Christ as my Savior. Even though I regularly repented of any sin I was aware of, I continued to feel guilty. I started feeling guilty during childhood when my father was sexually abusing me because I thought something must be wrong with me for him to want to do what he did to me.

I think I became addicted to guilt. I didn't feel right if I didn't feel wrong. I know now that this was the work of the devil. He was lying to me and making me feel a false sense of guilt. If you struggle with guilt or condemnation, please remember that when Jesus forgave our sins, He also took away any guilt, blame, or shame we are tempted to feel. When we do something wrong, confess it, and ask for forgiveness, God removes the sin and remembers it no more (Hebrews 8:12). The law of the Spirit of life in Him sets us free from the law of sin and death.

The fact that you feel guilty doesn't mean that you are guilty. Have you repented? Are you sorry for your sin? If so, then any guilt you feel is a lie from the devil, and I urge you to ignore the feeling and believe God's Word.

Confession: *I refuse to receive false guilt from the devil. When I repent of sin, it is completely forgiven and forgotten, and there is no more condemnation.*

NO LONGER I WHO LIVE

I have been crucified with Christ [in Him I have shared His crucifixion]; it is no longer I who live, but Christ (the Messiah) lives in me; and the life I now live in the body I live by faith in (by adherence to and reliance on and complete trust in) the Son of God, Who loved me and gave Himself up for me.

GALATIANS 2:20

Jesus died so we would no longer have to live to and for ourselves, but so we would be free to live to and for Him (2 Corinthians 5:15). God does not want us to be selfish and self-centered, and His Word teaches us that we are to die to self and live for Him. This is a process and requires a great deal of help from the Holy Spirit. We are born selfish, but thankfully we are born again generous. Once we receive the new life He offers us, we have the choice to continue being selfish or to be generous.

No one can be happy and selfish at the same time. We are only happy when we obey God and serve Him through helping others. One way we prove our love for Jesus is by helping people who are hurting. Jesus asked Peter three times if he loved Him, and each time Peter replied that he did. The first time Jesus answered, "Feed My lambs"; the second time, He said, "Tend My sheep"; and the third time, He said, "Feed My sheep" (John 21:15–17 NKJV). All were a way of saying "Help My people."

We live in a world of need and pain, and although we cannot do all that needs to be done, we can and should do our part. The worst thing we can do is nothing!

Confession: *When I become aware of someone who is hurting, I will do my best to help them.*

THE HOLY SPIRIT HELPS US DO WHAT WE SHOULD DO

For I do not do the good I want to do, but the evil I do not want to do—this I keep on doing. Now if I do what I do not want to do, it is no longer I who do it, but it is sin living in me that does it.

ROMANS 7:19–20 NIV

We have everything we need to live the life God wants us to live (2 Peter 1:3), but we must learn to follow the guidance of the Holy Spirit. Once we are born again, we may sometimes feel we are two people, and at times we do what we don't want to do—and we don't do what we do want to do. We see in today's scripture that this also happened to the apostle Paul, and we know there is hope for us. Even after we become Christians, we can still do the wrong things we have always done, but the good news is that we also have the ability to do the right things, and the Holy Spirit will help us. We are no longer slaves to sin (Romans 6:6 NIV).

Galatians 5:16 does not say "Try not to walk in the flesh so you can walk in the Spirit," which is what most of us do. It says that if we walk in the Spirit, we will not fulfill the lusts of the flesh. In other words, if we focus on doing the right things, there will be no room for the wrong things. When we focus on the positive, we will have victory. In relationships, if we focus on everything we find wrong with the other person, we will not be able to love them. But if we focus on what is good in them, we will soon pay little attention to what we don't like as much.

Confession: *I will focus on the positive things in life and the positive things about people. I will follow the Holy Spirit and not do what the flesh wants to do.*

THERE'S A WAR GOING ON

For we are not wrestling with flesh and blood [contending only with physical opponents], but against the despotisms, against the powers, against [the master spirits who are] the world rulers of this present darkness, against the spirit forces of wickedness in the heavenly (supernatural) sphere.

EPHESIANS 6:12

We are in a war, but our warfare is not against other human beings. It is against the devil and his demons. Our enemy, Satan, attempts to defeat us with strategy and deceit through well-laid plans and deliberate deception. The devil is a liar. Jesus calls him "the father of lies and of all that is false" (John 8:44). He lies to you and me. He tells us things about ourselves, about other people, and about circumstances that simply are not true. He begins by bombarding our mind with a cleverly devised pattern of little nagging thoughts, suspicions, doubts, fears, wonderings, reasonings, and theories. He moves slowly and cautiously (after all, well-laid plans take time), determined to deceive us. We should always remember that the devil is very patient.

The enemy has studied human beings for a long time, and his warfare against us has a strategy. He knows our likes, dislikes, insecurities, weaknesses, and fears, and what bothers us most. He is willing to invest any amount of time it takes to defeat us. But be encouraged today because Jesus came to destroy the works of the devil (1 John 3:8). God lives in us by the Holy Spirit. He lives in us and is greater than the enemy who is in the world (1 John 4:4).

Confession: *The enemy may try to deceive me, but I know that God, who is in me, is greater than the enemy, who is in the world.*

RIGHTEOUSNESS

And he [Abram] believed in (trusted in, relied on, remained stead-fast to) the Lord, and He counted it to him as righteousness (right standing with God).

GENESIS 15:6

No matter how many good or right things we do, they will never make us righteous before God. The only thing that can do that is faith. Second Corinthians 5:21 is a wonderful scripture that says, "For He made Him who knew no sin to be sin for us, that we might become the righteousness of God in Him" (NKJV). Romans 3:22 states that righteousness is given to those who believe in Jesus Christ.

In the world, we have to do what is right to be right. But in God's kingdom, we can never do enough right to pay for what we have done wrong. Since this is the case, God sent His Son Jesus to pay for our sins and give us God's righteousness. All we need to do is believe this. This truth is so good that it is hard to believe, but it is true because God's Word tells us it over and over (Romans 3:22; 5:19).

Confession: I am the righteousness of God in Christ. I put my faith in Jesus and am a joint heir with Him. I get what He earned and deserved as a gift simply for believing God.

HOW TO AVOID SIN

I will meditate on Your precepts and have respect to Your ways [the paths of life marked out by Your law].

PSALM 119:15

The Bible teaches us to meditate day and night on God's Word. If we do this, it will become part of us and guide us in such a way that we won't sin against God (Psalm 119:11). How does this work? Here's an example from my experience: Yesterday I found out something that made me start to worry and feel disappointed. My daughter was coming to my house, and I asked her not to come because I needed to spend some time with God and get direction about what had happened.

I sat down and began to ponder all the scriptures I know about not worrying and trusting God to take care of me. I prayed, asking God to strengthen me to do what is right in this time of trial. It took a couple of hours, but I soon sensed that faith was winning the battle and I was free from the worry and disappointment.

We all have trials in life. I have them, just as you do. When I face them, I tell myself to do exactly what I tell you to do. Our answers are the same. Trust God and do good (Psalm 37:3), and He will solve your problems.

Confession: *I will meditate on God's Word and trust Him, and this will help me do what is right.*

TRY TO KEEP THINGS IN PERSPECTIVE

Why, my soul, are you downcast? Why so disturbed within me? Put your hope in God, for I will yet praise him, my Savior and my God.
PSALM 42:11 NIV

When we lack proper perspective, we may consider minor situations to be major crises or view significant situations as "no big deal." Either tendency—exaggerating things or minimizing them—can lead to problems, so we need to do our best to see things as they really are.

I know a young man who spent many years trying to prove he was right in every disagreement. He habitually argued and became angry. This happened so often that he lost a lot of friends. He simply was not enjoyable to be with. After this continued for a period of years, I finally began to notice a big change in him. He wasn't argumentative if someone had a different opinion from his or did not want to do something his way. I asked him what had made him change, and he said, "I've discovered that being right is highly overrated." He had gained the proper perspective on being right and realized it wasn't worth the turmoil he experienced when trying to prove a point.

I encourage you to look at the whole of life instead of focusing on one thing that may be upsetting you. Thinking excessively about our problems only makes them appear larger than they really are. When you experience something upsetting, take time to intentionally recall the good things you enjoy in life. King David did this during times of depression, and this helped him keep things in perspective (Psalm 42).

Confession: *I make every effort to keep things in their proper perspective.*

LETTING GO

However, I am telling you nothing but the truth when I say it is profitable (good, expedient, advantageous) for you that I go away. Because if I do not go away, the Comforter (Counselor, Helper, Advocate, Intercessor, Strengthener, Standby) will not come to you [into close fellowship with you]; but if I go away, I will send Him to you [to be in close fellowship with you].

JOHN 16:7

We sometimes think God isn't working and wonder why. But if we try to do His job, He remains on standby until we give the situation completely to Him. He is a gentleman and won't interfere without an invitation. Perhaps God isn't working in a situation because our timing is off, we are out of His will, or we are operating with the wrong motive.

If God isn't giving us the breakthrough we ask for, it may be because He is using the circumstance as a tool to work something in us. The best thing we can do when we are trying to make something happen and feel frustrated because it isn't is to let it go and give it completely to God, trusting that He will do what is right and good for us.

The situations we think are terrible are often best for us, but we don't see this until later. We live life forward, but we understand backward.

Confession: *I will let go of things I am not qualified to handle and let God show Himself strong in my life.*

TRIALS WITH A PURPOSE

For we do not want you to be unaware, brothers, of the affliction we experienced in Asia. For we were so utterly burdened beyond our strength that we despaired even of life itself. Indeed, we felt that we had received the sentence of death. But that was to make us rely not on ourselves but on God who raises the dead.

2 CORINTHIANS 1:8–9 ESV

When we face any kind of difficulty, we usually wonder why and what its purpose is. In today's scripture, Paul and his companions were under such pressure that they despaired of life itself, but that this happened so they would rely on God instead of themselves.

Sometimes we won't depend on God unless we have no other choice, but for God to work through us, He must keep us trusting Him and relying on Him for all things. We may not know what the purpose is, but even when we don't, we should trust Him. God is good, and anything He allows in our life is designed to work for good eventually.

God kept Paul usable by allowing a thorn in his flesh. Even though Paul asked three times for God to remove it, God simply promised him the grace to deal with it (2 Corinthians 12:7–9 NKJV). Paul said that he was given this thorn, a messenger from Satan to keep him from being prideful, because of the greatness of the revelations he had been shown. Pride was one of Paul's problems, and God made sure it didn't reappear and make him of no use to His purpose.

Confession: *Even when things are confusing and seem unfair, I trust God to work them out for good.*

COMING TO THE END OF YOURSELF

For as the heavens are higher than the earth, so are My ways higher than your ways and My thoughts than your thoughts.

ISAIAH 55:9

We all have a lot of fleshly energy, and we often use it to try to fix our own problems, to change ourselves and others, or to alter our circumstances. This frustrates us because it doesn't work. It often takes a while for us to accept that it doesn't work and come to the end of ourselves in terms of trying to do things in our own strength. God wants us to trust Him, and He won't work in our lives any other way. Our access to His help is through faith alone.

I may be trying to open a jar and struggle with the process until I finally give up and ask Dave to do it for me. A simple example such as this may help you understand how we struggle to do things ourselves, but finally give up and ask God to do it for us. If nothing is happening as you try to solve your problems, perhaps God is waiting for you to come to the end of yourself and humbly ask Him to do for you what you cannot do by yourself.

It took me many years to reach this point, but I finally did. And when I did, I was able to enter God's rest. Now I can say, "If God doesn't do it, then I don't want it!"

Confession: *I turn myself and all that needs to be done in my life over to God. I will do anything He tells me to do, but I refuse to take action without His help and direction.*

SILENCING THE ACCUSER

Then I heard a strong (loud) voice in heaven, saying, Now it has come—the salvation and the power and the kingdom (the dominion, the reign) of our God, and the power (the sovereignty, the authority) of His Christ (the Messiah); for the accuser of our brethren, he who keeps bringing before our God charges against them day and night, has been cast out!

REVELATION 12:10

Satan loves to accuse us and make us feel guilty, but we overcome Him by the blood of Jesus and the word of our testimony. How do we overcome by the word of our testimony? This means that when he comes against us with accusations, we come against him with God's Word. We say things like "I'm forgiven, and God has forgotten my sin and there is no condemnation for those in Christ" (see Isaiah 43:25; Romans 8:1). Or we say, "I am the righteousness of God in Christ" (see 2 Corinthians 5:21).

We should use the shield of faith to quench all the fiery darts of the enemy (Ephesians 6:16). Satan is a liar, and his favorite thing to do is deceive us into believing God has not forgiven us when He has. He loves to make us feel guilty because when we do, we are weakened and not of much use to God. Jesus talked back to the devil (Luke 4:4, 8, 12), and we should too. Don't just stand idly by and listen to his lies. Remind him that you are more than a conqueror (Romans 8:37) and that he is already defeated (1 John 3:8 kjv).

Confession: When Satan comes against me with accusations, I will remind Him that I am forgiven and that he is a defeated foe.

FOCUS ON LOVING OTHERS

But whoever has this world's goods, and sees his brother in need, and shuts up his heart from him, how does the love of God abide in him? My little children, let us not love in word or in tongue, but in deed and in truth. And by this we know that we are of the truth, and shall assure our hearts before Him. For if our heart condemns us, God is greater than our heart, and knows all things. Beloved, if our heart does not condemn us, we have confidence toward God.

1 JOHN 3:17–21 NKJV

Instead of being concerned about performing perfectly to try to earn God's love, I recommend realizing that God already loves you and focusing on loving others in practical ways. Love is not theory or words; it is action. We have a heart of compassion, but we can close it and remain selfish if we choose to. If we do so, then the love of God that has been placed in us by the Holy Spirit (Romans 5:5) will not remain active, because love must flow to stay alive.

I believe that God gives us many opportunities to help people, but we must recognize and take advantage of them. It is more blessed to give than to receive (Acts 20:35), and when we have an opportunity to help someone and do it, we do ourselves a favor. The most important commandments in the Bible are to love God, to love ourselves, and to love others (Mark 12:30–31). If we focus on loving God and people, then we won't have to worry so much about sin. Most sin is caused by pride and selfishness, but love closes the door to both. Generous people are happy people. Think about who you know that you might be able to help in some way and do it.

Confession: *I take every opportunity that God gives me to help others.*

EMPOWERED THROUGH PRAISE

No unbelief or distrust made him waver (doubtingly question) concerning the promise of God, but he grew strong and was empowered by faith as he gave praise and glory to God.

ROMANS 4:20

When doubt and unbelief attack our minds, we can begin praising and thanking God. This will strengthen us and shut the door to doubt. When King David was experiencing some depression and a downcast soul, he spoke to himself, saying, "Why so disturbed within me? Put your hope in God, for I will yet praise him, my Savior and my God" (Psalm 42:5 NIV).

Part of the definition of *praise* in the biblical Greek is "fair speaking, fine speeches"[9] or flattering speech. It is to "tell a tale"[10] about the goodness of God.

When the devil attacks, one of the quickest ways to get rid of him is to remember and speak aloud of the good things God has done for you. Keep a book of remembrance in which you record the mighty acts God has done on your behalf. When you have a book like this, you will find that the pages will fill up fast, and it will be a great resource for you to turn to when you need to do war with Satan.

Confession: When doubt attacks my mind, I will remember all the great and mighty things God has done for me. I will rehearse them aloud, and Satan will flee.

DON'T SETTLE FOR LESS THAN GOD'S BEST

And Terah took Abram his son, Lot the son of Haran, his grandson, and Sarai his daughter-in-law, his son Abram's wife, and they went forth together to go from Ur of the Chaldees into the land of Canaan; but when they came to Haran, they settled there. And Terah lived 205 years; and Terah died in Haran.

GENESIS 11:31–32

Often people have a goal in mind, but they settle for less than what they really want. Abraham's father, Terah, was told to go to Canaan, but he settled in Haran. He lived 205 years and died where he settled. I think this is a sad story, but it is the story of many people. Too often many people will settle for a spouse they have doubts about simply because they are afraid of being lonely all their life. I did that, and it gave me five years of misery. Because of impatience and fear, people often settle for something inferior instead of waiting for God's best. Don't make that mistake!

Sometimes when we get hurt in life, we park at the point of our pain and never progress beyond it. But God offers us healing and restoration if we want it. We don't have to get stuck in a moment. Your entire life is not ruined because of one sad event that was unfair or painful.

Take this promise from God and go forward: "For I will restore health to you, and I will heal your wounds, says the Lord, because they have called you an outcast, saying, This is Zion, whom no one seeks after and for whom no one cares!" (Jeremiah 30:17). Even if no one else cares for you, God does, and He can work miracles out of anyone's biggest mistakes!

Confession: *I refuse to settle for less than God's best.*

THE FIERY FURNACE OF LIFE

Nebuchadnezzar then approached the opening of the blazing furnace and shouted, "Shadrach, Meshach and Abednego, servants of the Most High God, come out! Come here!" So Shadrach, Meshach and Abednego came out of the fire.

DANIEL 3:26 NIV

Shadrach, Meshach, and Abednego were thrown into a fiery furnace because they refused to bow to and worship the idol Nebuchadnezzar had set up. But "the fire had not harmed their bodies, nor was a hair of their heads singed; their robes were not scorched, and there was no smell of fire on them" (Daniel 3:27 NIV). They went through a very difficult situation that should have left them damaged, but because God was with them, they were not harmed. They emerged without any evidence that they had gone through such a terrible ordeal.

I feel this is the way my life has been. I was sexually abused by my father and abandoned to the abuse by my mother. Due to the fear of being lonely, at the age of eighteen, I married the first man who asked me. That was a disaster that caused a great deal of pain in my life. But to look at my life now, no one would ever think I had such a rough beginning. God has healed my wounded soul, and He will heal you also.

Just as the king told the young men to "come out" of the fiery furnace, God is saying to you that it is time to come out of the past and be made whole.

Confession: *My soul is being healed. God will do such a work that there will be no evidence that I was ever hurt.*

HAVE HOPE: GOD IS DOING A NEW THING

There is surely a future hope for you, and your hope will not be cut off.

PROVERBS 23:18 NIV

God loves new things. He does not want us to get stuck in the pain of our past. Forget the past and let today be the first day of the rest of a wonderful new life. Be filled with hope, which is the expectation of something good. God makes us new (2 Corinthians 5:17), and He gives us a new heart and a new spirit (Ezekiel 11:19).

His mercies are new every morning (Lamentations 3:22), and thankfully we don't have to drag the mistakes of yesterday with us. Are you living in the past? If so, it is time to let it go, stir up your hope, and start fresh. No matter how bad your past may have been, God can work it out for your good (Romans 8:28).

The greatest gift God has given you is the moment you have right now. Don't miss this moment because you are regretting yesterday or worrying about tomorrow. God is "I AM" (Exodus 3:14). He is here now in your life to make it wonderful if you will receive it.

Confession: *I refuse to be trapped in the past. This is the day the Lord has made, and I will rejoice and be glad in it (Psalm 118:24).*

BROKEN HEARTS ARE HEALED

He heals the brokenhearted and binds up their wounds [curing their pains and their sorrows].

PSALM 147:3

The promise of healing is wonderful. I was brokenhearted and had a wounded soul because of the abuse I suffered in my childhood through my early twenties. If we have a wound on our leg or arm, we can go to the doctor and get it taken care of, but only God can heal us on the inside. He alone can heal the brokenhearted. If our heart is wounded, we often wound others. That's what I did. The pain inside of me manifested every day in the way I felt about myself and the way I treated other people.

The person with a wounded soul will think wrong, feel wrong, and do wrong things. However, God can renew our minds and teach us to think as He does. He can heal our emotions and help us learn to live by His Word instead of according to how we feel, and He can help us want to do His will instead of our own. The healing of the soul is a journey that is often long and painful, but it is also wonderful and amazing.

I write from experience when I tell you that no matter what has happened to you, God will give you a double blessing for your former trouble (Isaiah 61:7), and what happened to you will help other people get through their pain.

Confession: *Instead of being depressed about the pain of my past, I am being healed and will use my experience to help others.*

GOD WANTS YOU HEALED AND PROSPEROUS

Beloved, I pray that you may prosper in every way and [that your body] may keep well, even as [I know] your soul keeps well and prospers.

3 JOHN 2

God doesn't want us to prosper beyond our level of spiritual maturity, but His will for us is to mature spiritually, be healed and healthy, and have our needs met. God also wants us to prosper so we will be able to help other people.

We don't serve God to get things, because things can never keep us happy. We serve God because we love Him, and if we put Him first, He will add everything we need (Matthew 6:33). Prosperity without God can be dangerous, for what does it profit a person if they gain the whole world and yet lose their own soul (Matthew 16:26)? Don't ever compromise your conscience and do things you know are wrong simply to gain a position, power, or material possessions. If you do, you will be tormented inwardly, and the things you have will never make you happy.

Serve God wholeheartedly, and let Him give you what He knows you can handle while keeping Him first in your life.

Confession: *I serve God because I love Him, and I only want what He wants me to have.*

GOD WILL TAKE CARE OF YOU

There is no fear in love [dread does not exist], but full-grown (complete, perfect) love turns fear out of doors and expels every trace of terror! For fear brings with it the thought of punishment, and [so] he who is afraid has not reached the full maturity of love [is not yet grown into love's complete perfection].

1 JOHN 4:18

Worry and anxiety are rooted in the fear that we won't be taken care of or that something bad will happen to us. The assurance that you will be taken care of and that God will protect you is found in today's scripture. If we are afraid of not being taken care of, we need to grow in the knowledge that God loves us unconditionally, perfectly, and everlastingly. This knowledge usually takes time to develop because we have difficulty believing that God could or would love us, due to our imperfections. Actually, it is because of our imperfections that God sent Jesus to die for us and take the punishment we deserved because of our sin.

I had to spend several years studying God's love for me in order to get my mind completely renewed in this area. Because my father abused me sexually and my mother abandoned me to his evil behavior, I was convinced that if I didn't take care of myself, nobody would take care of me. However, God is not like people, and we cannot judge how He will treat us according to how others have treated us.

Let me encourage you to pray and ask God to help you grow in the revelation and understanding of how much He loves you.

Confession: *God loves me perfectly, and He helps me when I have problems.*

SHAKE IT OFF

But Paul shook the snake off into the fire and suffered no ill effects.
ACTS 28:5 NIV

I want to share a story with you today.

> One day a farmer's donkey fell into a well. The animal cried piteously for hours as the farmer tried to figure out what to do. Finally, he decided the animal was old and the well needed to be covered up anyway; it just wasn't worth it to retrieve the donkey. He invited all of his neighbors to come over and help him. They all grabbed a shovel and began to shovel dirt into the well. At first, the donkey realized what was happening and cried horribly.
>
> Then to everyone's amazement, he quieted down. A few shovel loads later, the farmer finally looked down the well. He was astonished at what he saw. With each shovel of dirt that hit his back, the donkey was doing something amazing. He would shake it off and take a step up.
>
> As the farmer's neighbors continued to shovel dirt on top of the animal, he would shake it off and take a step up. Pretty soon, everyone was amazed as the donkey stepped up over the edge of the well and happily trotted off!

Life will shovel dirt on you. The key to getting out of the well is to shake it off and take a step up. We can get out of the deepest wells simply by never giving up.

Confession: *When life throws dirt on me, I will shake it off and take a step up.*

FROM THE PIT TO THE PALACE

Moreover, He called for a famine upon the land [of Egypt]; He cut off every source of bread. He sent a man before them, even Joseph, who was sold as a servant. His feet they hurt with fetters; he was laid in chains of iron and his soul entered into the iron.

PSALM 105:16–18

In Genesis chapters 37 and 39–50, we read that Joseph suffered many unfair situations. His brothers were jealous of him; they sold him into slavery and told his father a wild animal had killed him. He became the head of the house for Potiphar, one of Pharaoh's officers. Potiphar's wife wanted Joseph to sleep with her, and when he refused, she had him thrown in prison, where he remained for years. There, God promoted him, and he had authority over the other prisoners. He helped a cupbearer get out of prison by interpreting a dream for him, and asked the cupbearer to remember him when he was free, but when the cupbearer left prison, he forgot about Joseph.

Through these circumstances, Joseph kept a good attitude and continued trusting and obeying God. In every situation, God gave him favor and promoted him. Eventually, Joseph interpreted one of Pharaoh's dreams, and he was so impressed that he put Joseph in a high administrative position in his government. Joseph went from the pit to the palace!

If someone mistreats you, keep a good attitude and continue helping other people, and God will give you favor and reward you for your faithfulness to Him.

Confession: *I will keep a good attitude no matter how I am treated, and I believe God will give me favor and promote me.*

STAY FOCUSED WHEN THINGS DON'T GO ACCORDING TO PLAN

Let your eyes look straight ahead; fix your gaze directly before you.
PROVERBS 4:25 NIV

No matter how well we plan, things rarely go exactly as we anticipate. Some of the interruptions we deal with could be avoided if we stood more firmly on our decisions, but many cannot be. If I don't accomplish what I want to do today, I simply plan to do it tomorrow. At the same time, I also try to learn from experience how I can better stay on track. I want to allow interruptions that cannot be avoided, but I don't want to allow random distractions and unnecessary things to get me off course.

You and I cannot expect other people to keep us on track and moving toward our goals, because that is something we do for ourselves each day, and we should not blame the people who interrupt us if we are not willing to take responsibility for allowing their interruption. We may not be able to keep someone from calling us at an inconvenient time, but we don't have to answer the phone or, if we must take the call, get into a long conversation that isn't necessary.

Some people are naturally gifted at staying focused, but anyone can improve through practice. Our relationship with God is not based on our plan for the day or how organized we are, He loves us unconditionally. But living life with purpose and with a plan is the only way we will end up being the people we truly want to be and enjoying the best life we possibly can.

Confession: *I am diligent to stay focused and to live life on purpose.*

STOP BLAMING OTHERS FOR YOUR PROBLEMS

And the man said, The woman whom You gave to be with me—she gave me [fruit] from the tree, and I ate. And the Lord God said to the woman, What is this you have done? And the woman said, The serpent beguiled (cheated, outwitted, and deceived) me, and I ate.
GENESIS 3:12–13

Blaming others for our problems is a way to avoid responsibility, and people have done it since Creation. Being truthful with ourselves may be difficult, but it is the only pathway to freedom. The longer we blame, the longer we stay in bondage. We can blame people, we can blame the devil, we can blame the systems in which we live, but what we really need to do is take an honest look at ourselves.

God desires truth in the inner being (Psalm 51:6). I remember a woman who was getting married for the seventh time, and she asked our pastor to pray that this man would treat her right. She failed to realize that she was the common denominator in all seven marriages. Her husbands weren't the problem; she was. Until she faced this truth and took responsibility for herself, she would continue to have trouble.

No matter what we have done wrong, if we will admit it, be willing to turn from it, and ask the Holy Spirit to help us change, God will forgive us and help us make a fresh start.

Confession: *I will stop blaming others for my problems and take responsibility to fix them with God's help.*

BE PATIENT

But we all, with unveiled face, beholding as in a mirror the glory of the Lord, are being transformed into the same image from glory to glory, just as by the Spirit of the Lord.

2 CORINTHIANS 3:18 NKJV

As we study God's Word, we will be changed by the Holy Spirit, but this takes time. Today's scripture tells us we are being changed "from glory to glory," but there is time between each "glory," and unless we learn to wait with patience, we will not be happy. God is not in a hurry. He is more interested in doing a good job than in doing a quick job.

We cannot compare our rate of progress with anyone else's because we are all different, and God has a personalized, perfect plan for each of us. Spiritual maturity is a journey, and I encourage you not to be so focused on the destination that you don't enjoy the path to it. We all need to change, and it is fine for us to enjoy ourselves while God is changing us.

Be patient and celebrate your progress instead of mourning over how far you still need to go. God isn't concerned that you have not arrived yet; His only concern is that you keep making progress, even if that progress is slow.

Confession: *I will be patient on my journey toward being molded into the image of Jesus Christ, and I will enjoy myself while I make the trip.*

THE GREAT EXCHANGE

The Spirit of the Sovereign Lord is on me, because the Lord has anointed me to proclaim good news to the poor. He has sent me to bind up the brokenhearted, to proclaim freedom for the captives and release from darkness for the prisoners, to proclaim the year of the Lord's favor and the day of vengeance of our God, to comfort all who mourn, and provide for those who grieve in Zion—to bestow on them a crown of beauty instead of ashes, the oil of joy instead of mourning, and a garment of praise instead of a spirit of despair. They will be called oaks of righteousness, a planting of the Lord for the display of his splendor.

ISAIAH 61:1–3 NIV

What if you could take anything worn-out, ineffective, old, or no longer working to a store near you and exchange it for a brand-new one at no cost? Wouldn't that be wonderful? Jesus offers us an exchanged life. We give Him our sins, and He gives us His righteousness (2 Corinthians 5:21). We give him our ashes, and He gives us His beauty. We give him our grief and mourning, and He gives us His joy (Isaiah 61:3). He takes our old life and gives us a new one (2 Corinthians 5:17).

The Bible mentions many things we can exchange, yet many of us keep hanging on to the old stuff. If you haven't visited the exchange store, it's time to start going there regularly.

God will encourage you if you are discouraged, He will comfort you if you are sad or hurting, and He will exchange your weakness for His strength.

Confession: *I visit God's exchange store regularly because He has everything I need.*

DAILY RENEWAL

Therefore we do not become discouraged (utterly spiritless, exhausted, and wearied out through fear). Though our outer man is [progressively] decaying and wasting away, yet our inner self is being [progressively] renewed day after day.

2 CORINTHIANS 4:16

We all want to be strong physically, but what about being strong in our inner being? If you are strengthened inside, you can make it through anything that comes against you from the outside. For example, one way to stay young is to think young. Age is a number, but "old" is an attitude. Even as our body gets older our inner being can be daily renewed. In the amplification of Ephesians 3:16, Paul prayed for the church to be strengthened in the inner being by the Holy Spirit indwelling their innermost being and personality.

We feed our physical bodies food daily to stay strong. In the same way, we need to feed our inner being with God's Word, prayer, and meditation on the promises in His Word. Worship and praise also strengthen us. We need to think with the mind of Christ and make sure our thoughts line up with God's Word. For example, don't think "I can't" thoughts. Instead, believe you can do anything God asks you to do (Philippians 4:13). Stay positive and full of hope. And remember that laughter does good like a medicine (Proverbs 17:22).

Confession: *My body may grow old, but my inner being will stay young and renewed.*

YOU CAN THINK YOU'RE RICH YET BE POOR

For you say, I am rich; I have prospered and grown wealthy, and I am in need of nothing; and you do not realize and understand that you are wretched, pitiable, poor, blind, and naked.

REVELATION 3:17

Having an abundance of things and a lot of money is not what makes a person rich. Sometimes people who have a lot financially and materially are the poorest of all but don't realize it. What makes us truly rich is an intimate relationship with God through Christ, knowing God's Word, helping other people, and being rich in faith.

Many people who are financially well off are very unhappy, but they don't have to be. God wants us to prosper financially, but only as our soul prospers (3 John 2). I pray regularly that God will never give me more than I can handle without keeping Him first in my life. No matter how much merchandise you own or money you have, be sure to keep in mind that nothing this world offers can keep you happy for long unless you have Jesus in your life.

Confession: I am rich in faith and in the knowledge of God's Word.

THE KINGDOM WITHIN

Nor will people say, Look! Here [it is]! or, See, [it is] there! For behold, the kingdom of God is within you [in your hearts] and among you [surrounding you].

LUKE 17:21

Jesus is the King of His kingdom, and He should rule there. In practical terms, this means our thoughts, attitudes, motives, and plans should be subject to His will. What have you been thinking about? If you feel sad or depressed, you'll find that your thoughts are negative and hopeless. If your thoughts are not in agreement with God's thoughts (His Word), you can reject wrong thoughts and choose better ones. When I learned that I could do my own thinking and that I didn't have to think only about whatever fell into my head, it was life-changing for me.

Jesus lives in us, and we should keep the atmosphere in our inner being one where He is comfortable. If we are full of anger, unforgiveness, fear, or worry, He is uncomfortable, and this makes us uncomfortable. Sometimes we feel downcast and don't understand why. The next time this happens to you, take an inventory of your thoughts, attitudes, and motives—and you are likely to find the source of your problem.

Confession: I will pay attention to what is going on inside of me. The kingdom of God is in me, and I want to provide an atmosphere in which God will be comfortable.

YOU ARE GOD'S HOME

That Christ may dwell in your hearts through faith; that you, being rooted and grounded in love.

EPHESIANS 3:17 NKJV

We believe by faith that God dwells in us. He makes His home in our hearts. God is love, and that means we are full of His love. In today's scripture, Paul teaches us to be rooted and grounded in God's love. A revelation of how much God loves us is one of the most valuable things we can have. God's love casts out fear (1 John 4:18), and if we know He loves us, then we also believe He will always take care of us.

Having the confidence that God will meet all our needs—no matter what they are—allows us to eliminate the stress of worry and enter the rest of God.

The doctor I have had for twenty-seven years just told me she is moving to another state, and I was very disappointed. She knows my body, and over the years we have built a great working relationship. After I heard this news, I began worrying. But as I remembered that God has promised to always take care of me, I knew His care includes finding me a new doctor that is just right. You can trust God to meet any need you have. Ask and keep on asking and you will receive (Luke 11:9).

Confession: I believe that God loves me and that He will meet any need I have.

YOUR REPUTATION

Now am I trying to win the favor of men, or of God? Do I seek to please men? If I were still seeking popularity with men, I should not be a bond servant of Christ (the Messiah).

GALATIANS 1:10

Our outer life is our reputation with people, but our inner life is our reputation with God. We can do things that are phony to impress people, but God always knows our true motives. There is no pretending with Him. I think most of us go through a phase in life when we are very concerned about what people think of us. When we do, we are in danger of becoming people-pleasers unless we realize that what God thinks of us is much more important than what people think.

Jesus made Himself of no earthly reputation and took on the form of a servant (Philippians 2:7). In reading the Bible, we clearly see that Jesus did not have a good reputation with most people. Even members of His own family thought He might be "out of His mind" (Mark 3:21). None of this concerned Him because He knew His own heart, and more than anything, He cared about being pleasing to God (John 8:29). You can save yourself much heartache by realizing that no matter what you do, there will always be some people who won't like or approve of you, but that doesn't matter if God does approve.

Confession: *I am not concerned about my reputation with people, but with God. I want to be a person who pleases God, not other people.*

OUR WORDS AND THOUGHTS

Let the words of my mouth and the meditation of my heart be acceptable in Your sight, O Lord, my [firm, impenetrable] Rock and my Redeemer.

PSALM 19:14

I pray today's scripture often because I know I need God to help me say and think the right things. James 3:8 says that no one can tame the tongue. No matter how hard we try, we cannot control our tongue without God's help. Words carry either the power of life or death, "and they who indulge in it shall eat the fruit of it [for death or life]" (Proverbs 18:21). If you take time to think about this, the power of words is amazing.

Our thoughts are as important as our words because they become our words (Matthew 12:34). What is in our heart eventually comes out of our mouth if it stays in our heart long enough. Words have power, and we can hurt people with what we say. Once we speak something, we can't undo what we have said. Happily, we can also help people with our words, but this begins with thinking good thoughts about people.

When you think of people, focus on their strong points and what they do to help you. This way, you will build people up instead of tear them down.

Confession: *I will focus on every good thing I can think about people and circumstances. Then positive words will come out of my mouth.*

YOU WILL KNOW THEM BY THEIR FRUIT

Likewise, every good tree bears good fruit, but a bad tree bears bad fruit. A good tree cannot bear bad fruit, and a bad tree cannot bear good fruit. Every tree that does not bear good fruit is cut down and thrown into the fire. Thus, by their fruit you will recognize them.

MATTHEW 7:17–20 NIV

If we see apples on a tree, we know it is an apple tree. If we see peaches, we know it is a peach tree. If we see people bearing good fruit, such as patience, love, kindness, joy, peace, and other good qualities, we know they are good people. But if we see someone being mean, angry, rude, or unkind to others, we know they are someone we probably should not get involved with.

The people we spend a lot of time with should be those whose behavior challenges us to live higher. If we are around someone a lot, we usually pick up some of their habits, so make sure you want to become like the people you spend a lot of time with. Spend time with people who will help you, not hurt you.

Being generous is very important to me, so I love spending time with generous people, because they provoke me to be even more generous. Psalm 1:1 in the Amplified Bible, Classic Edition, tells us not to sit down inactive with those who are ungodly or mockers. It also states we are not to live in the counsel of the ungodly. Choose your friends wisely!

Confession: I am careful about who I spend time with because I want to be with people who will challenge me to be a better person.

KNOW YOUR OWN HEART

The heart is deceitful above all things, and it is exceedingly perverse and corrupt and severely, mortally sick! Who can know it [perceive, understand, be acquainted with his own heart and mind]?

JEREMIAH 17:9

The idea that our own hearts can deceive us is a bit frightening. How can this happen? I believe we are deceived by making excuses instead of being truthful with ourselves. The amplification of James 1:22 says that if we hear the Word but don't act on it, we are deceived by reasoning that is contrary to the truth.

Knowing our own hearts and being honest with ourselves concerning our motives is very valuable. It helps us to avoid making mistakes that eventually cause us a great deal of heartache. It is good to know our strengths, but it is also good to know our weaknesses. God will strengthen us in our weaknesses, but I believe we need to admit them first.

To be deceived means to believe a lie, and we know that the devil is a liar (John 8:44). But if we believe a lie, even though it is a lie, it becomes our truth. How many lies to do you think you believe? Take some time today to pray about this and give it some serious thought.

Confession: I want to know my own heart and never deceive myself. I will not make excuses for doing things I think are wrong.

THE TESTING OF OUR FAITH

My brethren, count it all joy when you fall into various trials, know-ing that the testing of your faith produces patience.

JAMES 1:2–3 NKJV

Today's scripture tells us to rejoice when we experience testing and all kinds of trials because they work good things in us. One thing they do eventually is work patience. Patience is not the ability to wait; it is how we behave while we wait. Do you wait with a good attitude or with frustration and anger?

The fact that something hurts or is uncomfortable doesn't mean it isn't good for us. I'm sure you have heard the saying "no pain, no gain." We love the gain but hate the pain. God gives us a measure of faith (Romans 12:3 NKJV). He gives us enough for everything He wants us to do in life, but our faith only becomes strong through use. When our faith is tested, we find out how strong it really is.

When you are being tested with trials or temptations, stay strong and pass your tests. Stay joyful, remain at peace, and be thankful for all God has done for you—and soon you will experience victory and be stronger in faith than you were before.

Confession: *When my faith is tested, I remain at peace because I know God loves me and will meet my every need.*

ASK IN FAITH WITH NO DOUBT

But let him ask in faith, with no doubting, for he who doubts is like a wave of the sea driven and tossed by the wind. For let not that man suppose that he will receive anything from the Lord; he is a double-minded man, unstable in all his ways.

JAMES 1:6-8 NKJV

When you have a decision to make, pray in faith and ask God to guide you. As you wait on His leading, it may take a few days or longer, but soon you will settle on what you believe to be the right course of action. Be sure you have peace about it, be sure it agrees with God's Word, and don't let doubt confuse you and cause you to change your mind. A double-minded person is unstable. They cannot settle on anything, and they waste a lot of time in indecision.

When you have asked in faith and you sense God's leading, have confidence that you are led by God's Spirit and that you make good decisions. Don't let the devil steal your time through doubt. Learn how to doubt your doubts. When doubt knocks on your door, send faith to answer. If we are double-minded, we will not receive what we ask for from God.

Don't worry if you make a mistake, because we all make mistakes. That's how we learn.

Confession: *I make good decisions because I am guided by God's Spirit, and I am not double-minded. I don't let doubt steal my faith or my time.*

BE GOOD TO PEOPLE WHO ARE HURTING

Woe to you, scribes and Pharisees, hypocrites! For you tithe mint and dill and cumin, and have neglected the weightier matters of the law: justice and mercy and faithfulness. These you ought to have done, without neglecting the others.

MATTHEW 23:23 ESV

The scribes and Pharisees followed all the Jewish laws, yet Jesus called them hypocrites. Why? Because although they followed the rules, they mistreated people. They neglected to help those who were hurting. Jesus said they should have done both.

Under the new covenant, we are set free from the rules and regulations of the law, but not from the moral code that God instituted. The main thing God wants us to learn is to love Him and love one another (Mark 12:30–31). If we do that, we will please God.

A person may go to church twice a week, tithe, pray, and read their Bible, yet mistreat others. I know this because I did it for years. It's not what we do when people are watching that is important but what we do when no one is watching. Focus on walking in love, and you will fulfill God's law of liberty (James 2:12–14).

Confession: *I love to help people who are hurting, and my goal is to walk in love.*

DEDICATE YOUR INNER SELF TO GOD

The King's daughter is all glorious within; her clothing is interwoven with gold.

PSALM 45:13 NASB

Your inner self, what 1 Peter 3:4 calls "the hidden person of the heart," should be dedicated to God. We may dedicate a portion of our money, time, or many other things to Him, but our thoughts, attitudes, motives, and will are important for us to dedicate to God also.

Jesus told the Pharisees that they cleansed "the outside of the cup and of the plate" (meaning their outward behavior), "but inside you yourselves are full of greed and robbery and extortion and malice and wickedness" (Luke 11:39). He said to dedicate your inner self (Luke 11:41).

Have you dedicated your inner self to God? This commitment means you will work with the Holy Spirit to honor God with your thoughts, attitudes, motives, and decisions. Take some time to think about what goes on inside of you and dedicate your inner self to God.

Confession: *I dedicate my inner self to God. I want everything that goes on in me to glorify and please Him.*

WHAT ARE YOU FULL OF?

[That you may really come] to know [practically, through experience for yourselves] the love of Christ, which far surpasses mere knowledge [without experience]; that you may be filled [through all your being] unto all the fullness of God [may have the richest measure of the divine Presence, and become a body wholly filled and flooded with God Himself]!

EPHESIANS 3:19

Today's scripture challenges us to "become a body wholly filled and flooded with God Himself." This is my goal, and I pray it is yours, too. But I have found that I must decrease so He can increase (John 3:30). Too often I am full of myself, working hard to get what I want. We may blame every kind of problem on the devil, but self is our biggest problem. God's Word teaches us to die to self, and this is not a quick or easy process.

If we will forget about ourselves and what we want and live for God and His will, He will give us more than we could ever get for ourselves. I urge you to pray regularly about decreasing while God increases. Pray to be full of God's thoughts, His will, His attitudes, and His desires, and be empty of yourself.

This doesn't mean you never want anything for yourself, but instead of trying to get it for yourself, ask God for it. Psalm 37:4 says to delight ourselves in God, and He will give us the desires of our heart.

Confession: *I am full of God, not full of myself.*

GREAT THINKING, GREAT LIFE

Let the words of my mouth and the meditation of my heart be acceptable in Your sight, O Lord, my [firm, impenetrable] Rock and my Redeemer.

PSALM 19:14

One of the most life-changing revelations we can have is to find out that we can do something about our thoughts. We can practice "on-purpose thinking." We do not have to meditate on everything that pops into our minds; we can choose what we want to think about. We can choose power-enhancing thoughts—not power-draining thoughts. We can be deliberate about what goes on in our minds. We can break up with bad habits and form good habits. In fact, learning to think great thoughts on purpose is one of the keys to a great life.

We often allow ourselves to buy into the world's idea of a "great life." We may equate greatness with fame, fortune, athletic success, celebrity status, remarkable business or scientific achievements, or physical attractiveness. But none of these constitutes a truly great life. In fact, some of the most famous and wealthy people in the world seem to be some of the most miserable people. To really have a great life, I believe a person must have love, peace, joy, right standing with God, good relationships, and other qualities the world does not necessarily consider "great." Without them, how could anyone's life be great? Just think about it: What do we really have without peace and joy? Think great thoughts today and every day—thoughts of peace, joy, success, and love—and see how great your life will be.

Confession: *I think great thoughts, which lead to a great life.*

THE POWER OF SIMPLE PRAYERS

This is the confidence we have in approaching God: that if we ask anything according to his will, he hears us. And if we know that he hears us—whatever we ask—we know that we have what we asked of him.

1 JOHN 5:14-15 NIV

Some people fail to pray much because they see prayer as a complicated exercise or something they don't know how to do. But prayer is simply talking to God, just as we would talk to a good friend. I like to begin my prayers with praise and thanksgiving for God's goodness, and I thank Him for specific ways He has answered my previous prayers. I pray for people I know who are sick or have other problems, and then I ask God to help me with my day and anything else I need help with.

Prayer can be very simple. Don't try to "sound religious" when you pray; just be yourself. Embrace your uniqueness, and always remember that you don't have to pray like anyone else prays. Also, the length of your prayer is not as important as the sincerity of it. You can pray anytime, anywhere, about anything.

When Jesus' disciples asked Him to teach them to pray, He gave them what we call the Lord's Prayer (Matthew 6:9–13). It is a short and simple prayer you can use as a guideline to follow when you pray if you desire to do so. Today's scripture teaches that some things are God's will and some are not. When we aren't sure, it is wise to pray and then say "I ask this, Lord, if it is Your will."

Confession: *When I pray, I simply talk to God.*

LET YOUR LIGHT SHINE

Let your light so shine before men that they may see your moral excellence and your praiseworthy, noble, and good deeds and recognize and honor and praise and glorify your Father Who is in heaven.

MATTHEW 5:16

The world is a dark place, but God's kingdom is filled with light. That light was in Jesus and is in us (John 1:9). Light is the only thing that swallows up darkness. You can go into a totally dark room and turn on the light, and suddenly the dark is gone. Today's scripture teaches us not to hide our light, but to let it shine and give glory to God.

I believe God strategically places each of us in a part of the world to be a light in a dark place. Your place might be your neighborhood, where you work, or where you shop. It might be anywhere in the world. I believe God has His people everywhere, and all we need to do is turn on our lights.

Glorifying God with our behavior is equivalent to turning on the light. Being good to people, giving to the poor, doing random acts of kindness, and forgiving people who hurt us are all examples of turning on your light. Let's all do our part and work with God to swallow up all the darkness in the world.

Confession: *The light of the world lives in me, and I choose to go out into my section of the world and let my light shine.*

SELF-CONSCIOUS

For we [Christians] are the true circumcision, who worship God in spirit and by the Spirit of God and exult and glory and pride ourselves in Jesus Christ, and put no confidence or dependence [on what we are] in the flesh and on outward privileges and physical advantages and external appearances.

PHILIPPIANS 3:3

To be self-conscious means to be excessively or uncomfortably aware of one's appearance or manner. Being overly self-conscious is born out of a lack of confidence and an excessive desire for others to think well of us. We can all have confidence if our confidence is in Jesus and not in what we look like, what others think about us, what our position is in the world or the church, our level of education, or many other things.

What does your confidence come from? We all want to look our best and do our best, and this is good, unless it becomes obsessive. I can't get my confidence from the number of people who watch me on television or how many come to my conferences. Of course, I want the numbers to be strong, but if they aren't, I don't have to lose my confidence if I place it in who I am in Christ. Sure, I feel good if I get compliments on my hair, my clothing, my teaching, and other things. But what if I do a teaching and don't get any compliments, or if I get a new outfit and don't get any compliments? If I lose my confidence in those situations, my confidence is in the wrong place. Do your best and leave the rest to God. Let your confidence be in Jesus.

Confession: *I am confident in Christ and His love for me. I want to look and do my best, but I am not overly self-conscious.*

DON'T BE TOO HARD
ON YOURSELF

*I care very little if I am judged by you or by any human court;
indeed, I do not even judge myself. My conscience is clear, but
that does not make me innocent. It is the Lord who judges me.
Therefore judge nothing before the appointed time; wait until the
Lord comes. He will bring to light what is hidden in darkness and
will expose the motives of the heart. At that time each will receive
their praise from God.*

1 CORINTHIANS 4:3–5 NIV

Are you too introspective and too hard on yourself? Paul writes
in today's scripture that he wasn't concerned about the judg-
ments of other people, and he left judgment up to God.

I spent years being too hard on myself and feeling guilty
every time I made any kind of mistake or even thought I might
have made a mistake. I was insecure due to the abuse in my
childhood, and I had to learn to find my security in Christ
alone. I still occasionally remind myself not to judge myself.
The Bible does tell us to examine ourselves (2 Corinthians
13:5–7), but this is different than judging yourself and pass-
ing sentence on yourself. The Holy Spirit is the one who will
convict us if we have done something wrong, but He doesn't do
this so we will feel condemnation. He only does it so we can let
Him help us improve.

Perhaps you need to give yourself a break. You may even
need to give others a break, because if we are too hard on our-
selves, we tend to be too hard on others also.

Confession: *I trust God to let me know when I have done
something wrong. Even then, I avoid being self-critical and too
focused on my faults.*

RECEIVE CORRECTION WELL

He was oppressed and He was afflicted, yet He opened not His mouth; He was led as a lamb to the slaughter, and as a sheep before its shearers is silent, so He opened not His mouth.

ISAIAH 53:7 NKJV

Jesus was not concerned about His reputation, so He felt no need to try to defend Himself when He was accused of something. He knew His own heart and trusted Himself and everything to God. If we are not insecure, we will also be able to do this.

As an employer, it is difficult when I need to ask someone to do something a little differently than they have been doing it, and they immediately try to defend themselves or their methods. That kind of behavior complicates something that could be simple. Proverbs 12:1 says those who hate correction are stupid. Correction is simply giving direction about how something should be done in the future and should not be taken as a personal attack.

I very rarely offer any kind of correction, new direction, or suggestion to improve something and hear only a simple "Thank you for sharing that." Life would be a lot easier if we could all be secure and confident and receive correction appropriately.

Confession: *I am secure and confident in Christ, and I receive correction with a gracious attitude.*

BE HUMBLE AND
LET GOD EXALT YOU

Therefore humble yourselves [demote, lower yourselves in your own estimation] under the mighty hand of God, that in due time He may exalt you.

1 PETER 5:6

To be humble means to be low-lying or to remain under. We are to stay under God's mighty hand and trust that He will exalt us in due time. If we are humble, we don't think more highly of ourselves then we ought to (Romans 12:3). The humble appreciate correction; they don't reject it and try to justify their actions. Lucifer's sin was pride. He wanted to lift his throne above the throne of God. But he was cast out and down to the lowest place (Isaiah 14:12–15).

When you are invited to an event, take the lowest seat and wait for the host to move you forward instead of taking a front-row seat and suffering the embarrassment of being asked to move back. True promotion only comes from the Lord (Psalm 75:6–7). I once met an agent who wanted me to become his client with the promise of bringing in large amounts of people to hear me speak and getting me invitations to all kinds of speaking events. Although my flesh wanted to do this because I was weary of waiting on God to promote me, deep in my heart I knew it would be wrong for me to do.

The afternoon after he made this offer, I lay across my bed and committed to God to wait on Him no matter how long it took. God did promote me in His timing and has given me more opportunities than any human being could have ever given me.

Confession: *I humble myself under God's hand and wait on Him to promote me.*

ENJOY LIFE

The thief comes only in order to steal and kill and destroy. I came that they may have and enjoy life, and have it in abundance (to the full, till it overflows).

JOHN 10:10

Do you simply try to survive, or do you truly enjoy your life each day? I pray you do enjoy your life, because most days are ordinary. We go to work, take care of our home responsibilities, care for our children, attend church, and go through our other routines. If we know how to enjoy God, we can enjoy life even when it isn't perfect.

Enjoyment was not part of my childhood or teen years. Even as an adult, for a long time, I didn't know what it was like simply to enjoy life. When I realized God wanted me to enjoy my life, I had to learn how to do it. I had spent most of my time working because I thought work and accomplishment got me acceptance. Work is part of a balanced life, but if we overdo work without fun or rest, we will eventually burn out and become unhappy, and we may end up sick.

When I talk about enjoying life, I am not speaking of taking vacations, going shopping, or buying a new car or home. I am talking about being able to say with the psalmist, "This is the day the Lord has made; we will rejoice and be glad in it" (Psalm 118:24 NKJV). Notice that he writes "we will." Something can always steal our joy if we let it, but we don't have to. Life is our gift from God, so let's enjoy it fully.

Confession: *I will enjoy my life on ordinary days as well as special days. The joy of the Lord is my strength (Nehemiah 8:10).*

GOD IS MY PORTION

And the Lord said to Aaron, You shall have no inheritance in the land [of the Israelites], neither shall you have any part among them. I am your portion and your inheritance among the Israelites.

NUMBERS 18:20

I remember a time when I was weary of working all the time and seemingly getting nothing out of it except fatigue. I was working for God, but I said to Him, "When will I get something for myself out of this?" He answered, saying, "I am your portion; you get Me!" Of course, we all have God. He wants a special relationship with each of us, but in today's scripture, God says Aaron will receive no portion of the Promised Land, but that God Himself would be his portion.

God did eventually do many wonderful things for me, but I believe He tested me to see if I could be content with Him alone as my portion in life. Could you be content with that? Sometimes the more things we have, the more they take us away from God. The psalmist writes, "My flesh and my heart may fail, but God is the strength of my heart and my portion forever" (Psalm 73:26 NIV). Whatever portion God gives to you, be sure to enjoy it and realize that He always does what is best for us. What we have may vary in different seasons of life, but always know that God is our provider and will give us what we can handle.

Confession: *I trust God to give what He knows is best. He is my portion, and that is more important than anything else.*

SELF-DETERMINATION

*Except the Lord builds the house, they labor in vain who build it;
except the Lord keeps the city, the watchman wakes but in vain.*

PSALM 127:1

There is no doubt that we need to be determined if we want
to live a life that pleases God. The world, the devil, and even
our own flesh pressure us to compromise and live according
to self-will. Self-determination is good when it is in balance,
but no matter how strong-willed we are, we must be dependent
on God in all things, trusting Him to enable us to do what
we need to do. Jesus says, "Apart from me you can do nothing
(John 15:5 NIV).

Our scripture for today states that if we try to build any-
thing without the Lord, it will be in vain. We can build it, but
it won't last, and it won't bring joy and peace. We need to live a
"with God" life, one in which we seek His presence continually
and invite Him to be involved in everything we do. God wants
to be our partner in life, not merely someone we visit weekly for
an hour on Sunday mornings.

Elijah may have been physically strong, yet he said that his
strength was in the Lord (Isaiah 40:29; 1 Kings 18:46). Sam-
son had supernatural strength as he obeyed the Lord, but when
he became disobedient, he lost his strength, although he did
not know the Lord had left him (Judges 16:20). Be determined
to be dependent on God in all things.

Confession: *I am determined to follow God's will, but I know that
my strength is in Him.*

AVOID PETTINESS

Have nothing to do with godless myths and old wives' tales; rather, train yourself to be godly. For physical training is of some value, but godliness has value for all things, holding promise for both the present life and the life to come.

1 TIMOTHY 4:7–8 NIV

Looking back, I now realize how much time I wasted being angry over silly, petty things that really made no difference compared to what is truly important in life. I remember arguing with Dave and getting angry over which route was best to take to the hardware store. I remember arguing over which actor was in a movie we were watching. I remember staying angry for days because Dave played golf on a day when I wanted him to stay home with me. I wasted many days in self-pity, focused on only myself and what people were not doing for me.

Let us put aside foolish, time-wasting things and give ourselves to things that really matter and are truly important. Trade self-pity for compassion, which will move you to help someone who is hurting. Trade anger and offense for forgiveness and peace. Trade pride for humility. Trade self-will for God's will.

The next time you are tempted to get angry and waste a day feeling sorry for yourself, ask yourself if it is silly and simply a waste of time. If so, spend the time you would have wasted on negative emotions on what is truly important in life and will produce lasting fruit.

Confession: *I don't waste my time being angry about petty, silly things that bear no good fruit and do not please God.*

HOW TO EXPERIENCE GOD'S PEACE

Do not be anxious about anything, but in every situation, by prayer and petition, with thanksgiving, present your requests to God. And the peace of God, which transcends all understanding, will guard your hearts and your minds in Christ Jesus.

PHILIPPIANS 4:6–7 NIV

Many of us find ourselves nervous, unsettled, or fretful at times. Such feelings and comments are symptoms of anxiety, and anxiety produces no good fruit in our lives. When we have anxiety, we spend today trying to figure out tomorrow or fearing or dreading it. Anxiety is inconsistent with trusting God. Anxiety is rooted in fear, and it is Satan's method of stealing the peace that Jesus died to give us. Because we are afraid, we try to take care of situations ourselves. This causes us to worry and reason as we try to come up with solutions. We cannot enjoy peace of mind if we constantly think about how to solve our problems.

Today's scripture not only instructs us not to be anxious, but it also tells us *how* to experience God's peace. I truly believe that if we can understand the power of this Scripture passage, we will find the answer to anxiety. Any time I have a problem, my first instinct may be to worry, but after doing that for a few minutes I remind myself that I have often traveled the road of worry, and it has never once gotten me to my desired destination, which is peace. This morning, remind yourself not to be anxious about anything.

Confession: *Instead of worrying, I pray, I am thankful, and I let God's peace guard my heart and mind.*

EXPECT THE BEST

Joshua son of Nun and Caleb son of Jephunneh, who were among those who had explored the land, tore their clothes and said to the entire Israelite assembly, "The land we passed through and explored is exceedingly good."

NUMBERS 14:6–7 NIV

One of the world's largest shoe manufacturers sent two market researchers, independent of each other, to an underdeveloped nation to find out whether that country was a viable market for them. The first researcher sent a telegram to the home office that said "No market here. Nobody wears shoes." The second researcher sent a telegram back home that said "Unlimited potential here—nobody has any shoes!"

I'm sure the second researcher went on his trip expecting to send good news to his employer—and he did. He could have viewed the fact that everyone he saw was barefoot as an obstacle or a challenge, as the other researcher did, and then his attitude would have been negative. But because he anticipated the best, he saw the situation in a positive light.

In any situation, the habit of negative expectation needs to be broken. Twelve spies went into Canaan to see if it would be good for the Israelites. Ten spies gave a negative report because giants would need to be defeated for God's people to enter the land. But Joshua and Caleb gave a positive report focused on the goodness of the land and their trust that God would lead the Israelites into it. Life holds many challenges, but most of them can be overcome with a positive outlook that expects the best and trusts God.

Confession: *No matter what my circumstances, I expect the best.*

STAY STRONG WHEN YOU FACE TEMPTATION

All of you must keep awake (give strict attention, be cautious and active) and watch and pray, that you may not come into temptation. The spirit indeed is willing, but the flesh is weak.

MATTHEW 26:41

We all have areas in our lives that are weaknesses for us, and we are wise to pray regularly that when tempted in these areas we will stay strong and resist temptation. We often think of ourselves more highly than we ought to and assume we won't make the wrong choice, but Jesus teaches us to pray that we don't come into temptation.

Jesus needed His disciples to stay awake and pray with Him as He experienced agony in the garden of Gethsemane regarding going to the cross and taking our sin upon Himself. He told them their spirit was willing, but their flesh was weak, and that they should pray not to enter into temptation. But they all fell asleep.

When Jesus told Peter that he would deny Him, Peter didn't believe it (Matthew 26:31–35), but he did end up denying that he knew the Lord three times (Matthew 26:69–75). Had Peter been humble and prayed, perhaps he could have avoided such offensive words.

Prayer takes only a few moments, and it can help us avoid hours of agony over the sins we could have avoided had we simply prayed.

Confession: *I know I have weaknesses, and I pray that when I am tempted, I will be strong enough in the Lord not to let them control me.*

PRAY YOUR WAY THROUGH THE DAY

Pray at all times (on every occasion, in every season) in the Spirit, with all [manner of] prayer and entreaty. To that end keep alert and watch with strong purpose and perseverance, interceding in behalf of all the saints (God's consecrated people).

EPHESIANS 6:18

Extended times of prayer are good, but it's also good to pray and ask God to help you with anything you deal with throughout the day. Prayer does not need to be long to be effective; it simply needs to be sincere. James 4:2 says, "You do not have, because you do not ask." And Luke 11:9 says, "Ask and keep on asking and it shall be given you." You can never ask for too much. God wants to help you in all you do, no matter what it is.

Each day is an opportunity to also pray for other people. We may hear of someone who is struggling, and instead of saying "Oh, that's too bad," we can pray. We may see a sin in their life, and instead of judging or gossiping, we can pray.

I am so grateful for all the people who pray for me. I know I could not do what I do without their prayers to strengthen me and encourage me. One of the greatest gifts we can give anyone is to pray for them.

Confession: *I love to pray—to pray for others and to pray about everything I do.*

STAY HAPPY

*A happy heart is good medicine and a cheerful mind works heal-
ing, but a broken spirit dries up the bones.*

PROVERBS 17:22

Recently my daughter-in-law sent me a video of our youngest
grandchild, Brody, who is three years old, saying, "Don't worry,
be happy. That's all!" I think he has the formula for a healthy
and happy life. Depression and discouragement drag us down,
and I think they may open us up for disease. But the joy of the
Lord is our strength (Nehemiah 8:10), and a cheerful heart is
medicine (Proverbs 17:22 NIV). Just imagine how much better
you might feel if you laughed more.

There are many things in the world these days to make us
sad, but if we put our trust in God, we can relax and not worry
about them. Take every opportunity you can to laugh. Find
clean comedians and watch their programs. Look up funny
things children do and watch their videos. Laugh at yourself
more instead of getting upset every time you drop or spill
something. You need to clean it up anyway, so what good will it
do to get angry about it?

Take my grandson's advice: "Don't worry, be happy. That's all!"

Confession: *I will focus on laughing more, because laughter is
like medicine and brings healing.*

CHOOSE YOUR THOUGHTS CAREFULLY

We demolish arguments and every pretension that sets itself up against the knowledge of God, and we take captive every thought to make it obedient to Christ.

2 CORINTHIANS 10:5 NIV

It's amazing how quickly and completely our thoughts can change our moods. Negative thinking quickly steals our joy and causes bad moods. When our thoughts are down, everything else goes down with them—our moods, attitudes, self-esteem, and many other things. People who tend to think and speak negatively are usually unhappy and rarely content with anything for very long. They probably do not realize they could be happy if they would simply change the way they think. We must stop merely waiting for something good to happen and take action to ensure that something good will happen.

I am truly amazed when I consider the fact that we can make ourselves happy or sad by what we choose to think, and the longer I live, the more I'm amazed by the fact that my mind so profoundly affects my moods. I still need to fight the battle in my mind, and I doubt anyone reaches the point of being entirely "battle-free." But we can continually make progress.

God has given us the fruit of self-control (Galatians 5:22–23), which means we do not have to allow our thoughts to be out of control, but we can be intentional in our thinking. We can control what we think. God allows us to make choices about our thoughts, and we must choose carefully.

Confession: *I choose my thoughts carefully, knowing how powerfully they affect my moods.*

PRIORITIZE PLEASING GOD

But just as we have been approved by God to be entrusted with the gospel...so we speak, not as [if we were trying] to please people [to gain power and popularity], but to please God who examines our hearts [expecting our best].

1 THESSALONIANS 2:4 AMP

We can all be tempted to please other people because we want them to accept us. Wanting acceptance and not wanting to be rejected is normal. But when we give in to the pressure to please people instead of pleasing God, we allow them to control us instead of letting Him lead us. This will keep us from fulfilling our God-ordained destiny.

For years, I tried to avoid rejection by trying to please people and, therefore, allowed them to control me. Eventually, I discovered they were much more interested in getting what they thought was best for them than in helping me do what was best for me. They were using me to make them happy but had no desire to see me happy too. When God called me into ministry, the people I thought were my friends almost immediately rejected me. I felt deeply hurt, but I am grateful that God helped me choose Him over them.

I thank God that I no longer live a life of pretense, trying to win the favor of people who did not genuinely care about me. Your true friends will be sincerely interested in you, want the best for you, and do all they can do to help you become all God wants you to be. They will encourage you to please Him, not them.

Confession: *I prioritize pleasing God over pleasing people.*

MEDITATE ON GOD'S WORD

This Book of the Law shall not depart out of your mouth, but you shall meditate on it day and night, that you may observe and do according to all that is written in it. For then you shall make your way prosperous, and then you shall deal wisely and have good success.

JOSHUA 1:8

To meditate means to roll something over and over in your mind and perhaps to mutter it softly. If you know how to worry, then you know how to meditate. To worry is to meditate on your problems, but proper meditation is to think about God's Word. The more you think about His Word, the more you will get from it, and it will become part of you. The scriptures you have meditated on will come back to you at times when you need them.

Psalm 37 talks about not fretting over evil people, and verse 3 tells us to trust God and do good. I have taught on and thought about this scripture many times, and when I am dealing with a problem or a person who is frustrating, it often comes to mind and reminds me to stay focused on trusting God and helping other people.

If you hide God's Word in your heart, it will keep you from sinning (Psalm 119:11). Today's scripture promises that if we meditate on the Scriptures day and night, all we do will prosper. This sounds good to me—don't you agree? God's Word is full of power, and the more of it we know, the more powerful we will be.

Confession: *I will meditate on God's Word regularly, and I will have success.*

MAKE NO PROVISION FOR THE FLESH

But clothe yourself with the Lord Jesus Christ (the Messiah), and make no provision for [indulging] the flesh [put a stop to thinking about the evil cravings of your physical nature] to [gratify its] desires (lusts).

ROMANS 13:14

If we live according to the flesh, it is because we have set our mind on the things of the flesh. Likewise, if we live according to the Spirit, it is because we have set our mind on the things of the Spirit. I like to say it this way: "Where the mind goes, the man follows."

If you are trying to lose weight, thinking about a hot fudge sundae is not the way to victory. If you think about it long enough, you will go get one and eat it. If you desire to be obedient to God's Word and forgive anyone who has abused or mistreated you, then you need to stop thinking and talking about the evil things they did to you. Our thoughts eventually come out of our mouths in the form of words, and they affect our attitudes and our actions.

We often waste our time and wear ourselves out trying to do the right thing while we are thinking the wrong thing, and this will never work. Think right first, and doing right will follow.

Confession: I set my mind on the things of the Spirit, and I will walk in the Spirit.

BE EXCELLENT

For His divine power has bestowed upon us all things that [are requisite and suited] to life and godliness, through the [full, personal] knowledge of Him Who called us by and to His own glory and excellence (virtue).

2 PETER 1:3

God is excellent in all He does, and He desires for us to do everything we do with excellence. Excellence is not perfection; it's doing the best you can with what you have. You might have a car that is ten years old, but you can keep it clean and well serviced.

Excellence is one of the principles on which Joyce Meyer Ministries was established, and we still strive for excellence over forty years later. Our offices are kept clean, the bathrooms are always clean, and the grounds and surrounding property are well manicured and as beautiful as we can make them. If we represent God, we should always do the best we can in all we do. Perhaps you are a person who likes to dress casually, and that is fine, but you can still look nice. Casual doesn't mean sloppy. If you do a job, always do it right and finish what you start.

Our manners should also be excellent. Train yourself to always say "please" and "thank you." Be quick to say "I'm sorry," if you think you have hurt someone or done something you should not have done. Have and maintain a standard of moral excellence for your life, and don't compromise on it. This doesn't mean you need to be legalistic or that you can never have fun; it just means to do what you believe Jesus would do.

Confession: *I am a person who pursues excellence in all I do. God is excellent, and I represent Him the most excellent way I can.*

DO ALL THINGS WITHOUT COMPLAINING

Do everything without grumbling or arguing, so that you may become blameless and pure, "children of God without fault in a warped and crooked generation." Then you will shine among them like stars in the sky.

Almost everywhere I go these days, I hear people complaining. When we complain, we remain where we are. It does not help us make progress, nor does it remove our problems. It makes us and the people around us feel worse than we already do, not better. When we complain, it makes our situation seem worse than it is.

The Israelites complained during the forty years they spent in the wilderness trying to get to the Promised Land, and this was one reason it took them so long to get there. The trip was an eleven-day journey, but they wandered for forty years, murmuring, complaining, blaming, feeling sorry for themselves, being negative, and doing other things that kept them in bondage.

Complaining is a sin. We certainly don't complain by faith, and Romans 14:23 says that whatever is not of faith is sin. The opposite of complaining is being thankful. Gratitude glorifies God, but complaining does not. We all have more to be thankful for than to complain about, but if we complain long enough, all we will see is what is wrong with life and the people in it, and we will miss all the good things. Starting today, ask God to help you be thankful and to say so (Psalm 100:4).

Confession: *I am a thankful person, and I say so to God and to people. I focus on my blessings, not my problems.*

LIVE TO PLEASE GOD

I am able to do nothing from Myself [independently, of My own accord—but only as I am taught by God and as I get His orders]. Even as I hear, I judge [I decide as I am bidden to decide. As the voice comes to Me, so I give a decision], and My judgment is right (just, righteous), because I do not seek or consult My own will [I have no desire to do what is pleasing to Myself, My own aim, My own purpose] but only the will and pleasure of the Father Who sent Me.

JOHN 5:30

Today's scripture is powerful and contains many lessons for us. Please spend time reading and rereading it and think about everything Jesus says in it.

If we want to be led by God's Spirit, we must listen with our heart for what He is saying and be discerning about the direction He wants us to take. Decide that your answer to God will always be "Yes, Lord," before He even asks you to do or not to do something.

The wise way to live is to follow God's will. He is always right in all He says and does, and everything He asks of us is always for our good. Even if what He asks is difficult or challenging, if you are willing to do it, He will give you the grace and the strength to obey Him.

Confession: I want God's will, not my own will. I will listen for His voice and follow His leading.

HAVE A CLEAR CONSCIENCE

Therefore I always exercise and discipline myself [mortifying my body, deadening my carnal affections, bodily appetites, and worldly desires, endeavoring in all respects] to have a clear (unshaken, blameless) conscience, void of offense toward God and toward men.

ACTS 24:16

If you have ever had a guilty conscience—and I think everyone has—then you know how miserable it makes you feel. At least, it makes me feel miserable. Our conscience informs us when we are doing or have done something that isn't right. I'm sure it always convicts us in time for us to stop what we are about to do before we sin, but we don't always listen.

A guilty conscience is the hardest pillow in the world to try to sleep on. One of the things the Holy Spirit does for us is convict us of sin and convince us to do the right thing. But if we ignore our conscience long enough it becomes seared (hardened). When this happens, discerning how God feels about our actions becomes more and more difficult for us. We should do all we can do to keep a tender conscience toward God.

Paul told Timothy that deacons must hold the mystery of faith with a clear conscience (1 Timothy 3:9 esv), and this is excellent advice for all of us. A guilty conscience and faith simply do not go together. Thankfully, if we have sinned, we can repent and receive God's forgiveness, but it is even better to do the right thing before we end up with a guilty conscience.

Your conscience is your friend, and it will keep you out of trouble if you will listen to it.

Confession: *I am thankful for my conscience, and I strive to keep a clear conscience.*

ENJOY THE QUIET

He who has knowledge spares his words, and a man of under-standing has a cool spirit.

PROVERBS 17:27

To keep a cool spirit means to be at peace. Restraining our words will greatly help us do that. Excessive talking gets us stirred up inside, and people who talk too much will ultimately say things they should not say. Being quiet on the inside is peaceful and aids us in hearing from God. Outer silence helps us maintain inner silence. I think we live in a very noisy world.

I love quiet and total silence. It restores my soul. I try to have one or two hours of silence every day. I might read and then think a little, but I do it in the quiet. I don't like it when I go to a restaurant to eat and the music is so loud that I can't hear the people with me when they speak. I love music, but at a decibel I can enjoy, not one so loud it makes me want to leave the room.

Due to the technological devices we keep around us, we constantly hear dings, rings, beeps, and other things letting us know that someone is trying to contact us. And most of us, including me, are not very good at ignoring them. Instead, we interrupt what we are doing so we can see what they want. Let's be courageous and turn off all the sounds just for a couple of hours and enjoy the quiet. Some people are so addicted to noise that this may be difficult at first, but if you have a problem in this area, I encourage you to press through and learn to enjoy the quiet.

Confession: *I love outer and inner silence. It helps me hear from God and know what's in my own heart.*

STOP ALLOWING YOURSELF TO BE UPSET

Peace I leave with you; My [own] peace I now give and bequeath to you. Not as the world gives do I give to you. Do not let your hearts be troubled, neither let them be afraid. [Stop allowing yourselves to be agitated and disturbed; and do not permit yourselves to be fearful and intimidated and cowardly and unsettled.]

JOHN 14:27

We don't need to ask God to give us peace because He has already given it to us. Jesus left us His special peace, but we must learn how to stop letting ourselves get upset and fearful. I have learned that the devil "sets us up to get upset." He knows what rattles us and can easily arrange for those things to happen. We are wiser than he is, but we need to use the wisdom God has given us and not keep going around and around the same mountain, making the same mistakes repeatedly.

Peace is wonderful. I hate strife, anger, arguing, and harsh disagreements—and I think until we do hate them, we won't avoid them. Proverbs 6:16 says there are "six things the Lord hates," and "seven are an abomination to Him." The seventh is "he who sows discord among his brethren" (Proverbs 6:19). Ephesians 6:15 mentions shoes of peace (NLT), and we are to put them on. This means to walk in peace all the time, and it doesn't happen automatically. We have to learn to sense when we are starting to get upset and stop it before it reaches a full roar.

God has given us self-control, and it will help us stay in peace if we learn how to recognize the symptoms of getting upset.

Confession: *I stay peaceful all the time, because when I have peace I have more power.*

THINK BEFORE YOU SPEAK

Be not rash with your mouth, and let not your heart be hasty to utter a word before God. For God is in heaven, and you are on earth; therefore let your words be few.

ECCLESIASTES 5:2

"Think before you speak" is good advice for all of us. Once words are spoken, we cannot take them back. I think slowing down would help us in this area. We move fast, talk fast, make fast decisions, and rush around multitasking. It is no wonder we find ourselves saying things we wish we hadn't said.

Can you even imagine Jesus being in a hurry? I can't. He was the epitome of peace always. Nothing rattled Him, upset Him, or provoked Him to say things that were foolish.

The amplification of John 14:30 says that when He knew the time was drawing near for Him to begin His suffering, He told his disciples He wouldn't be talking with them much more because the "evil genius" was coming, and "he has no claim on Me." I think Jesus realized that He would be under great pressure, and He needed to be quiet so He didn't say anything the devil could use against Him. Isaiah 53:7 says that when He was oppressed and afflicted, He didn't open His mouth.

When we are under pressure, we need to use the same wisdom Jesus used. Don't just try to think before you speak; pray daily that you will do it.

Confession: *I always think before I speak. When I am under pressure, I don't open my mouth.*

PATIENT OR PROUD?

Better is the end of a thing than the beginning of it, and the patient in spirit is better than the proud in spirit. Do not be quick in spirit to be angry or vexed, for anger and vexation lodge in the bosom of fools.

ECCLESIASTES 7:8-9

The patient person waits on God when He says to wait, but the proud person takes his own actions and refuses to wait. Many never see the fulfillment of their dreams and visions, because they have no patience. They think of ways to hurry things along, but this only causes problems. When we do this, we engage in "works of the flesh."

Works of the flesh are so tempting because we can come up with all kinds of ideas that sound as though they will work. In fact, they might work for someone else. But if God is trying to do something in you, or for you, or through you, He won't let your plan succeed, no matter how good it is. He wants us to lean entirely on Him and follow His lead.

Jesus was meek, and He teaches us to take on that same meek spirit (Matthew 11:28–30). Meekness is not weakness; it is strength under control. Jesus allowed Himself to go to the cross; no one forced Him into being crucified. He told Peter in the garden of Gethsemane that if He wanted to, He could call twelve legions of angels and they would rescue Him (Matthew 26:53). He also knew that if He called the angels, God's will would not be fulfilled. Are you willing to wait on God so His will can be completely fulfilled in your life?

Confession: *I am patient, and I wait on God so His will can be done in my life.*

DILIGENCE

The plans of the diligent lead to profit as surely as haste leads to poverty.

PROVERBS 21:5 NIV

Good things usually don't come easily or quickly. People who want to succeed at anything in life need to be diligent. Diligence is careful and persistent work. It is constant effort and exertion to accomplish what we undertake. Jesus says we should count the cost before beginning to build something to see if we have what it will take to finish (Luke 14:28–30). Some people do finish what they start, but many do not. When God called me into the ministry and I had a dream to teach His Word all over the world, I certainly had no idea how much work it would take. But anything worth having is worth working for.

A diligent person sees what needs to be done, and they do it and do it and do it until they get the desired result. They don't stop because they get tired of doing it or because no one else is doing it. They don't stop because it isn't popular with their friends, and they don't stop because it takes longer than they expected. They may want to stop, but something in them (their diligent spirit) won't let them quit.

Few people today are willing to start at the bottom and work their way to the top. They have an attitude of entitlement and want to be given what those who have gone before took years to earn. I don't think we can really appreciate anything we have if we didn't have to exert the effort to get it. Don't be afraid of hard work, and don't expect everything to be given to you. Be diligent, and you will eventually succeed.

Confession: *I am diligent. I work hard and don't give up on anything until it is finished.*

WHAT ARE YOU EXPECTING?

And therefore the Lord [earnestly] waits [expecting, looking, and longing] to be gracious to you...Blessed (happy, fortunate, to be envied) are all those who [earnestly] wait for Him, who expect and look and long for Him [for His victory, His favor, His love, His peace, His joy, and His matchless, unbroken companionship]!

ISAIAH 30:18

God is looking and waiting for someone who is looking for and expecting Him to be good to them. You may think expecting God to do good things for you, give you favor, and promote you would be improper because you know you don't deserve it. You're right, but we receive from God according to our faith, not according to our perfection.

I like to start each day saying "I am expecting something good to happen to me and through me today." We know we should wait on God, but this doesn't mean we sit passively and expect nothing. It means to expect something good to happen at any moment. We may be physically still, but we can be active spiritually at the same time. God wants to do more for you than you can imagine, but He is waiting for you to expect Him to do it.

Growing up, I experienced many bad and painful things and came to expect more of what I'd always had. I felt this way in my relationship with God until I learned that my negative expectations were making me anxious and unhappy. Start expecting something good from God each day.

Confession: *I am expecting something good to happen to me and through me today.*

GOD IS SLOW TO ANGER

The Lord is compassionate and gracious, slow to anger, abounding in love.

PSALM 103:8 NIV

I grew up with a father who was easily angered. The slightest little thing could make him angry, and much of the time, I didn't even know what I had done to irritate him. I understand now that he was angry because he felt guilty about his life, but I didn't understand that as a child. As a result, I came into my relationship with God expecting Him to be like my father was, so I was often fearful that God was angry with me about something. Even if I was not aware of anything I had done wrong, the devil could convince me there was something.

God is not like people, and He is slow to anger, quick to forgive, compassionate, and abounding in love (Numbers 23:19; Psalm 103:8, 145:8–9; 1 John 1:9). Our anger does not promote the righteousness that God desires, and neither would His. We serve a gracious God who is anxious to forgive us. All we need to do is receive the forgiveness Jesus has provided through His death and resurrection.

I have good news today: God is not mad at you. I wrote an entire book on this subject, and I recommend you read it if you struggle in this area. I once was uncomfortable in God's presence due to my fear of His being angry, but now I am very comfortable with Him, even if I have sinned. I know that He loves me, He is not angry with me, and He is full of forgiveness.

Confession: *I know God loves me and that He is slow to anger, compassionate, and ready to forgive.*

GOD'S GRACE IS SUFFICIENT

And lest I should be exalted above measure by the abundance of the revelations, a thorn in the flesh was given to me, a messenger of Satan to buffet me, lest I be exalted above measure. Concerning this thing I pleaded with the Lord three times that it might depart from me. And He said to me, "My grace is sufficient for you, for My strength is made perfect in weakness." Therefore most gladly I will rather boast in my infirmities, that the power of Christ may rest upon me.

2 CORINTHIANS 12:7-9 NKJV

Paul was given what the Bible refers to as a "thorn in the flesh." We don't know for sure what it was, but we do know that it was irritating and uncomfortable, and Paul wanted to get rid of it. He asked the Lord three times to remove it, but God said, "My grace is sufficient for you." He reminded Paul that He had enabled him to bear the trouble. This thorn was given to Paul to keep him from being prideful because of the greatness of the revelations God was giving him.

It is important for us to be humble if we want God to use us. Often when He is using someone in a major way, they start out humble and thankful but gradually begin to think more highly of themselves than they should. When this happens, God must do something. He will first try to change them, but if they won't change, He will remove them from their position.

Always remember that we are nothing without God and can do nothing of any value without Him (John 15:5).

Confession: *I want God to keep me humble so He can use me as He sees best.*

SIN AND GRACE

But then Law came in, [only] to expand and increase the trespass [making it more apparent and exciting opposition]. But where sin increased and abounded, grace (God's unmerited favor) has surpassed it and increased the more and superabounded.

ROMANS 5:20

It is interesting to note that the only reason God gave the Law was to show us that we couldn't keep it and needed a Savior. All the Law does is increase sin. But the good news is that where sin abounds, grace superabounds because grace is greater than sin.

If we love God, we will always do our best not to sin, but it is good to know that when we do sin, His grace is greater than our sin. Grace is undeserved favor, and I like to describe it also as God's power to enable us to do what we need to do. It is not an excuse to sin and get away with that sin. It is the power to overcome sin and say no to it.

God's grace is wonderful beyond comprehension. It is what changes us into the image of Christ as we learn to rely on it instead of relying on ourselves. Max Lucado said it well: "Grace is the voice that calls us to change and then gives us the power to pull it off."[11] And Saint Augustine said, "For grace is given, not because we have done good works, but in order that we may be able to do them."[12]

Confession: *I'm grateful that where sin abounds, grace abounds much more, and I depend on God's grace to help me in all situations.*

HOPE IS POWERFUL

Against all hope, Abraham in hope believed and so became the father of many nations, just as it had been said to him, "So shall your offspring be." Without weakening in his faith, he faced the fact that his body was as good as dead—since he was about a hundred years old—and that Sarah's womb was also dead.

ROMANS 4:18–19 NIV

You and I may desire many things, even pray and believe God for them, but beyond what we believe for, we believe in Someone. That Someone is Jesus. We don't always know what is going to happen in life, but we do know that as we walk with Him, it will work out for our good (Romans 8:28). This means we can have a positive, faith-filled attitude in every situation.

You may be living in the midst of a big problem or some adverse circumstances today. I encourage you to reread today's scripture and remember that Abraham, knowing full well that he and Sarah should not have been able to have a biological child, still stayed strong in his faith in God. He was very positive about a very negative situation.

According to Hebrews 6:19, hope is the anchor of the soul. It is the force that keeps us steady in times of trial. Don't ever stop hoping, and refuse to be afraid or discouraged. I can't promise that things will always turn out exactly the way you want them to or that you'll never be disappointed. But even in disappointing times, you can hope, be positive, believe God is working for your good, and keep your faith strong.

Confession: *I know that hope is powerful, and I choose to be hopeful in all situations.*

DON'T WASTE TODAY REGRETTING YESTERDAY

They seldom reflect on the days of their life, because God keeps them occupied with gladness of heart.

ECCLESIASTES 5:20 NIV

One thing you don't want to do is get up in the morning, realize you basically wasted yesterday, and then waste today feeling guilty about the poor choices you made yesterday. Zig Ziglar said, "Worrying does not take away tomorrow's troubles, it takes away today's peace."[13]

One day this week I had my prayer time in the morning, as I always do, and I fully intended to stay in close fellowship with God all day. But when evening came, I realized I had stepped out of my office after my prayer time and hadn't even thought about the Lord the rest of the day because I was busy, busy, busy! I started feeling guilty, or perhaps just disappointed in myself, when God reminded me not to waste the present regretting the past. His mercies are new every morning, and we can always begin again (Lamentations 3:22–23).

The next evening, I was amazed at how often the Lord was in my thoughts and what great fellowship we had all day, but I strongly believe that I would have missed that opportunity if I had continued in my regrets. I was reminded that God is with me even when I am not consciously aware of Him, that He understands that I am growing, and He sees my heart. And the same is true for you.

Confession: *I do not spend the present filled with regrets about the past.*

ALL THINGS ARE POSSIBLE

*For with God nothing is ever impossible and no word from God
shall be without power or impossible of fulfillment.*

LUKE 1:37

There are many things we think we cannot do, but all things
are possible with God. We should never say "That's impossi-
ble." I look back at my life, and I know that what God has done
in me and through me would be impossible without Him. But
He can do anything and will do more than we can imagine if
we will have the courage to ask Him to. When I was in school,
I barely got a passing grade in English, yet I have written more
than 140 books without any professional writing training at
all. This sounds impossible, I know, but it is a good example of
God doing the impossible.

Don't be afraid to ask for big things. God will never be
angry with you because you ask for too much. I figure that the
worst thing that can happen if I ask for too much is simply that
I won't get it. Hebrews 4:16 tells us to come boldly to God's
throne and receive mercy and grace. We can do this even after
we have sinned and repented.

You and I do not deserve anything God has done for us,
but we should be exceedingly thankful for what He has done. I
believe that the more thankful we are, the more God will want
to do for us. Start today being bolder than ever in your asking
and more generous than ever in your gratitude.

Confession: All things are possible with God, so I will pray boldly
and be excited to see what He will do.

GOD PRESERVES ME IN TROUBLE

Though I walk in the midst of trouble, you preserve my life; you stretch out your hand against the wrath of my enemies, and your right hand delivers me.

PSALM 138:7 ESV

We all walk through troubled times in life, but sadly, not everyone knows they can go to God and receive the help they need. God protects, defends, and delivers us from our enemies. He even tells us that the battle is not ours but His (2 Chronicles 20:15). God created us with His own hand carefully and uniquely, and He will not forsake the work of His hands. You belong to God. You were bought with a precious price—the blood of Jesus. It is wonderful to know that if God is for us, it doesn't matter who is against us (Romans 8:31).

When you are having trouble, if you begin to feel fear, spend some time waiting on God, because your salvation comes only from Him. As you quietly wait on God and seek Him in your heart, you will feel the assurance that He is with you and will meet your need. He won't tell you how or when, but you can rest in His love and be assured that He won't forsake you.

God's job is to do what needs to be done, and our job is to trust Him. Practice saying aloud, several times a day, "God, I trust you." Remember things He has done for you in the past, and they will encourage your faith to believe He will do again what you need Him to do.

Confession: I trust God, and He meets my needs. He created me, and He will not forsake the work of His hands.

LIVING IN THE TRUTH

Rather, let our lives lovingly express truth [in all things, speaking truly, dealing truly, living truly]. Enfolded in love, let us grow up in every way and in all things into Him Who is the Head, [even] Christ (the Messiah, the Anointed One).

EPHESIANS 4:15

Jesus says that He is the Truth (John 14:6), and the Holy Spirit is the Spirit of Truth who guides us into all truth (John 16:13). And Psalm 51:6 says that God desires truth in the inner being. John 8:31–32 is one of the first scriptures I learned, and it says that if we are Jesus' disciples, we will continue in His Word and know the truth—and the truth will make us free. I had many bondages in my life, and when I read this verse, being free sounded very good to me.

For more than forty-five years I have continued in God's Word and experienced freedom after freedom from the lies of Satan, which had deceived me and held me in bondage. God's Word is truth, and learning truth is the only way we can recognize lies.

Be truthful with yourself about your motives and actions. And be truthful with your family and friends. Good relationships cannot be built on lies. Being totally truthful is sometimes challenging, because telling the truth may mean that you will suffer for doing so, but God will reward you. Remember to always speak the truth in love and be kind in the way you say things.

Confession: *I am always truthful in everything I say and do.*

GIVE THOUGHT AND
STUDY TO GOD'S WORD

Be careful what you are hearing. The measure [of thought and study] you give [to the truth you hear] will be the measure [of virtue and knowledge] that comes back to you—and more [besides] will be given to you who hear.

MARK 4:24

The more we study and think about God's Word when we read or hear it, the more understanding we will have about what we have read or heard. In short, we'll get from God's Word what we put into it. Today's scripture tells us that the amount of thought and study we devote to the Word will determine the amount of virtue and knowledge that will come back to us.

Sadly, some people do not read or study the Bible at all, and many Christians do not delve into God's Word deeply. Then they wonder why they struggle so much, why they don't seem to hear God's voice clearly, and why they feel unable to overcome some of the situations they face. I believe many people are not spiritually powerful because they don't put much effort into the study of the Bible. They may hear others teach and preach the Word, listen to podcasts, or read the Bible occasionally, but they are not seriously dedicated to making the Word a major part of their lives, including spending time thinking about it.

I encourage you today to evaluate how much time you spend in God's Word and make adjustments if needed. The more you give to it, the more you'll get from it.

Confession: *I invest my time and energy in serious study of God's Word.*

GOD TAKES CARE OF HIS OWN

Your God has commanded your strength [your might in His service and impenetrable hardness to temptation]; O God, display Your might and strengthen what You have wrought for us!

PSALM 68:28

One thing we all need is strength. We need physical strength and good health, as well as a strong mind and spirit. I am so grateful that God promises us His strength, not just in today's scripture but in many others. Jesus says we can come to Him and be refreshed when we feel weak or overwhelmed (Matthew 11:28–30).

Perhaps you have health problems and also have a lot of responsibility, so you are not sure how you will do all you need to do. I can promise that you are stronger than you think you are. It is amazing what we can go through and still come out victorious. Keep putting one foot in front of the other, and you will make it. Don't think too far ahead, and think about all that could go wrong or how difficult you think it will be. Live life one day at a time, and God will give you the grace you need for today. When tomorrow comes, He will give you grace for that day.

We need mental strength so we don't faint in our minds, meaning we won't give up mentally and think *I can't do this.* Most of all, we need spiritual strength, because a person's strong spirit will sustain them through pain and trouble (Proverbs 18:14). I've had my share of pain and trouble, yet God enabled me to do everything I needed to do. He will do the same thing for you if you trust Him.

Confession: *God has commanded strength for me, and I will never quit or give up.*

HOW TO KEEP GOING
WHEN THE GOING GETS TOUGH

*Looking away [from all that will distract] to Jesus, Who is the Leader
and the Source of our faith . . . and is also its Finisher [bringing it to
maturity and perfection]. He, for the joy [of obtaining the prize] that
was set before Him, endured the cross, despising and ignoring the
shame, and is now seated at the right hand of the throne of God.*

HEBREWS 12:2

Determination and discipline keep us going when the going
gets tough in life. Facing difficulties helps us keep our eyes on
the prize, practice good habits until they become natural for
us, and resist being easily distracted by painful or frustrating
situations.

As Christians, our determination is driven by something
far greater than sheer will. We must have the help of the Holy
Spirit, which is always available to those who ask and believe.
It is our greatest source of strength and power, enabling us to
overcome obstacles and live a life of purpose. If you tend to
give up easily, begin to make a change by praying that God
will work determination in you. Believe that He has heard and
answered you, and then step out in faith, trusting that the feel-
ings you desire will come as you keep moving forward.

Sadly, some people say they don't feel like doing what is
right. I doubt that Jesus "felt" like dying for the sins of man-
kind, but He did. He was determined to make the ultimate
sacrifice because He relied on the power of God to enable Him,
and He looked forward to the joy on the other side of the pain.

Confession: *I choose to be determined, with the Holy Spirit's
help.*

YOU ARE SPECIAL

But you are a chosen race, a royal priesthood, a dedicated nation, [God's] own purchased, special people, that you may set forth the wonderful deeds and display the virtues and perfections of Him Who called you out of darkness into His marvelous light.

1 PETER 2:9

We all want to feel we are special. I remember feeling chosen and special in grade school when I got picked for the softball team. Our son Daniel has four boys. He takes "dad and son" trips with each of them at least once a year, and this makes them feel so special. If you have children, take time to make them feel special.

God, too, wants each of us to know that we are special. You are chosen and royal in God's eyes. Don't just read today's scripture, but meditate on it and believe it is for you. Maybe you have never been made to feel special or chosen, but you are.

As God's special, chosen child, you are no longer to walk in darkness, but to walk in the light. You are God's representative, and it is important that you walk with your head held high and display His character wherever you are. How we feel about ourselves helps determine how we behave. If we feel bad about ourselves, we will act bad; but knowing we are chosen by God and given His favor causes us to want to do our very best in every situation.

Confession: *I am chosen, royal, and special to God.*

SET YOUR MIND AND KEEP IT SET, PART 1

And set your minds and keep them set on what is above (the higher things), not on the things that are on the earth.

COLOSSIANS 3:2

In today's scripture, the apostle Paul gives us valuable instruction about our thinking. He clearly tells us to think about things that are important to God ("the higher things") and that doing so will always fill our minds with good thoughts.

"Setting" your mind is probably one of the greatest and most beneficial things you can learn to do. To set your mind means to make up your mind firmly. Wet concrete can be moved with ease and is very impressionable before it dries or sets. But once it does set, it is in place for good. It cannot be easily molded or changed.

The same principle that applies to concrete applies to setting your mind. To set your mind is to determine decisively what you will think, what you believe, and what you will or will not do—and to set it in such a way that you cannot be easily swayed or persuaded otherwise. Once you set your mind according to the truth of God's principles for a good life, you need to keep it set and not allow outside forces to reshape your thinking. Setting your mind does not mean being narrow-minded and stubborn. We should always be open to learning, growing, and changing, but we must consistently resist the temptation to conform our thoughts to the world and its ideas. To set your mind on things above means to be firm in your decision to agree with God's ways of living, no matter who may try to convince you that you are wrong.

Confession: *I set my mind and keep it set on things above.*

SET YOUR MIND AND KEEP IT SET, PART 2

And set your minds and keep them set on what is above (the higher things), not on the things that are on the earth.

COLOSSIANS 3:2

I want us to continue thinking about setting our minds and keeping them set on the things of God. When I began to conform my way of thinking and living to God's Word, I met with a great deal of opposition and had to be firm in my decision. For example, I discovered that when I tried to be positive, it was not received well by those who had a habit of being negative. They told me I was trying to live a fairy tale and that real life wasn't as positive as I believed it to be.

Sadly, I had to realize that Satan would even use my closest friends to try to prevent me from making progress. They simply did not understand, and human nature usually tries to find fault with what we don't understand. I had to know for sure that God was leading me, and I had to be firm in my resolve to think right thoughts so I could see right results in my life.

Setting your mind and keeping it set is so important because there's not much hope of being able to resist temptation if you don't make up your mind ahead of time concerning what you will do when you are tempted. You will be tempted; that's just a fact of life. So, it's important to think ahead of time about situations that can pose problems for you. If you wait until you are in the middle of a situation to decide whether or not you will stand firm, then you are sure to give up.

Confession: *I will set my mind ahead of time to focus on the things of God. This will help me resist temptation.*

USE YOUR TIME WISELY

Look carefully then how you walk! Live purposefully and worthily and accurately, not as the unwise and witless, but as wise (sensible, intelligent people).

Each one of us gets the same amount of time: twenty-four hours a day, seven days a week. Why is it that some people do so much with their lives, while others do very little or nothing at all? It isn't a lack of luck, or growing up in a dysfunctional family, or not getting to go to college. It is all about the choices we make. Have a meeting with yourself and ask yourself how many things you are doing that are just a waste of time. Anger is a waste of time; jealousy is a waste of time; murmuring and complaining are wastes of time. These negative emotions and behaviors take your time and energy and produce no good fruit.

Someone recently told me that 80 percent of people hate their job. If this is true, why do people do it? Because of money. We all need money, but we should also ask ourselves if we would be better off making a little less money and doing what we would truly enjoy instead of doing something we hate because it pays a little more than a job we would love and enjoy.

If you want a job you are not trained to do, why not start getting the training you need now? Don't get to the end of your life and look back and have nothing but regrets. Make the changes you need to make now—before you run out of time.

Confession: *I use my time wisely and do not waste it. I put my time into what will produce good fruit in my life.*

PREPARING FOR THE UNEXPECTED BRINGS PEACE

Let the peace of Christ [the inner calm of one who walks daily with Him] be the controlling factor in your hearts [deciding and settling questions that arise]. To this peace indeed you were called as members in one body [of believers]. And be thankful [to God always].

COLOSSIANS 3:15 AMP

It is wise to leave some room for the unexpected as you prepare for each day. For years, one of my self-induced problems was that I didn't leave space in my schedule for unexpected things. I planned activities with no time between commitments—a recipe for stress. I ended up rushed and impatient because people and situations disrupted "my" plan.

I was not fond of ten-minute intervals between commitments that didn't leave me enough time to do anything worthwhile. I viewed them as wasted time until I realized I needed those moments to breathe, regroup, and organize my thoughts. Small chunks of downtime provide opportunities to thank God or just talk with Him about your day. If things are not going well, they may allow you to hear from Him about ways to be productive and make the most of the day.

If we leave no time between appointments and commitments, what happens when we get delayed in heavy traffic? What if we are delayed by a last-minute phone call we truly need to take? Unexpected events do arise. Sometimes they are positive, and sometimes they cause unwanted pressure. The simple act of preparing and planning for the unexpected can bring a great deal of peace into your world.

Confession: *I prepare for the unexpected so I can live in peace.*

THE VALUE OF EXPERIENCE

Happy (blessed, fortunate, enviable) is the man who finds skillful and godly Wisdom, and the man who gets understanding [drawing it forth from God's Word and life's experiences].

PROVERBS 3:13

Wisdom is one of our greatest needs. God has given us wisdom, but we must use it. I like to define wisdom as doing now what you will be happy with later in life. Today's scripture tells us that we draw wisdom from the Word of God and from life's experiences. Each situation we go through teaches us something. It may teach us what we should not do in the future, or it may teach us what we should do in the future.

Hebrews 5:8 says that Jesus gained experience through the things that He suffered, and this equipped Him to be the author of salvation. Experience equips us, and in my estimation, it is even more important than education. Education is very important but having head knowledge about something and having experience applying it are two different things.

Be thankful for the experiences you've had because God can use them to help you or someone else in the future. I have had a lot of painful experiences in my life, and I have a lot of experience watching God's promises come to pass as I have placed my trust in Him. I use what I have learned and experienced to help other people who are hurting. Don't waste your pain. Use it for your gain or for someone else's gain in the future.

Confession: Each situation I go through gives me wisdom for the future and equips me for what I am called to do.

YOU HAVE THE ADVANTAGE

Little children, you are of God [you belong to Him] and have [already] defeated and overcome them [the agents of the antichrist], because He Who lives in you is greater (mightier) than he who is in the world.

1 JOHN 4:4

We have an enemy called the devil, and he is always looking for openings in our life through which he can attack us and make us miserable. He has power, but as believers, we have more power than he does because the One who is greater than the enemy lives in us. Think about and be conscious of the fact that Jesus lives in you, and think of the advantage that gives you. He is with you to guide you, to love you, and to comfort you when you are sad. He also helps you fight your battles, and with Him on your side, you will win them.

"All things are possible with God" (Matthew 19:26), and you belong to Him, so you can expect Him to help you with whatever you need. You are never alone because He is with you always and will guide you "even unto death" (Psalm 48:14 KJV). The first thing you should do when trouble comes is pray and ask God to guide you. It is dangerous to get upset and begin acting without having secured the wisdom and help of God.

Sometimes God will show you what to do, and at other times He will lead you to wait on Him and let Him fight the battle for you (Exodus 14:14). You are more than a conqueror (Romans 8:37) and have already defeated the enemy. Don't live in fear, because you have what it takes to be a winner in life.

Confession: *Jesus lives in me, and I have already defeated the enemy.*

FORGIVEN AND CLEANSED

If we [freely] admit that we have sinned and confess our sins, He is faithful and just (true to His own nature and promises) and will forgive our sins [dismiss our lawlessness] and [continuously] cleanse us from all unrighteousness [everything not in conformity to His will in purpose, thought, and action].

1 JOHN 1:9

We all sin, but it's very simple to have our sins forgiven. All we need to do is admit them and receive the forgiveness Jesus provided when He died on the cross for our sins. God continually cleanses us from all unrighteousness. This promise that God will forgive our sins is not a one-time opportunity only; we can receive it again and again.

"If we say that we have no sin, we deceive ourselves" (1 John 1:8 NKJV). "For all have sinned and fall short of the glory of God, and all are justified freely by his grace through the redemption that came by Christ Jesus" (Romans 3:23–24 NIV). Don't waste today feeling guilty about the sins you committed yesterday. Admit them, receive forgiveness, and press on to what God has for you today.

The gospel is good news. Jesus came to save us all from our sins and to take all the guilt that comes with them. Most of the world's news is bad news, but we have good news all the time when we believe and receive the promises of God in His Word.

Confession: *I quickly admit my sins and receive the forgiveness God so freely offers me.*

GOD WON'T BE LATE

The Lord does not delay and is not tardy or slow about what He promises, according to some people's conception of slowness, but He is long-suffering (extraordinarily patient) toward you, not desiring that any should perish, but that all should turn to repentance.

2 PETER 3:9

We like to do everything fast and get answers to our questions quickly, but God is not in a hurry. We may think He is working slowly, but this is only because we look at time differently than He does. We want to get a job done, but He wants to get it done right.

God is long-suffering and extraordinarily patient with us, and this truth makes me very glad. He may not be early in providing our breakthrough, but He will never be late. Paul and Silas were in jail still singing at midnight (Acts 16:25) when God suddenly caused an earthquake to shake the jail and the doors flew open. When the jailer awoke and saw all the doors opened, he was frightened, but Paul told him not to worry because the prisoners were all still there. Paul stayed to preach the gospel to the jailer, and as a result, the jailer and his entire household were saved. God seemed to be late, but Paul and Silas trusted Him so much that they were still singing, and something wonderful came out of the long wait.

Are you waiting on God to do something in your life? If so, keep singing and know that He will come through at the right time and the result will be good.

Confession: *No matter how long it takes for God to bring my breakthrough, I will wait patiently because I know His timing is perfect.*

WHAT WE THINK DETERMINES WHAT WE DO

I know and am convinced (persuaded) as one in the Lord Jesus, that nothing is [forbidden as] essentially unclean (defiled and unholy in itself). But [none the less] it is unclean (defiled and unholy) to anyone who thinks it is unclean.

ROMANS 14:14

The apostle Paul did not believe meat offered to idols could be tainted because he knew idols were nothing more than wood or stone. He also understood that many people did not share his perspective. He advised them not to eat the meat if they thought it was unclean. He knew that eating meat they considered defiled would affect their conscience as though the meat had actually been unclean. In other words, in a sense, perception is reality.

The more I think about Romans 14:14, the more amazed I am by the depth of Paul's insight. He understood that what people think determines what they do. This principle was true regarding meat offered to idols in ancient times, and it is true today in any area of life. For example, people who think they'll never get a good job are not likely to get one. People who think they can never do anything right tend to make lots of mistakes and have a high rate of failure. People who consider themselves accident-prone seem to have one accident after another.

We can never move beyond what we think and believe. When we believe lies, our minds can actually limit us and even keep us from doing what God created us to do. But, if we will contend for the truth, embrace the truth, and build our lives on the truth, we will succeed.

Confession: *I contend for, embrace, and build my life on the truth.*

FIGHT THE GOOD FIGHT OF FAITH

Fight the good fight of the faith; lay hold of the eternal life to which you were summoned and [for which] you confessed the good confession [of faith] before many witnesses.

1 TIMOTHY 6:12

There will be times of trouble when we must stand our ground and continue trusting God even when it is difficult, and those are the times we must "fight the good fight of the faith." During these seasons of life, worry and anxiety bombard our minds, and we must keep meditating on God's Word and remembering past victories.

We may even need to talk to ourselves. I do this regularly. I may say something such as "Joyce, you don't have to worry about this or try to figure it out. God is faithful, and He will give you the answer to your problem. Stand your ground and remain firm in your faith because all things are possible with God" (see Matthew 19:26).

When negative thoughts assault your mind, the mental attack will cease if you declare the promises of God. You cannot think two thoughts at once, so thinking on the good things will push the negative things out of your mind, though you may have to repeat this process many times. Remember that the devil won't give up easily, but you can outlast him if you are determined to do so.

Confession: *I declare the promises of God and continue to trust Him in times of trouble. I fill my mind with good things so there will be no room for bad things.*

BEAR GOOD FRUIT

But the fruit of the [Holy] Spirit [the work which His presence within accomplishes] is love, joy (gladness), peace, patience (an even temper, forbearance), kindness, goodness (benevolence), faithfulness, gentleness (meekness, humility), self-control (self-restraint, continence). Against such things there is no law [that can bring a charge].

GALATIANS 5:22-23

God want us to bear the fruit of the Spirit, listed in today's scripture. Fruit is given in seed form when the Holy Spirit comes to live in us, but we must work with Him to develop each fruit. I believe the fruit of the Spirit is even more important than the gifts of the Spirit (1 Corinthians 12:1–11) because the world needs to see the fruit of our relationship with God flowing through us.

The first fruit listed in Galatians 5:22 is love, and everyone wants to be loved. People are looking for love, and if we develop it, they can see it flowing through us. Love is not a feeling we have for a person, but it is seen in treating them well. Jesus tells us to be good to our enemies so they will see our good works and glorify God who is in heaven (Matthew 5:16, 43–48).

Study the fruit of the Spirit and practice it in your life. The more you practice it, the more it will develop. Love is the most important thing in the world. First, we should love God with all of our heart, soul, mind, and strength, and then, we should love our neighbors as we love ourselves (Luke 10:27).

Confession: *I practice the fruit of the Spirit by loving God and people.*

KEEP YOUR MIND ACTIVE

Be alert and of sober mind. Your enemy the devil prowls around like a roaring lion looking for someone to devour.

1 PETER 5:8 NIV

Passivity is a dangerous problem, because God's Word clearly teaches that we must be alert, cautious, and active. Some believers are so ruled by their emotions that an absence of feeling is all they need to stop doing what they know to do. They praise God, give to others, and keep their word if they feel like it—and if they don't feel like it, they don't.

An empty, passive mind can be easily filled with ungodly thoughts. Believers who have a passive mind and don't resist wrong thoughts often take them as their own, not realizing that evil spirits can inject ungodly thoughts into their minds because there is empty space to fill.

There are active sins, and there are passive sins. In other words, there are wrong things that we do, and there are right things that we don't do. For example, a relationship can be destroyed by thoughtless words, but it can also be destroyed by the omission of kind words that should have been spoken but never were. People who are passive don't think they are doing anything wrong when they fail to invest in a relationship, but problems arise because they are not doing anything to help it grow.

Let's be active in our relationships with others and in our relationship with God, not allowing empty space in our minds.

Confession: *I do not allow empty space in my mind, and I am not passive. I fill my mind with God's Word.*

CHOOSE TO BELIEVE

So too the [Holy] Spirit comes to our aid and bears us up in our weakness; for we do not know what prayer to offer nor how to offer it worthily as we ought, but the Spirit Himself goes to meet our supplication and pleads in our behalf with unspeakable yearnings and groanings too deep for utterance.

ROMANS 8:26

God often gives us faith for things our minds can't seem to grasp. The mind wants to understand everything—the why, when, and how of situations. When God doesn't give us understanding or insight into certain things, we are tempted to refuse to believe. When we walk with Him, sometimes we sense things in our hearts, but our minds fight against what we know because they don't understand. I choose to believe what God's Word says and what I believe He speaks to my heart, even if I don't understand why, when, or how it will come to pass in my life.

The devil finds many ways to keep us from moving forward into all the good things God wants to do in and through our lives. He can be creative and persistent as he tries to keep us from moving forward. But Jesus came to earth to destroy the works of the devil (1 John 3:8). In addition, He has given us the Holy Spirit as our Helper (John 14:26). He will always help us do what God calls us to do and be who God has created us to be. And as today's scripture teaches us, He even intercedes (pleads) for us.

With the Holy Spirit's help, we can choose to believe everything God wants us to believe, even when we don't understand it, knowing that God always intends the very best for us.

Confession: *I choose to believe God's Word and to believe what He speaks to my heart.*

THE BEAUTY OF PATIENCE

I waited patiently for the Lord; he turned to me and heard my cry.
PSALM 40:1 NIV

Patience has been the most difficult fruit of the Spirit for me to develop. It means to be long-suffering with people and to have mercy and an even temper. Most of us know people who are difficult for us to get along with. This doesn't mean there's something wrong with them; it simply means they are different than we are. Instead of rejecting them or trying to change them, God wants us to love them and be patient with them.

When it is difficult for us to be patient with someone, we should remember that someone else is struggling to be patient with us. Paul said he had learned how to be all things to all people (1 Corinthians 9:19–23). I think this is beautiful, because he was saying that he was willing to adapt and adjust to others in order to win them to Christ, or perhaps just to get along with them.

Who do you have a hard time being patient with? I can almost guarantee that it's someone who is not like you are. You may be fast, and they are slow; you may always be on time, and they are habitually late; you might be a quiet person, and they talk incessantly. We make a mistake when we try to change people to be what we want them to be. God wants us to love people the way they are (not the way we want them to be), to focus on their good qualities, and to believe the best about everyone. We should endeavor to be who God wants us to be and be patient with everyone else.

Confession: *I am patient with all people.*

GIRD UP YOUR MIND

Therefore gird up the loins of your mind, be sober, and rest your hope fully upon the grace that is to be brought to you at the revelation of Jesus Christ.

1 PETER 1:13 NKJV

In biblical times both men and women wore long skirtlike outfits. Had they tried to run in those clothes, they probably would have gotten tangled up in the fabrics and stumbled. When they needed to move quickly, they would gird up their clothing, meaning that they gathered the material of their garments and pulled it up so they could walk or run freely.

When the Bible tells us to "gird up the loins" of our minds, I believe it means to get our minds off of everything that would cause us to stumble as we run the race God has set before us. I think it may also refer to concentrating on the task at hand rather than allowing our thoughts to wander all over the place. Focus and concentration are both real challenges in our world today. We have a great deal of information coming at us all the time, and keeping our minds on what our purpose is requires great determination and even practice.

You may wake up and fully intend to start your day by spending time with God in prayer and Bible study. Then you intend to finish three specific projects that day. You need to go to the grocery store, do some car maintenance, and finish cleaning out a closet. Your intentions are good, but if you don't focus on those projects, you will surely be pulled away by other things or people. Girding up your mind is another way of saying "Stay focused on what you need to do."

Confession: *I concentrate on what I need to do so I can accomplish it without losing focus.*

BREAK BAD HABITS AND DEVELOP GOOD ONES

For if you are living according to the [impulses of the] flesh, you are going to die. But if [you are living] by the [power of the Holy] Spirit you are habitually putting to death the sinful deeds of the body, you will [really] live forever.

ROMANS 8:13 AMP

We all have habits—good and bad. Our harmful habits need to be broken and replaced with good ones. I believe the best way to do this is to focus on making good habits instead of on breaking bad ones. When we have good habits, there's no room for bad ones. Bad habits are not broken simply because we want to break them; we must break them on purpose by using our energy to develop good ones.

I found thirty-three references in the Amplified Bible, Classic Edition, to the word *habitually*. This tells me that God expects us to form good habits. Establishing the habits necessary for success requires consistency, especially in our thought life. Thinking and doing the right things a few times do not equal success, but habitually doing them will produce a life worth living. It may not be easy, but I believe it will be worth the effort. Try it for thirty days, and see if you agree. Don't get discouraged if at first you feel you are making little or no progress in developing new habits. Remember that habits take time. The person who never gives up always sees victory.

Confession: *I am diligent to form good habits that will leave no room for bad habits.*

SELF-CONTROL IS YOUR FRIEND

For the grace of God has appeared that offers salvation to all people. It teaches us to say "No" to ungodliness and worldly passions, and to live self-controlled, upright, and godly lives in this present age.
TITUS 2:11-12 NIV

Did you groan a bit when you saw the title of today's devotion? Some people view self-control as difficult, something that leads to suffering, but the truth is that self-control is your friend. It is the only thing that will help you be what you truly want to be and have what you want to have. We cannot simply wish good things into our lives; we must train ourselves in ways that will help us have them. If you want to lose some weight, you will have to be a little hungry for a while until your body adjusts to eating less food. You will be uncomfortable for a while, but later you will get what you want and be happy that you used self-control.

Hebrews 12:11 says that no discipline for the present time seems joyous, nevertheless later "it yields a peaceable fruit of righteousness to those who have been trained by it." We need to use self-control in every area of our lives. Be an investor, not a gambler. A gambler doesn't do a good thing but hopes to get a good result. An investor does the hard thing in the beginning, knowing that, in the end, the result will be positive.

What do you want out of life? Are you disciplining yourself and using self-control so you will have it someday? If not, you will never have it. Anyone can have a great life if they are willing to do the right things to have it.

Confession: *I love self-control, and it is my friend.*

DON'T COMPLAIN, GIVE THANKS

Give thanks in all circumstances; for this is God's will for you in Christ Jesus. Do not quench the Spirit.

1 THESSALONIANS 5:18–19 NIV

No one has to tell us to complain. It is a natural fruit of the flesh, but we frequently need to be reminded to give thanks. God answers prayers, but He doesn't answer complaints. I believe that all complaining does is quench the Spirit, and *to quench* means to stop or to extinguish.

We are to do everything "without grumbling or arguing," according to Philippians 2:14 (NIV). The next verse, Philippians 2:15, states that if we will eliminate these bad habits from our lives, we will be seen like stars shining out brightly in a "warped and crooked generation" (NIV). Everywhere I go, I hear people complaining, but when I meet someone who is thankful, I think, *That person is probably a Christian.*

Can you be inconvenienced without complaining? If any of us could make it through one entire day without complaining about anything at all, it might fall into the category of a miracle. Complaining seems to be our default setting for anything that is even mildly inconvenient.

I strongly believe that gratitude is a form of spiritual warfare. We can defeat Satan if we are thankful to God and say so, but we cannot defeat him with complaining and grumbling.

Confession: With God's help, I do not complain; instead, I am grateful.

SIMPLY PASSING THROUGH

*Beloved, I urge you as aliens and strangers [in this world] to abstain
from the sensual urges [those dishonorable desires] that wage war
against the soul.*

1 PETER 2:11 AMP

Do you ever feel a sense of dissatisfaction and have no idea
why? I do, and in seeking God for answers, He let me know
through Scripture that I will never be completely satisfied until
I am home in heaven with Him. We are aliens and strangers
in this world. We are simply passing through it. Our hearts
long for home. Right now, as I write this, I have been on an
extended trip, and I am longing for my home. The trip has been
enjoyable, but it isn't home.

The Bible says we have eternity in our hearts (Ecclesiastes
3:11). Those who belong to Christ have a God-given awareness
that there is more than we experience here in this life. Inwardly,
we long for our heavenly home. Most days I tell the Lord that
I am looking forward to coming home to be with Him. I am
happy to be here however long God wants to use me, but I am
not clinging to this world or dreading to leave it.

I try to imagine what heaven will be like, but all I can do is
imagine. The Bible gives us a few glimpses of what it will look like.
But I think about things like how it will be to live in an atmo-
sphere of perfect love and no longer be trapped in a fleshly body,
to be totally satisfied and to see Jesus and walk and talk with Him.
God tells us there are rewards waiting for us in heaven, and I am
excited to see what they are. Enjoy your time on earth, but always
realize it is not the best there is, because the best is yet to come!

Confession: *I'm just passing through this world and looking
forward to my heavenly home.*

GOD'S WORD MAKES YOU WISE

Blessed are those who find wisdom, those who gain understanding, for she is more profitable than silver and yields better returns than gold.

PROVERBS 3:13–14 NIV

I believe we can summarize good judgment, right discernment, and knowledge with one word: *wisdom.* Wisdom is one of the most valuable assets we can have. It is the correct use of knowledge. What good is knowledge if we don't know how to apply it wisely? I say, "Wisdom is doing now what you will be satisfied with later." We may not always feel like doing what is the wise thing, but if we do it anyway, we will eventually be glad we did.

In order to operate in wisdom, we must know God's Word and take our time making decisions, so we know we are making wise ones. Wisdom stands at the intersections of life, calling out to us to follow her (Proverbs 1:20–21).

Hebrews 12:11 says that no discipline seems joyous when we are going through it, but later on "it yields a peaceable fruit of righteousness to those who have been trained by it." Do you care about later on? Many people live only for the moment without thinking seriously about the future and how their current actions will affect it. This kind of thinking is unwise because "later on" always comes, and it brings the results of decisions we have made in the past. Once we have those results, it is too late to go back and undo what we have done.

Confession: *I use wisdom and do now what I believe I will be satisfied with later.*

YOUR BREAKTHROUGH IS COMING

For this light momentary affliction is preparing for us an eternal weight of glory beyond all comparison.

2 CORINTHIANS 4:17 ESV

Paul calls our earthly troubles light, momentary afflictions compared to the glory we are to receive. When I go through trying times, it helps to remind myself that they will pass. "This cannot last forever" is what I tell myself. I think of other things that I thought I would not survive, yet I did. The devil whispers in our ear that certain things will last forever, but they won't.

Christ is your strength, and no matter how bad your current situation may look, God loves you and has already planned your escape to a safe landing place. In addition, you will learn something from your trial that will help you later in life. Keep your eyes on the prize of heaven and the glory that awaits you there.

When we go through hard situations, they make us able to endure the next tough time with more ease. Each time we experience God's deliverance, it is easier to know that it will also be there the next time we need it. Enter God's rest today. Your breakthrough is coming!

Confession: *When I go through difficult times, they never last because God always provides a way out.*

STAND FIRM IN FREEDOM

Now the Lord is the Spirit, and where the Spirit of the Lord is, there is freedom.

2 CORINTHIANS 3:17 ESV

God's Word promises us freedom, but what kinds of things can we expect to be free from?

- We are free from sin (John 8:36; Romans 6:6, 14, 18, 22).
- We are free from guilt (Psalm 32:5; Hebrews 10:22).
- We are free from the fear of other people (Proverbs 29:25; Hebrews 13:6).
- We are free from comparing ourselves with other people (Galatians 6:4).
- We are free from the fear of what others think (Galatians 1:10).
- We are free from the fear of death (Psalm 23:4; John 14:1–3; Hebrews 2:14–15).

The people Jesus sets free are free indeed! (John 8:36). "It is for freedom that Christ has set us free. Stand firm, then, and do not let yourselves be burdened again by a yoke of slavery" (Galatians 5:1 NIV). Stand firm against the devil when he attempts to put you in bondage again. It took me a long time to break free from guilt, because it had been a part of my life as long as I could remember. Gaining freedom in some areas takes longer than others, but if you stick with God's Word, asking the Holy Spirit to help you, you will enjoy freedom in every area where you were once in bondage.

Confession: I am free and I will stand firm in my liberty and not be enslaved again to the bondage I have put off.

PRISONERS OF HOPE

Return to the stronghold [of security and prosperity], you prisoners of hope; even today do I declare that I will restore double your former prosperity to you.

ZECHARIAH 9:12

A prisoner of hope is so sure that there is hope (a positive expectation that something good is going to happen), that it can never be taken away from them. The devil hates it when we are full of hope. He wants us full of negativity and doubt. But we can be prisoners of hope who will receive double what we have lost. I call this getting "double for your trouble."

I don't think we can have faith if we don't first have hope. Put your faith in God that something good is coming your way. Trust Him with all your heart, and don't doubt. Hope never disappoints, according to Romans 5:5. Even if you don't get exactly what you want, you will get what is best for you, because God is good! "'For I know the plans I have for you,' declares the Lord, 'plans to prosper you and not to harm you, plans to give you hope and a future'" (Jeremiah 29:11 NIV). No matter what has happened to you or what is happening now, God has a good future planned for you, one that is full of hope.

"May the God of hope fill you with all joy and peace in believing, so that by the power of the Holy Spirit you may abound in hope" (Romans 15:13 ESV). This is one of my favorite scriptures, and I turn to it when I seem to have lost my joy. A loss of joy and peace means that you have stopped believing. But the God of hope will fill you once again as you trust Him.

Confession: *I am full of hope, and I believe something good is going to happen to me.*

DON'T SPEND TODAY
WORRYING ABOUT TOMORROW

So do not worry or be anxious about tomorrow, for tomorrow will have worries and anxieties of its own. Sufficient for each day is its own trouble.

MATTHEW 6:34

As I mentioned earlier, anxiety occurs when we spend today trying to get answers for tomorrow. It's like when the Israelites tried to collect the next day's manna on the current day (Exodus 16:16–20). This breadlike substance that God provided for their daily nourishment became rotten and began to stink if people hoarded it. Some individuals have what they would call "rotten, stinking lives" because they don't know how to live one day at a time, believing and trusting that God is in control.

We often tell God what we can and cannot do. When we have problems, we assure Him we just cannot take any more, but He knows what we can endure. He will never allow us to be tempted beyond what we can bear, and He will always provide a way out (1 Corinthians 10:13).

We don't have to have all the answers to all our problems, because God has them, and He is with us. At just the right time, He will reveal what we should do. Be assured that God is in control, that He is good, and that He loves you more than you could ever understand.

Confession: *I live one day at a time and trust God with the rest.*

SLOW DOWN AND PRAY

Teach me good judgment (discernment) and knowledge, for I have believed and trusted and relied on Your commandments.

PSALM 119:66 AMP

It is important for us to operate in wisdom, and it's also important for us to operate in discernment, which helps us know the difference between good and evil, and between right and wrong. I pray for discernment on a regular basis. Discernment is deeper than emotion or human thought, and if we seek it, we will make right decisions that lead us into a life we can enjoy.

We have all made decisions based on emotions and later regretted them. Most of us live fast, busy lives, and the only way to have good judgment, wise discernment, and knowledge is to slow down. The more quickly we make decisions, the more likely we are to make bad ones. Often it is best to sleep on a decision and see if you feel the same way the next morning as you felt the night before. Another good exercise is to try to think about the consequences your decision will create in your life.

I love dogs, and more than once I have purchased a puppy based on emotions and then had to give it away because my lifestyle is too busy for me to do the work a puppy requires. I like the emotional and fun side of having one, but I don't really want the work. Everything we enjoy in life comes with responsibility, and we must consider both enjoyment and responsibility when making decisions.

Confession: *Before I make a decision, I slow down and pray.*

SENSITIVITY TO THE HOLY SPIRIT

And do not grieve the Holy Spirit of God [do not offend or vex or sadden Him], by Whom you were sealed (marked, branded as God's own, secured) for the day of redemption (of final deliverance through Christ from evil and the consequences of sin).

EPHESIANS 4:30

We should be sensitive to the Holy Spirit, who is very gentle like a dove and does not like to be in an atmosphere of strife and arguing. I heard a story about a man who had pigeons and occasionally doves that nested on his windowsill. One day he and his wife were arguing, and he noticed the doves flew away, but the pigeons stayed.

The Holy Spirit is one of the most precious gifts we have. As believers, He lives in us and is our Teacher and Comforter (John 14:26). When you are hurting, you can ask the Holy Spirit to comfort you. The Holy Spirit is our guide, and if we follow His guidance, we will have a lot less trouble in our lives. It is important to the Holy Spirit that we are respectful not only to Him, but also to all the people we deal with in our lives.

The reverential fear of God is a good type of fear, a respectful awe, and we should have this kind of fear of offending the Holy Spirit. Reverential fear keeps us walking in obedience to God. Some of the things that offend the Holy Spirit are listed in Ephesians 4:31 and include "bitterness, rage and anger, brawling and slander, along with every form of malice" (NIV).

Confession: *I make every effort not to grieve or offend the Holy Spirit. He is gentle like a dove, and I want Him to be comfortable living in me.*

DO NOT QUENCH THE HOLY SPIRIT

Do not quench (suppress or subdue) the [Holy] Spirit.

1 THESSALONIANS 5:19

To *quench* means to suppress or subdue. We don't want to do this to the Holy Spirit, because we need Him working in our lives. We need greater sensitivity to the Holy Spirit, so we don't want to hurt Him by hurting one another. Sensitivity has two meanings: One has to do with being easily hurt, and the other has to do with being aware of the needs and emotions of others.

The way we treat people is the measure of many things—our character, our spiritual maturity, the depth of our love for God and others, and the level of anointing (power) God will release in our lives. Let us pray for and practice sensitivity in the way we treat others. Jesus referred to Himself as "gentle (meek) and humble (lowly)" (Matthew 11:29). We should desire to be the same and practice being gentle. It seems to me that the world we live in today is harsh, and we should resist becoming like it.

To treat people well, we must slow down. The faster we go in life, the more likely we are to hurt people and not even be aware we have done it. I know I am guilty of this, and although I have improved with God's help, I still have a long way to go. We should never use people to get things, but instead follow the leading of the Holy Spirit and use the things we do have to be a blessing to other people.

Confession: I don't want to quench the Holy Spirit. I want to be sensitive to what offends Him and avoid it, so I will make every effort to be kind and gentle with all people.

A GREATER GENTLENESS

Let your gentle spirit [your graciousness, unselfishness, mercy, tolerance, and patience] be known to all people. The Lord is near.

PHILIPPIANS 4:5 AMP

Ephesians 5:10 says, "And try to learn [in your experience] what is pleasing to the Lord [let your lives be constant proofs of what is most acceptable to Him]." Today's scripture tells us that God wants us to be gentle, which means considerate or kind; not harsh, or severe, or violent; easily managed or handled. Gentleness is one of the nine fruits of the Spirit. Gifts are given, but fruit must develop, grow, and ripen.

The fruit we purchase in a grocery store is often picked green and then receives a burst of gas called ethylene to force it to ripen. No wonder it usually doesn't have much taste. Natural ripening takes time and is a process, but the fruit tastes better. Due to greed in our society, we have found ways to work around nature's ripening process, even though it ruins the product.

There are too many unripe believers who are picked for use but are not able to do anyone any real good. They look good on the outside, but experience with them proves not to be good on the inside. I urge you to go through whatever process the Holy Spirit wants to take you through, no matter how long it takes. Don't be in such a big hurry to get where you are going. Instead, learn to enjoy the journey and be gentle toward yourself and others.

Confession: *I am patient and allow the fruit of the Spirit to ripen in my life, especially gentleness.*

POWER UNDER CONTROL

Now the man Moses was very meek (gentle, kind, and humble) or above all the men on the face of the earth.

NUMBERS 12:3

It is interesting that when God chose someone to lead the Israelites through the wilderness toward the Promised Land, He chose the meekest man on earth. Meek and gentle people are not weak, as some might suppose. They are people who have great power but know how to keep it under control. Psalm 18:35 says, "You have also given me the shield of Your salvation, and Your right hand has held me up; Your gentleness and condescension have made me great."

Moses was not gentle when he fled Egypt. He was crude and insensitive. But he changed in the wilderness over a period of forty years, and in today's scripture we see a man who prays and pleads for the ignorant. After Naomi had wrongfully accused him and was stricken with leprosy, Moses cried to the Lord, "Heal her now, O God, I beseech You!" (Numbers 12:13).

When the Israelites grumbled and complained against Moses and Aaron, they fell on their faces and prayed for them (Numbers 14:1–5). Wisdom is a great gift that God has given us, and James 3:17 says that it "is first of all pure (undefiled); then it is peace-loving, courteous (considerate, gentle). [It is willing to] yield to reason." Let's seek to develop gentleness in our lives.

Confession: I am gentle and meek, so I walk in wisdom and treat people the way God would treat them.

BE ENCOURAGED

Why are you cast down, O my inner self? And why should you moan over me and be disquieted within me? Hope in God and wait expectantly for Him, for I shall yet praise Him, my Help and my God.

PSALM 42:5

Discouragement destroys hope, and without hope, we give up. God knows we will not overcome our problems if we get discouraged, and I believe that's one reason He tells us in His Word not to be discouraged or dismayed and not to fear (Joshua 1:9; Deuteronomy 31:6), but to "take courage" and to "be strong" (Psalm 27:14; 31:24). He wants us to be encouraged, not discouraged.

One way to stop discouragement is to examine your thought life. What kind of thoughts have you been thinking? Have they sounded something like this: *I'm not going to make it; this is too hard. I always fail; nothing ever changes. I'm tired of trying. I may as well give up*? If this example represents your thoughts, no wonder you get discouraged. Discouraging thoughts will plunge you into discouragement.

Instead of thinking negatively, think like this: *Well, things are going slow, but, thank God, I'm making some progress. I made mistakes yesterday, but today is a new day. You love me, Lord. Your mercies are new every morning. I refuse to be discouraged. Father, help me choose right thoughts today.* I'm sure you can already feel the victory in this type of cheerful, positive, God-like thinking. Change your thinking and be encouraged.

Confession: *I choose thoughts that will encourage me, and I refuse to be discouraged.*

HAVE YOU BEEN IN THIS PLACE LONG ENOUGH?

The Lord our God said to us in Horeb, You have dwelt long enough on this mountain.

In Deuteronomy 1:2, Moses points out to the Israelites that their journey to the border of Canaan (the Promised Land) should have taken only eleven days, yet it took them *forty years* to get there. Then in verse 6, he says, "The Lord our God said to us in Horeb, You have dwelt long enough on this mountain."

Have you dwelt long enough on the same mountain? Have you, in a way, spent what feels like forty years trying to do something that should have taken much less time? Have you been in debt long enough? Have you been overeating long enough? Have you held on to a grudge or to unforgiveness long enough? Have you put the pursuit of your dreams on hold long enough? Have you let anger control you long enough? Let today be the day you decide to move forward in God's plans and promises for your life. Even if you take just one tiny step in that direction, do *something* to get yourself off the mountain you've been on too long. God has success and many good things in store for you, so move toward them.

I believe the Israelites took so long to make a fairly short trip because of a "wilderness mentality"—certain thought patterns kept them in bondage. If you feel stuck and cannot seem to get where you believe God is leading you, ask Him to show you how to adjust your thinking.

Confession: *I believe God has good things ahead for me, and I take steps each day to move toward them.*

A READY MIND

These were more noble than those in Thessalonica, in that they received the word with all readiness of mind, and searched the scriptures daily, whether those things were so.

ACTS 17:11 KJV

Today's scripture describes the Berean believers as "more noble" than the Thessalonian believers because "they received the word with all readiness of mind, and searched the scriptures daily." What is "readiness of mind"? I believe it means we are to have minds that are open to God's Word and His will for us, whatever it may be.

For example, recently a young person I know experienced the sorrow of losing a very good job. He was praying about whether the Lord would have him remain in the same career field or pursue something different. He wanted to remain in his field and hoped he would soon find a job doing what he had been doing. I advised him to have a "ready mind" in case things didn't work out that way. He asked, "Isn't that being negative?"

No, it isn't! Negativism would be to say "No one will ever want to hire me. I'll never have a good life." In contrast, being positive would be to say "I don't like that I got downsized at my job, but I'm going to trust God. I hope I can stay in this field, and I'm going to pray for that to happen. But more than anything, I want God's perfect will for my life. If things don't turn out the way I want them to, I'll survive. I believe everything will work out for the best."

This is facing facts, having a ready mind, being open to change, and still being positive.

Confession: *I have a ready mind that is open to God's Word and His will.*

LETTING GO OF GUILT

Therefore, [there is] now no condemnation (no adjudging guilty of wrong) for those who are in Christ Jesus, who live [and] walk not after the dictates of the flesh, but after the dictates of the Spirit.

ROMANS 8:1

I know that many people suffer with guilt even after they have repented of their sins. I did, and it took a long time for me to realize that all I was doing was trying to pay for my sins by feeling guilty. But since Jesus had already paid for them completely, my time and energies were being wasted.

If you have a tendency to feel guilty even after you have truly repented of your sins, I urge you to take time to receive God's forgiveness and remember that He says He will not only forgive us, but also remember our sins no more (Hebrews 8:12). If He can forget them, so can we.

If you feel condemned, it is not coming from God. It is either the devil, or you are doing it to yourself, so please accept God's complete forgiveness and start enjoying your life.

Confession: *I am completely forgiven of all my sins, and I will not receive condemnation or guilt because it is not from God.*

GREAT FAITH

The apostles said to the Lord, Increase our faith (that trust and confidence that spring from our belief in God).

LUKE 17:5

Many people pray for great faith, but they don't understand that it doesn't happen instantly. Faith grows little by little. It develops as we step out to do new things or as we take steps of obedience when God leads us in ways we don't understand. Faith becomes great over time and as we gain experience with God. Like muscles in the body, faith grows stronger as it is exercised.

When the disciples said to Jesus, "Increase our faith." He responded, "If you have faith as small as a mustard seed, you can say to this mulberry tree, 'Be uprooted and be planted in the sea,' and it will obey you" (Luke 17:6 NIV). I believe Jesus meant that if they had faith, they would do something to prove it. He also meant that a little faith can accomplish great things. Let me explain.

One way we demonstrate our faith is through taking action, often when we don't know what the outcome will be. In Luke 17, the apostles were doing nothing, yet they wanted great faith. Sometimes God does not want us to take action because He wants us to trust and wait for Him to act on our behalf. But even trusting God is active, not passive. We should be active in trusting Him, praying, studying and confessing His Word, and worshipping Him while we wait for Him to move. We should also be prepared to do anything He asks us to do.

Confession: *I am growing in faith each day.*

Do you have a real relationship with Jesus?

God loves you! He created you to be a special, unique, one-of-a-kind individual, and He has a specific purpose and plan for your life. And through a personal relationship with your Creator—God—you can discover a way of life that will truly satisfy your soul.

No matter who you are, what you've done, or where you are in your life right now, God's love and grace are greater than your sin—your mistakes. Jesus willingly gave His life so you can receive forgiveness from God and have new life in Him. He's just waiting for you to invite Him to be your Savior and Lord.

If you are ready to commit your life to Jesus and follow Him, all you have to do is ask Him to forgive your sins and give you a fresh start in the life you are meant to live. Begin by praying this prayer . . .

Lord Jesus, thank You for giving Your life for me
and forgiving me of my sins so I can have
a personal relationship with You. I am sincerely
sorry for the mistakes I've made, and I know
I need You to help me live right.
Your Word says in Romans 10:9, "If you declare
with your mouth, 'Jesus is Lord,' and believe
in your heart that God raised him from the dead,
you will be saved" (NIV).

I believe You are the Son of God
and confess You as my Savior and Lord.
Take me just as I am, and work in my heart,
making me the person You want me to be.
I want to live for You, Jesus, and I am so grateful
that You are giving me a fresh start in my
new life with You today.

I love You, Jesus!

It's so amazing to know that God loves us so much! He wants to have a deep, intimate relationship with us that grows every day as we spend time with Him in prayer and Bible study. And we want to encourage you in your new life in Christ.

Please visit joycemeyer.org/salvation to request Joyce's book *A New Way of Living*, which is our gift to you. We also have other free resources online to help you make progress in pursuing everything God has for you.

Congratulations on your fresh start in your life in Christ! We hope to hear from you soon.

NOTES

Unless otherwise noted, Scripture quotations are taken from the Amplified® Bible, Copyright © 1954, 1958, 1962, 1964, 1965, 1987 by The Lockman Foundation. Used by permission. www.Lockman.org.

Scripture quotations marked NIV are taken from the Holy Bible, New International Version®, NIV®. Copyright ©1973, 1978, 1984, 2011 by Biblica, Inc.™ Used by permission of Zondervan. All rights reserved worldwide. www.zondervan.com The "NIV" and "New International Version" are trademarks registered in the United States Patent and Trademark Office by Biblica, Inc.™

Scripture quotations marked NKJV are taken from the New King James Version®. Copyright © 1982 by Thomas Nelson. Used by permission. All rights reserved.

Scripture quotations marked AMP are from the Amplified® Bible. Copyright © 2015 by The Lockman Foundation. Used by permission. www.lockman.org.

Scripture quotations marked ESV are taken from The Holy Bible, English Standard Version. ESV® Text Edition: 2016. Copyright © 2001 by Crossway Bibles, a publishing ministry of Good News Publishers.

Scripture quotations marked KJV are taken from the King James Version of the Bible.

Scripture quotations marked NASB are taken from the New American Standard Bible® Copyright © 1960, 1962, 1963, 1968, 1971, 1972, 1973, 1975, 1977, 1995 by The Lockman Foundation. Used by permission.

Scripture quotations marked NLT are taken from the Holy Bible, New Living Translation, copyright ©1996, 2004, 2007, 2013, 2015 by Tyndale House Foundation. Used by permission of Tyndale House Publishers, Inc., Carol Stream, Illinois 60188. All rights reserved.

1. F. B. Meyer, *The Secret of Guidance* (Fleming H. Revell Company, 1896), 23.

2. BrainyQuote, https://www.brainyquote.com/quotes/blaise_pascal_159858.

3. Blake Stilwell, "The Real-Life Murphy and How 'Murphy's Law' Came to Be," Military.com, June 10, 2022, https://www.military.com/history/real-life-murphy-and-how-murphys-law-came-be.html.

4. *The Westminster Shorter Catechism*, question 1 (Assembly of Divines, 1648), https://www.apuritansmind.com/westminster-standards/shorter-catechism.

5. A. B. Simpson, "The Spirit of Love," in *Walking in the Spirit* (Christian Alliance Publishing Company, 1889).

6. Erwin W. Lutzer, "D. L. Moody, An Unlikely Servant," Moody Church Media, January 19, 2014, https://www.moodymedia.org/sermons/-/d-l-moody-unlikely-servant.

7. BrainyQuote, https://www.brainyquote.com/quotes/zig_ziglar_381975.

8. BrainyQuote, https://www.brainyquote.com/quotes/corrie_ten_boom_135203.

9. "Eulogia," Bible Hub, https://biblehub.com/greek/2129.htm.

10. "Epainos," Bible Hub, https://biblehub.com/greek/1868.htm.

11. Max Lucado, *Grace: More Than We Deserve, Greater Than We Imagine* (Thomas Nelson, 2014), 8.

12. St. Augustine, *On the Spirit and the Letter* (Society for Promoting Christian Knowledge, 1925), 53.

13. AZ Quotes, https://www.azquotes.com/quote/855992.

ABOUT THE AUTHOR

Joyce Meyer is one of the world's leading practical Bible teachers and a *New York Times* bestselling author. Joyce's books have helped millions of people find hope and restoration through Jesus Christ. Joyce's program, *Enjoying Everyday Life*, is broadcast on television, radio, and online to millions worldwide in 110 languages.

Through Joyce Meyer Ministries, Joyce teaches internationally on a number of topics with a particular focus on how the Word of God applies to our everyday lives. Her candid communication style allows her to share openly and practically about her experiences so others can apply what she has learned to their lives.

Joyce has authored more than 140 books, which have been translated into more than 160 languages, and over 41 million of her books have been distributed worldwide. Bestsellers include *Power Thoughts*; *The Confident Woman*; *Look Great, Feel Great*; *Starting Your Day Right*; *Ending Your Day Right*; *Approval Addiction*; *How to Hear from God*; *Beauty for Ashes*; and *Battlefield of the Mind*.

Joyce's passion to help people who are hurting is foundational to the vision of Hand of Hope, the missions arm of Joyce Meyer Ministries. Each year Hand of Hope provides millions of meals for the hungry and malnourished, installs freshwater wells in poor and remote areas, provides critical relief after natural disasters, and offers free medical and dental care to thousands through their hospitals and clinics worldwide. Through Project GRL, women and children are rescued from human trafficking and provided safe places to receive an education, nutritious meals, and the love of God.

JOYCE MEYER MINISTRIES

U.S. & FOREIGN OFFICE ADDRESSES

Joyce Meyer Ministries
P.O. Box 655
Fenton, MO 63026
USA
(866) 480-1528

**Joyce Meyer Ministries—
Canada**
P.O. Box 7700
Vancouver, BC V6B 4E2
Canada
(800) 868-1002

**Joyce Meyer Ministries—
Australia**
Locked Bag 77
Mansfield Delivery Centre
Queensland 4122
Australia
+61 7 3349 1200

**Joyce Meyer Ministries—
England**
P.O. Box 8267
Reading RG6 9TX
United Kingdom
+44 1753 831102

**Joyce Meyer Ministries—
South Africa**
P.O. Box 5
Unit EB06, East Block,
Tannery Park
23 Belmont Road
Rondebosch, Cape Town,
South Africa, 7700
+27 21 701 1056

**Joyce Meyer Ministries—
Francophonie**
29 avenue Maurice Chevalier
77330 Ozoir la Ferriere
France

**Joyce Meyer Ministries—
Germany**
Postfach 761001
22060 Hamburg
Germany
+49 (0)40 / 88 88 4 11 11

**Joyce Meyer Ministries—
Netherlands**
Postbus 55
7000 HB Doetinchem
The Netherlands
+31 (0)26 20 22 100

Joyce Meyer Ministries—Russia
P.O. Box 789
Moscow 101000
Russia
+7 (495) 727-14-68

Other Books by Joyce Meyer

Books by Dave Meyer
Life Lines